ADAP

EDEN

Oregon's Catholic Minority
1838–1986

Patricia Brandt
Lillian A. Pereyra

WSU
PRESS

Washington State University Press
Pullman, Washington

Washington State University Press
PO Box 645910
Pullman, Washington 99164-5910
Phone: 800-354-7360
Fax: 509-335-8568
E-mail: wsupress@wsu.edu
Web site: wsupress.wsu.edu

Library of Congress Cataloging-in-Publication Data

Brandt, Patricia.
    Adapting in Eden : Oregon's Catholic minority, 1838-1986 / by Patricia Brandt and Lillian A.
Pereyra.
        p. cm.
    Includes bibliographical references and index.
    ISBN 0-87422-253-2 (pbk. : alk. paper)
        1. Catholic Church. Archdiocese of Portland in Oregon—History. 2. Catholic Church—
Oregon— History. 3. Oregon—Church history. I. Pereyra, Lillian A., 1920- II. Title.

BX1417.P65 B73 2002
305.6'20795–dc21   2002151812

Table of Contents

Acknowledgments

This study would not have been possible without assistance from many sources. First of all, we wish to express our deep gratitude to the Oregon Catholic Historical Society for their moral support and for sponsoring publication of this history. Various archivists who made their holdings available are due special thanks, including Mary Grant-Doty, Archivist for the Archdiocese of Portland in Oregon; Sister Rosemarie Kasper, S.N.J.M., former Archivist for the Oregon Province of the Sisters of the Holy Names of Jesus and Mary; Jacqueline Dougherty, former Archivist for the Indiana Province of the Congregation of the Holy Cross; Fr. Hugh Feiss, O.S.B., former librarian at Mount Angel Abbey Library; and anonymous archivists at the National Archives and the Bureau of Catholic Indian Missions. We are especially grateful to Ed Langlois of Oregon Catholic Press who not only encouraged us to research and write about Oregon Catholic history but also opened their photo archives to us.

Many others have encouraged and supported us, notably Rev. Arthur Schoenfelt, C.S.C., who helped financially in getting this project started; Cecilia Baricevic, who provided background information on Catholic Charities; Sister Pauline Rose Waibel, S.S.M.O., who shared her research on the missionary activities of the Sisters of St. Mary of Oregon; and Dr. James Strassmaier, retired Head of the Oral History Department of the Oregon Historical Society, who provided the equipment for the oral interviews that provided substantial information for the latter part of this history. And a big thank you to the interviewees who honestly and patiently answered the many questions asked of them. Also, thanks to the many authors whose published works provided valuable background information.

We want to acknowledge the editorial assistance of the special committee of the Archdiocesan Historical Commission which included the two authors and James Strassmaier, Joseph Schiwek Jr. and Brother Donald Stabrowski, C.S.C., who were originally charged with producing this history.

Staff members of Washington State University Press have gone out of their way to assist in publishing this book, especially Glen Lindeman and our editor, Nancy Grunewald.

Finally, we want to thank Mary and Joseph for their constant guidance and intercession.

Patricia Brandt and Lillian Pereyra

Francis Norbert Blanchet (1795–1883)
Archbishop of Oregon City (1846–1880)
Oregon Catholic Press

Chapter One

An Improbable Dream

ATHOLICISM CAME TO THE PACIFIC NORTHWEST at a measured pace. Spanish sailors in Bruno de Heceta's 1775 expedition were the first Catholics to set foot in the Oregon country, and a short-lived Spanish colony attempted settlement at Neah Bay in 1792. Nearly two more decades passed before Catholics made another tentative venture into the region. Several French Canadians from the American Astor expedition of 1811–12 settled in the Willamette Valley, and trappers and mountain men joined them for part of each year, with their Indian women and families.[1]

The planting of the first definably Catholic community in the Northwest came about through the Hudson's Bay Company, which in 1821 extended its operations to the Columbia River. Merging with its rival, the North West Company, Hudson's Bay strengthened British claims to land along the river, held jointly with the United States under an 1818 treaty. The British government and company directors had already privately conceded to Americans the land south of the Columbia, although the treaty provided that citizens of either nation could settle anywhere within the territory. Anticipating the arrival of Americans, the company moved its headquarters from Astoria across and up the river to Fort Vancouver in 1824.

That same year, the man who would assist in the actual establishment of the Catholic community, Dr. John McLoughlin, arrived as chief factor at the new fort. McLoughlin's parents were Catholic, and he had been baptized as an infant; but his maternal grandfather, an Anglican, raised him in that church. At the age of fourteen, John began the study of medicine as physician's apprentice and received his medical license five years later. Starting his career with the North West Company as a doctor, he gradually worked up to the position of chief trader. In the negotiations at the merger of North West Company with Hudson's Bay Company, McLoughlin impressed the directors enough to maintain his status in the merged company. After several minor assignments, McLoughlin was appointed chief factor of the Columbia District.[2]

McLoughlin, "the virtual emperor of the Oregon country," was a man well over six feet tall, powerfully built, with an untamed mane of prematurely white hair and piercing blue eyes. He was a successful businessman, organized, honest, and flexible; but he struggled with an uncontrollable temper and irascible disposition. He was known to burst out in impetuous and regrettable rages. When the British government gave Hudson's Bay Company (HBC) exclusive trading rights in the Northwest, it also granted criminal and civil jurisdiction, so McLoughlin held almost absolute power. Paternalistic but humane, the factor was generous to those who came to the fort in need—including, in time, American Protestant missionaries. One of the duties he assumed was the spiritual care of the Catholics under his charge, personally conducting Catholic services and teaching prayers and catechism in French.[3]

The HBC charter required provision for the moral and religious improvement of Indians under its control, but compliance was cursory. Then the directors sent an Anglican, Rev. Herbert Beaver, who was unable to adapt to the conditions at the fort. Rev. Beaver considered the domestic arrangements of the French-Canadian trappers and their Indian women scandalous, and he included McLoughlin and his Indian consort in his condemnations. His tenure lasted only two complaint-filled years.[4]

In the meantime, McLoughlin encouraged retired French Canadian trappers and other company employees who had produced families through their alliances with Indian women to settle in the region on the Willamette River near present-day St. Paul. With earlier settlers, they formed a rudimentary community that became known as French Prairie. As early as 1833, McLoughlin wrote to Father Thomas Maguire, chaplain of his sister's Ursuline convent in Quebec, who carried to Rome the chief factor's proposal to found a Catholic mission on the Columbia. The French Canadians, mostly nominal Catholics, were firmly settled at French Prairie in 1834 when they wrote to Bishop Joseph Provencher of Red River, in present-day Manitoba, Canada, asking for priests. Like McLoughlin, they received no reply. The next year they tried again, and this time Provencher responded that he would see what could be done. Working with his superior, Bishop Joseph Signay of Quebec, Provencher led the attempt to find missionaries. As a partial response to the requests for priests, the Columbia area became part of the

Vicariate Apostolic of Red River in 1836. Trusting in a positive reply to their latest request for a priest, the French Canadians began building a log church at French Prairie, the first Catholic church in Oregon, thus establishing the earliest identifiable Catholic community in the Northwest.[5]

About the same time, another appeal for missionaries had been made, resulting in much broader consequences. A deputation of Flathead and Nez Perce Indians, who had learned of Catholicism from French Canadian trappers or Hudson's Bay employees, made their way to St. Louis in 1831 to request that "blackrobes" be sent to them. As with the French Prairie request, no priests were available. This incident received wide publicity, particularly in the religious press. The Indians' request galvanized the Methodist Church, among others, to respond to the petition with a missionary expedition. However, the Methodist missionaries sent to the Flatheads, Jason and Daniel Lee, passed the tribe's territory without contact. The Lees continued west to reach Fort Vancouver in 1834, only months after the French Canadians' first plea for priests had been sent to Canada.[6]

Abandoning their original goal of ministry to the Flatheads and accepting the suggestion of John McLoughlin, the Lees established a mission near the French Canadians and began ministering to their spiritual needs as well as evangelizing the Indians. In 1836 Marcus Whitman and other missionaries from the American Board of Commissioners for Foreign Missions set up a mission network among the Indians in the eastern part of the Oregon country. By 1838, the beginning of what would become a massive American migration created a significant Protestant presence in the region.[7]

Aware of these developments, McLoughlin supported the French Canadian requests for priests, but the Hudson's Bay Company, which controlled travel between Canada and Fort Vancouver, was reluctant to permit them into the area, fearing that the differences in religious doctrines would lead to violence. Finally, in 1838, McLoughlin convinced the directors that priests could help retain the loyalty of the French Canadians, now being proselytized by the American missionaries. In spite of serious reservations, HBC Governor George Simpson permitted Catholic missionaries to travel to the Cowlitz River area in 1838 with the annual supply train from Canada. The stipulation was that these priests were not to establish missions south of the Columbia, because of the belief that only the area north of the river would remain British territory when the border question was resolved.[8]

Even before formal approval was received, the bishop of Quebec selected Father Francis Norbert Blanchet to be his vicar general in a missionary territory on the Columbia. Newly ordained Father Modeste Demers was named to serve with Blanchet, but the negotiations went on so long that he seized the opportunity for a temporary assignment with the bishop of Red River.

Francis Norbert Blanchet, member of an old and distinguished French Canadian family, was born September 3, 1795, in the village of St. Pierre, Quebec. After being educated in the parish school, he and his younger brother, Augustine, enrolled together in the seminary at Quebec. Ordained in 1819, Francis first ministered in a wilderness parish in New Brunswick. Weather was wretched, travel was difficult, and living was hard, yet he maintained his zeal and good spirits. He worked closely with the Indians in his parish, and he knew firsthand the special problems involved in dealing with native peoples. Because he also served some British parishioners, Blanchet also learned English while in New Brunswick.[9]

A rather dour, stern, humorless man, Blanchet viewed his own abilities with pessimism. His visionary plans frequently overtaxed his resources. Nonetheless, by 1838 he was already a mature, earnest, devout, and widely experienced priest; he seemed ideally prepared for what was expected to be a demanding mission field. He had most recently served a relatively urban parish near Montreal, The Cedars, which was a gateway to the West for fur traders and *voyageurs*. Blanchet recognized the difficulties of the assignment and his earlier experiences contributed to his fear that the isolation would cause him to lose his faith. He remarked: "…[W]hen I consider the isolation in which the missionaries of the Columbia find themselves; the dangers and difficulties by which their mission will be surrounded; it seems to me that they will need a divine vocation with all the graces which accompany it; and even then, they will still have to fear that after having preached to others, they might be lost themselves."[10]

Leaving the final decision to his superiors, Blanchet learned before long that he would leave as soon as a replacement could be obtained for his parish. After several delays, which included missing his boat and having to pursue it along the bank for a day, on May 3, 1838, he left Montreal for Red River, where Father Demers waited eagerly with hope that he would join the group. Modeste Demers had been a priest for only two years, but he already had a taste of hardships in the untamed land at St. Boniface, a frontier settlement on the Red River. Like Blanchet, he was also French Canadian, born in St. Nicholas, Quebec, on October 11, 1809, and ordained in 1836 in Quebec. Zealous, agreeable, and pious, Demers was a youthful and enthusiastic partner for the older man.[11]

Before leaving the Red River territory, Blanchet met John McLoughlin, who was on his way to London. From the chief factor he learned how impatiently the Willamette settlers anticipated his arrival, and he knew what disappointment there would be when they learned he could not settle among them.[12]

The robust missionaries endured the same hardships as the *voyageurs* on the dangerous and exhausting journey to the Columbia. On October 13, 1838, the party reached the Oregon country at the foot of the Rockies, and the next day Father Demers offered the first Mass in the Pacific Northwest at what is now Big Bend, British Columbia. That afternoon, the group braved the dreaded Dalles of the Dead on the Columbia River, and twelve people drowned when their boat overturned in the rapids.[13]

Reaching Fort Vancouver far behind schedule in the late afternoon of November 24, Blanchet and the survivors greeted a throng that included only three representatives of the French Prairie settlers—Joseph Gervais, Stephen Lucier and Peter Beleque; the others had had to return home when the brigade was late. As Blanchet had expected, the French Prairie delegates were disheartened that the missionaries could not settle in their midst. The next day the new vicar general found space in the fort's schoolroom to offer what Blanchet recorded as the first Mass in the lower Oregon country, a High Mass of thanksgiving.[14]

Within two days, the missionaries inaugurated religious meetings for the Canadians and the Indians. However, obedient to the agreement with the company, Blanchet left for the Cowlitz River to establish a mission and start a church building there. Meanwhile, Demers continued work at Fort Vancouver. Both men discovered there was no familiar structure on which to build; this was a virtually virgin missionary land.[15]

Nothing in the HBC agreement prevented a visit to French Prairie, but it was several weeks before Blanchet could travel to the little church that had long awaited a priest. Blanchet arrived at French Prairie on the Saturday afternoon of January 5, 1839, and was greeted by most of the population, Indian and white. The next day, the French Canadians proudly escorted him to the site of their log church, with its lean-to for the priest's living quarters. Blanchet blessed the building that day, dedicating it to St. Paul, and celebrated the first Mass in the first Catholic church in what would become the State of Oregon.[16]

Active proselytizing of the Canadians by Protestants, which had led some from the Church, gravely concerned Blanchet, and he remained at French Prairie for a month. He designed his assemblies to teach the Catholic religion and encourage return to the faith, besides regularizing fur-trade marriages and insisting that husbands and wives live separately until they were properly married. Living in tents near the church, the Canadians became reacquainted with their childhood faith, some having been away from the Church so long

that they had forgotten their prayers and religious training. The French Canadians rallied around one of their own, raising Blanchet to the status of
leader, whether he wanted the honor or not. Before his return to Fort
Vancouver, Blanchet claimed 640 acres for a mission site on French Prairie,
hoping that the HBC would change its policy. It was obvious that the population needed continuous, dedicated, and vigilant attention to improve its
spiritual condition.[17]

After an extended missionary tour, Blanchet returned to Fort Vancouver
in September, 1839. James Douglas gave him the welcome news that the
Hudson's Bay Company had withdrawn its objections to a mission on the
Willamette—a change Blanchet attributed to the influence of John
McLoughlin during his recent visit to London. Armed with written permis-
sion, Blanchet left October 10 and took up residence in the church at St.
Paul. There were now two permanent missions in the vicariate, Cowlitz and
Willamette (or St. Paul, as it was soon known). The building of Catholic
communities was underway.[18]

After returning from his European trip, John McLoughlin continued to
take interest in Catholic affairs and, since his own beliefs were completely
compatible with Catholic teachings, it was perhaps inevitable that he would
be drawn back to the faith of his parents. Rather unexpectedly, McLoughlin
made his abjuration of heresy and was absolved of excommunication, and he
renewed his marriage vows and received the nuptial blessing from Blanchet
for his marriage to Marguerite Wadin in 1842.[19]

While Blanchet was on his first obligatory trip to Cowlitz, Demers remained at Fort Vancouver, conducting services and learning the Chinook jar-
gon, the trade language of the territory. He translated prayers and hymns so
Indians could be instructed, using songs during his services to attract not
only the music-loving French Canadians but also the Indians. The missionaries were encouraged to see that the Indians would flock to church, but the
amount of work to be done in converting them was overwhelming.[20]

A six-week visit with the Indians in the Cowlitz area early in Blanchet's
ministry emphasized to him the problem of explaining the mysteries of the
faith in a form the natives could understand and pass on. Blanchet devised a
stick with marks indicating events in religious history and spent a week teaching them so they could return to their tribes to spread the Gospel. The *sahale
stick* (stick from above) proved to be quite successful, but it was soon replaced
by a more easily reproduced chart depicting the fundamentals of salvation
and church history. Known as the "Catholic Ladder," the chart became an
important and popular tool in instructing both Indians and whites.[21]

The missionaries' orders emphasized their duty to serve the Indians of the region, and Blanchet zealously set about visiting Hudson's Bay Company forts and working on the evangelization of the tribes, using the Catholic Ladder. Both missionaries were out in the field most of the time, traveling on foot, boat, and horseback; over mountains, rivers, deserts, and marshes; in heat and cold, supported mainly by their prodigious devotion and robust physical endurance. Virtually no request for "blackrobes" was ignored. Continually expanding the boundaries of their mission, the two tirelessly traveled to areas near Nesqually, The Dalles, Walla Walla, Colville, Puget Sound and Okanogan, up the Columbia River, on the Willamette, at HBC forts, and in Indian villages.[22]

From the start, the Catholic and Protestant clergy were at odds; friction escalated as time went on, with bitter rivalry on both personal and theological levels. The Protestants protested the priests' presence, denounced their teachings, and decried their influence on the French Canadians. The priests, for their part, were concerned that their parishioners were being misled, and they would do anything to win them back. It became a favorite Catholic tactic to establish missions near Protestant stations and try to destroy their credibility, which of course antagonized the Protestants. Blanchet's visit to the Indians on the Clackamas River inspired this comment from the priest: "Minister Waller saw me enter into his sheepfold; I had the right to do it, as he is not a true shepherd."[23]

With animosity from the beginning, and intense—if misplaced—zeal on both sides, disputes arose frequently. However, the Catholic priests had the distinction of coming by invitation of their French Canadian congregation. They also had the advantage of being flexible and mobile, unencumbered by families or the need for settlements. The allure of vestments, crosses, rosaries, medals, and holy pictures, and the richness of Catholic services, appealed to the Indians in a way that was impossible for the Protestants to rival. Yet the result was that Catholics, especially those at St. Paul who already had a different nationality, culture, and language, became a separate community, isolated and distrusted.[24]

While Blanchet was determined to stay out of political affairs, the joint occupancy made that almost impossible. As a British citizen, Blanchet owed some allegiance to Hudson's Bay Company and to John McLoughlin for providing transportation and support for his mission. Whether the American Protestants' opposition was aroused more by their self-reinforced perception of the Catholic priests as agents of the British or by their innate hatred of Catholics is difficult to ascertain. Inevitably, political and religious opposition became entwined; to some degree Blanchet was, knowingly or innocently, used by Hudson's Bay Company.

Nowhere was the confusion of politics and religion more evident than in the formation of a government. While the Company's legal protection satisfied Blanchet and most of the French Canadians, the Americans rejected rule by any British body, and they also wanted their familiar political institutions and laws. In 1841, one of the French Canadians stole property from a Methodist missionary. Jason Lee thought that this situation required formation of a civil authority to punish the offender, but Blanchet preferred to handle the situation pastorally, punishing one of his flock for a sin. The argument was still in progress when Ewing Young, a wealthy stock raiser, died without a will in February, 1841. Members of the Methodist mission took it upon themselves to call a settlers' meeting to settle the estate, since no legal authority existed with power to handle the problem. The meeting minutes indicate that while the outward purpose of the settlers' meetings on February 17-18, 1841, was to decide on disposition of Young's estate, the Methodists also designed them to form a government. Blanchet very reluctantly attended the assembly and expressed his doubts about the legal basis of the meeting, especially with its expanded purpose. The settlers elected officers to deal with the estate problem—and the astonished priest found himself chairman of a seven-man committee charged with writing a constitution for a local government, apparently in an attempt to gain French Canadian support.[25]

At a subsequent meeting held in June in Blanchet's new living quarters at St. Paul, Blanchet rose to report, as the first order of business, that nothing had been done, and that he and his people were opposed to such government. He was quickly replaced as chairman. Support for the priest's opinion came not only from John McLoughlin but also from Lt. Charles Wilkes, on an exploring expedition for the U.S. government, whose opinion was sought. Eventually even Jason Lee came to agree with Blanchet.[26]

Whether Blanchet had the iron grip on the French Canadians' ideas and actions that the Americans supposed is debatable. Nevertheless, an assembly of Oregon settlers voted to form a provisional government on May 2, 1843, in a close contest reportedly split primarily by nationality. Surviving reports of the meeting raise questions about what actually happened; there is reason to believe that reputed French Canadian opposition was more against the idea of a large government with a governor, than against government itself. When those at the meeting agreed to a three-man executive committee, which was less threatening to McLoughlin's power and support, the French Canadians were mollified and approved the provisional government. As a matter of fact, one might make a case that Catholics helped to bring about a *modus vivendi* with a document written by Father Anthony Langlois, one of Blanchet's assistants, presented at the 1844 meeting to consider unsatisfactory aspects of the Provisional Government. "So important were the changes made in the Organic Laws and Articles of 1843 by the legislative committee of 1844 that something like a new constitution was then made."[27]

By 1845 it was becoming evident that Oregon would be incorporated into the United States as the population of Oregon swelled with the addition of over 3,000 new immigrants, most of them Americans. Father Demers commented, "Emigrants from the United States are arriving here in large numbers, some by sea, others by land, with their wagons, animals, horses, oxen, cows, etc., making a road across forests and mountains; nothing stops them—there is not, I think, a people like that one under the sun." Few were Catholics. Seeing the handwriting on the wall, the Oregon Catholics began the slow process of building social acceptance, breaking down the separation that kept them apart from their neighbors. Blanchet readily adapted to the American government that both he and John McLoughlin had begun to accept as inevitable.[28]

The increased American immigration did indeed decide the nationality of Oregon: it would be American, with a government established on American principles. The border dispute with Great Britain was settled in 1846. Oregon City, established by John McLoughlin in 1842, became the most important town as well as capital of the Provisional Government. By this time, there were so many in the white community needing spiritual guidance that it was difficult to spare priests to care for the Indians, most of whom now lived far from white population centers.[29]

For their first two years in Oregon country, the priests labored alone, with little contact with each other, much less other priests. Loneliness was their lot, and Blanchet lamented to the bishop of Quebec: "Your Highness may judge of the grief which we experience on seeing ourselves for so long separated one from the other, we who would so often have need of meeting to consult about our obstacles, and to revive our courage which continual difficulties tend to paralyze." When Demers returned to Cowlitz in the summer of 1840, he heard that priests were in the Rocky Mountain area, and he wrote to them on August 6. Only days later, the unknown missionary introduced himself in a letter to Blanchet as Father Peter De Smet, S.J. He was evaluating the possibility of finally starting a long-delayed mission among the persistent Flathead Indians and promised to visit the Columbia missionaries in the near future.[30]

By the spring of 1842, De Smet found time to travel to Fort Vancouver and St. Paul. Demers reported the meeting of Blanchet and De Smet: "No sooner had Father De Smet descried the Vicar General than he ran to prostrate himself at his feet, imploring his blessing; and no sooner had the Very Rev. Blanchet caught sight of the valiant missionary than he also fell on his knees, imploring the blessing of the saintly Jesuit." The three priests held a conference of immense historical significance at Fort Vancouver, to consider the future of the western missions and to decide where to focus their efforts, given the lack of personnel. They had no mandate from higher authority; they made decisions before asking permission to carry them out. An independent vicariate apostolic for Oregon, they decided, would make recruiting of missionaries easier, as well as solve political problems. De Smet would go to St. Louis and to Europe to find more workers, as well as financial and ecclesiastical support. Demers was selected to develop missions in New Caledonia (now British Columbia). This left the rest of the extensive mission to be cared for by Blanchet in their absence.[31]

Blanchet's heavy workload, which he had cited as a reason for disassociating himself from the incipient government, suddenly doubled with the loss of his companion. Bishop Signay tried to find additional missionaries, but there were many difficulties, including Hudson's Bay Company's refusal to take any more priests on their brigades to the West. Blanchet observed that Americans were crossing the Rockies to the Oregon country in increasing numbers, and he wondered if the time had not come for the mission to seek independence from Quebec, so he could get priests overland from St. Louis. Bishop Signay, coming to the same conclusion almost simultaneously, wrote Blanchet that he planned to ask Rome to remove the Columbia region from his care. Despairing of help from the HBC, Signay finally dispatched two priests to Oregon by ship, but with no others available, he was unable to send any additional priests.[32]

Hearing no particulars about these priests, Blanchet supposed that they were making the overland trek. He was overjoyed when Fathers Anthony Langlois and J. B. Bolduc arrived at Fort Vancouver on September 15, 1842, after a voyage of over a year. Blanchet wrote: "What can I say about the first interview, so filled with emotions of joy, of hope, of rejoicing, of complete happiness!" Their visit at St. Paul provided the occasion for the first High Mass in the territory with deacon and subdeacon, an unprecedented experience for the unsophisticated observers.[33]

With their arrival, the forces of the mission doubled, and Blanchet was suddenly thrust into the role of superior. He was at a disadvantage, being temporarily deprived of the assistance of the loyal Demers, off in New

Caledonia. Demers was virtually of one mind with his mentor, and plans were amicably decided mutually; but the new men were not as compliant and uncomplaining. Langlois had boundless zeal, but Blanchet needed him for less exciting service. Meanwhile, Bolduc became a peripatetic missionary to the Indians on the Cowlitz and elsewhere. He quickly succumbed to the lure of arduous missionary life, relishing the physically stressing travel and harrowing life-style. Later, when assigned to St. Paul, his ardor cooled, which he blamed on the devastation caused by liquor. Both Bolduc and Demers threatened to leave because of shiftless and drunken parishioners.[34]

The missionaries met better success with distant church officials, who recognized that population growth in Oregon would require changes in jurisdiction. Bishop Signay realized that the boundaries of his diocese were unsettled at the founding of the Oregon mission, although he assumed that they extended as far as the Pacific coast. West of the Mississippi, in what was to become the United States, the Catholic Church was vaguely under the authority of the bishop of St. Louis and his superior, the archbishop of Baltimore. When Oregon was held jointly by the United States and Great Britain, it was not clear which diocese—Quebec or St. Louis—was responsible for Oregon. Originally, when most Oregon Catholics were Canadians, Quebec authority seemed reasonable, but as time went on, a separate bishop for the Oregon country seemed to be the best solution. In consultation with the American bishops on this matter, Signay recommended a full bishopric with its seat at Fort Vancouver and Blanchet as bishop. The idea of an Oregon vicariate had been the principal item of discussion at the Fort Vancouver meeting with De Smet, and the Jesuit promoted it on his trip to the East Coast and Europe. Supported by Blanchet's correspondence, De Smet used personal contacts to place the topic on the agenda of the U.S. bishops when they met in a national council in Baltimore in May, 1843. The council did recommend a vicariate apostolic in the Oregon country; however, it ignored De Smet's suggestion that Blanchet be appointed its bishop, recommending a Jesuit vicar chosen from three candidates, one of whom was De Smet himself. The well-known Jesuit would likely have been appointed if the Jesuit Father General had not convinced the Pope that no exception to Jesuit rules should be made in this case. De Smet happened to be in Rome at just this time, and without doubt, he influenced his superior to oppose the appointment.[35]

The Holy See's decision became public in 1843, issued in three briefs: one designated the Oregon territory as a vicariate apostolic; a second named

Francis Blanchet bishop of Philadelphia *in partibus infidelium* (continuing the tradition of naming vicariates after ancient dioceses no longer in existence); and the third placed the new vicariate under the supervision of the bishop of Quebec. It took many months for the unwelcome news to reach Blanchet.[36]

After a vigorous campaign in Europe, De Smet at last embarked for Oregon in January, 1844, bringing with him five more Jesuits for the Oregon missions. Six Belgian Sisters of Notre Dame de Namur in the party were destined to be the first nuns in Oregon. If De Smet and his group sought the crown of martyrdom, they almost received it on this trip. The voyage around Cape Horn almost seemed cursed: provisions spoiled; eventually, rationing curtailed the already poor food supply; rats were rampant, and so vicious that they gnawed through a beam of the ship, almost causing a wreck. Hurricanes buffeted the vessel; when they landed in Chile, they were shaken by earthquakes. Crossing the Columbia bar was a nightmare, only to be followed by meeting unfamiliar and seemingly savage Indians at Astoria and dysentery at Fort Vancouver.[37]

Since De Smet's voyage took many months, Blanchet was led to believe that the party was traveling overland across the plains. Impatient at the delay of De Smet's recruits, and a firm believer that schools were essential to maintain and spread the faith, Blanchet could wait no longer for educational facilities after he received a donation from a wealthy Canadian, Joseph Larocque, in 1843. Preempting the facility intended for the nuns accompanying De Smet, Blanchet established St. Joseph's College (actually an elementary school) in St. Paul. Nearby, a replacement school began to rise for the anticipated sisters.[38]

Surprise and relief spread through the Oregon Catholic community when De Smet suddenly arrived by canoe at Fort Vancouver August 4, ahead of the reinforcements who arrived a day later on the ship *Indefatigable*. After the group arrived at the French Prairie settlement, the Jesuits selected land near the St. Paul mission claim and built a residence named for St. Francis Xavier on the lake they called St. Ignatius (now Connor's Lake), where De Smet envisioned a Jesuit headquarters for their western operations. Once the new mission was functioning, De Smet left for the Rocky Mountain missions and St. Louis.[39]

After quickly recovering from their exhausting trip, the Notre Dame nuns opened St. Mary's, or *Ste. Marie de Willamette*, the first academy for girls in Oregon, in their partially completed building. A dearth of carpenters forced the nuns to do most of the interior finishing. In supporting the school, many parents could pay only in produce or the loan of cows, so the nuns made do without money. These women, mostly raised in sheltered, middle-class comfort, spent so much time in heavy labor to support the school that their health suffered, along with their English lessons. By the second year, their agricultural enterprises began to produce income, especially from the sale of butter. As the population continued to grow, the sisters started another school in Oregon City (where Blanchet had moved in 1848), with classes held in Blanchet's residence, the "episcopal palace." Later, they expanded into an additional house on the riverbank. In spite of the many problems the sisters had to overcome, visitors to Oregon expressed amazement at the high quality of the Catholic schools.[40]

During Advent 1842, John McLoughlin platted a town on his claim at Willamette Falls that he named Oregon City. At McLoughlin's invitation, Blanchet selected land for a church and school in the new town. He was so impressed with the spectacular growth of Oregon City that in late February 1844 he personally traveled to the Cowlitz Mission to escort Demers south to a new assignment as pastor of St. John's parish in Oregon City. Demers celebrated his first Mass there in a rented building on March 3. The town continued burgeoning and in 1845 Demers started constructing a church.[41]

John McLoughlin, the most prominent layman in the region, retired from the Hudson's Bay Company in 1846 and moved to Oregon City, adding to the already bustling parish. Several notable converts entered the Church there about the same time: Dr. J.E. Long, secretary of the Provisional Government, and his wife; Peter H. Burnett, first chief justice of Oregon, later to become first governor of California; and others, including Walter Pomeroy, architect and builder of the Oregon City church.[42]

Father Demers, reporting on the 1846 dedication of St. John's Church at Oregon City—destined to become the cathedral—noted with pride: "My church at Oregon City was consecrated on February 8th last, Septuagesima Sunday, before a large gathering of Protestant Americans.... Little by little their prejudices are disappearing and they end up with taking a liking for a religion hitherto despised, even hated, because it was unknown."

Oregon City became so important that Blanchet moved the seat of his see there just before Christmas, 1848, living in a rented house because the sisters were using the rectory. He sincerely regretted leaving the friendly French Canadian atmosphere of St. Paul, his first home in Oregon, but the area was inconvenient and unlikely to grow.[43]

Oregon's first cathedral, St. John's, in Oregon City. *Archives of the Archdiocese of Portland*

New parishes were established in the Willamette Valley as church membership slowly increased. Besides the newly founded parish in Oregon City, Louis Vercruysse, S.J., one of De Smet's missionaries, settled at St. Louis on French Prairie in 1844 to establish a parish there. Blanchet himself said the first Mass in the Portland area on August 15, 1844, although the population was too small to justify even a chapel.[44]

＊＝＝＊

As church growth gathered momentum from the infusion of new personnel, the 1843 papal briefs, establishing the vicariate in the Oregon territory and naming Francis Blanchet vicar apostolic, at last arrived at St. Paul on November 4, 1844. He did not desire the honor, leaving the document unopened for several days. Blanchet protested both the recommendation and the appointment; even before the unsettling news of the appointment reached him, he had written to Bishop Pierre Turgeon, Signay's coadjutor: "I am already old and *hors d'age;* my powers diminish.... So, for the greater glory of God and in the interest of my fellow creatures, would it not be better that I live as I am, rather than to try to rise to become a useless and even a blamable leader." Bishop Signay urged Blanchet to take on the burden, and in the end he reluctantly accepted, deciding to go to Quebec for his consecration and from there to Europe and Rome. Blanchet sent his first pastoral letter on November 22, 1844, informing his people of the establishment of the vicariate apostolic. Before departing, he appointed Father Demers his vicar general, with orders to supervise an extensive construction program. Taking the first transportation available, Blanchet left on a ship bound circuitously for Canada by way of the Sandwich Islands and England.[45]

Five months after leaving the Columbia region, Bishop-elect Blanchet stopped briefly in England, then sailed on to Montreal. Disappointed in his intention to have his consecration in Quebec, he returned to Montreal, where, on July 25, 1845, Francis Norbert Blanchet was consecrated as vicar apostolic *in partibus Drasa,* changed from *Philadelphia* because of possible confusion. Bishop Ignatius Bourget of Montreal officiated at the impressive ceremony. After six weeks in Canada, Blanchet left for Europe to secure assistance, both financial and human, for his new diocese. Landing in England, he paid his mission's surprisingly massive debts, and found he was immediately poverty-stricken. His London agent had dropped digits in looking over his finances—instead of £39, his debt was £1397. By the time Blanchet reached Paris, he was so poor that he welcomed rescue by an Irish priest; this charitable man paid for Blanchet's trip to Belgium, where he recruited more Sisters of Notre Dame at Namur.[46]

On his arrival in Rome early in 1846, Blanchet met prominent churchmen who inspired him to launch an ambitious plan for his vicariate. He presented to the Sacred Congregation of the Propagation of the Faith (*Propaganda Fide*), the agency that supervised the American church, a grandly optimistic, sixty-page *Mémoire.* This document detailed the status and needs of the Oregon church, stressing the necessity for an ecclesiastical province in the Oregon country, with an archdiocese and seven subordinate dioceses, three of which demanded immediate activation.[47]

In vain, the skeptical secretary of *Propaganda Fide* protested that the cardinals would not discuss the plan without prior consideration by the Provincial Council of Baltimore, but Blanchet and his advisors insisted that the plan be considered immediately. Presenting only his own unsupported recommendations, Blanchet proposed himself as archbishop of Oregon City, with Modeste Demers as bishop of Vancouver Island. Blanchet declared his younger brother Augustine "eminently fit" to be bishop of Walla Walla.

Blanchet's vision of the Church in the Northwest was virtually a prophecy of what eventually developed, although much farther in the future than he had anticipated. While waiting for a final decision, the fledgling bishop traveled all over Europe, making known his needs. During a stop in Paris, Blanchet learned that Pope Pius IX, just elected after the sudden death of Pope Gregory XVI, had ratified virtually his entire audacious plan for Oregon, with the exception of several requests for episcopal control of religious communities. The vicariate became a province, the second in the United States; and the briefs of July 24, 1846, established the dioceses of Oregon City, Walla Walla, and Vancouver Island, and approved all his personnel assignments. To clarify matters, the new province was to be a part of the Church in the United States, since by terms of the treaty of June 16, 1846, the Oregon Country became American territory.[48]

American bishops were aghast when they heard the news; they had not been consulted by either Blanchet or Rome. The archbishop of Baltimore wrote to the bishop of Philadelphia for confirmation: "Should you know anything about the affair, and be at liberty to communicate it, you will much oblige me by letting me know whether there is any foundation for the report. The measure bears on its face a character of extravagance, but the source through which I have heard it is one of high respectability." Unabashed, Blanchet wrote to Archbishop Samuel Eccleston of Baltimore in September, 1846, confirming the existence of the new province and explaining his non-attendance at the 1846 Baltimore Council, which was intended to be the First United States Plenary Council.[49]

Rumors from Canada brought news of Blanchet's success to Oregon; Demers reported to Canada that they didn't know whether to laugh or cry. Calling the plan a monstrosity, the chagrined Demers lamented, "Humanly speaking this plan will make us the laughing stock of the Protestants in the country." When news of his appointment as bishop arrived in May, 1847, the thunderstruck priest at first thought of rejecting the honor and returning to Canada, but he resigned himself to the inevitable.[50]

During his sojourn in Europe, Blanchet realized that accumulated debts of at least 194,000 francs in the diocese would curtail development until they were paid. He immediately notified Father Demers that building should be postponed, but the warning arrived too late. During Blanchet's travels, the remaining missionaries had maintained or even increased their strenuous pace. The priest's house at Oregon City was finished, work on the church there went ahead, and a church was finally completed at Fort Vancouver. St. Paul also witnessed a flurry of activity, with an addition to St. Mary's school and a long-planned church constructed of bricks made at the site. In place of

1846 St. Paul Church, St. Paul, Oregon (before 1900 tower remodeling). *Oregon Catholic Press*

the absent Blanchet, Demers officiated at the laying of the cornerstone for the church rising at St. Paul, which all believed would be the cathedral. On November 1, 1846, he dedicated that building, the first brick church in Oregon, still standing today. All the while, it appears that the Oregon workers were unaware of the momentous changes in the status of the diocese until as late as March, 1847.[51]

More successful in recruiting both money and personnel for his new archdiocese than he had hoped, the new Archbishop Blanchet discovered last-minute problems that delayed his departure from Europe. He may have been a bit too successful in recruiting, since he left behind a group of three Brothers of the Holy Cross and their priest companion, literally, on the docks at Brest, when an unexpectedly large group of Jesuits filled the accommodations on the ship. At last, with a prayer of thanks, Blanchet and his band of twenty-one missionaries set sail for Oregon on the *L'Eoile du Matin* in February 22, 1847. There were seven additional Sisters of Notre Dame, as well as eight priests in the company. The Jesuits sent three lay brothers; completing the group were deacons Bartholomew Delorme and John F. Jayol and unordained cleric, Toussaint Mesplie. Although the voyage took almost six months, it was not unpleasant, with Mass offered every day on an improvised altar built over the relics of four saints that Blanchet was bringing to Oregon.[52]

Everyone rejoiced when they arrived safely at the Willamette—even though the ship ran aground near the mouth of the Willamette and the sisters had to be rescued by boat. For Blanchet it was a triumphal return, but he went first to say Mass in the humble Oregon City church suddenly transformed, by his presence, into a cathedral. Crowds attended the new archbishop as he traveled on to St. Paul for even more solemn liturgical rites. For almost three months there was a whirlwind of Catholic events in Oregon. While officially, St. John's Church in Oregon City was the cathedral, the archbishop's throne remained at St. Paul, where all important ceremonies took place. Shortly after his return to Oregon, Blanchet administered confirmation there. On September 19, also at St. Paul, J.F. Jayol, one of the two newly arrived deacons, became the first man to be ordained in Oregon, followed shortly by ordination of the other deacon, Bartholomew Delorme. Oregon's first episcopal consecration took place at St. Paul on November 30, 1847, when Modeste Demers was consecrated as first bishop of Vancouver Island. The modest ceremony, with only Archbishop Blanchet officiating, was quite appropriate for a diocese devoid of both priests and money.[53]

In the meantime, Bishop A.M.A. Blanchet of Walla Walla, the archbishop's brother, was consecrated in Montreal in September, 1846. He traveled across the country with a group of Oblates of Mary Immaculate, who planned to open Indian missions in his new diocese. Enthusiastically, Bishop Blanchet went directly to Fort Walla Walla, arriving in September, 1847. His appearance aroused the disapproval of Marcus Whitman, whose Protestant mission was not far away. Undeterred, A.M.A. Blanchet and his vicar general, Father John B.A. Brouillet, established the mission of St. Anne among the Cayuse Indians on November 27 in an Indian house near the Umatilla River. For some time, the Indians in eastern Oregon had been restless and upset about illnesses and the influx of white settlers, for which they blamed Dr. Whitman particularly. Only two days after the founding of St. Anne's, the Indians' pent-up bitterness exploded in violence when a group of them descended on the Whitman mission and massacred the Whitmans and eight others. Father Brouillet, just starting his missionary work for the Diocese of Walla Walla, came upon the bloody scene at Waiilatpu the next day. He helped bury the dead, and as he left, his warning to Rev. Henry Spalding saved the Presbyterian minister's life. News of the murders reached Oregon City on December 8, 1847, and from the first there were ugly rumors that the Catholics had fomented the slaughter. Bishop Blanchet tried to calm both Indians and whites, but eventually authorities convinced him to leave the area because of Indian threats against his life and Father Brouillet's.[54]

Henry Spalding, whom Brouillet saved from death at the time of the Whitman Massacre, showed his ingratitude by spinning wild tales designed to discredit Catholics, particularly Brouillet and Bishop Blanchet. Spalding blamed Catholics for the massacre and credited Whitman with saving Oregon for the United States. With the aid of willing partisans, his tales created a myth that was successsfully refuted only in the early twentieth century. Shortly after the massacre, a petition to expel Catholic clergy from Oregon was introduced in the Territorial Legislature. Although it did not pass, it indicated the seething anti-Catholic sentiment in the new territory. The Cayuse Indians found guilty of participating in the Whitman Massacre were executed in Oregon City in 1850. Archbishop Blanchet responded to their request for a priest, baptizing them shortly before their hanging. His action demonstrated his Christian charity, but it reinforced the association of Catholics with the massacre. Attempts to discredit Catholics and blame them for the events at Waiilatpu included widespread lies, fabrications, and misrepresentations.[55]

In the Cayuse War that followed the Whitman massacre, Bishop A.M.A. Blanchet was forced to take shelter with his brother at St. Paul. Amid the uproar, the archbishop insisted on observing the proprieties, but the ceremony investing him with the pallium, the symbol of his episcopal authority, at St. Paul on February 13, 1848, must have been very quiet. None of the participants noted the event in his journal, probably because the first Oregon Provincial Council—indeed, the first strictly provincial council in the United States—overshadowed it. The thrifty archbishop took advantage of having his two suffragan bishops and most of the priests in attendance at St. Paul. The fact that the three bishops had been trained in Quebec produced a similarity of liturgical thought. Nevertheless, the jumble of cultures among the faithful made it difficult to establish standard church practices. Wisely, the council confined itself to submitting petitions and suggestions, as well as advising the establishment of a new Diocese of Nesqually for Bishop Blanchet and recommending a new bishop for the war-torn Walla Walla Diocese.[56]

Soon after the council ended, word reached Bishop A.M.A. Blanchet that Indians at The Dalles were eager for priests, so he sent the newly ordained Louis Rousseau to explore the possibility of establishing a mission there. When the Cayuse Indians asked that the missionaries return, Bishop Blanchet started back to his mission at Walla Walla, only to be detained at The Dalles by the superintendent of Indian affairs. He settled there temporarily, joining Rousseau in building a log church as headquarters for St. Peter's Mission.[57]

Demonstrating the stability of the Church's new province, Archbishop Blanchet published the decrees of the first Provincial Council in a circular in December, 1848. Demers was sent to Rome to deliver a report, but due to unsettled conditions in Europe, Pope Pius IX did not give his approval until 1850. While rejecting the archbishop's afterthought addition to the council *acta* that northern California become part of the Oregon archdiocese, Rome did establish the Diocese of Nesqually in what is now western Washington on May 31, 1850, in response to the council's request. It was a timely change, since unsettled conditions continued in eastern areas of the territory. A.M.A. Blanchet transferred to the new diocese, establishing the seat of his see at Fort Vancouver in October, 1850. The Diocese of Walla Walla and its attached districts returned to F.N. Blanchet's jurisdiction while Rome considered a course of action.[58]

In spite of their advanced years and the long trip, Francis and Augustine Blanchet attended the First Plenary Council of Baltimore in 1852. It was a command appearance, since Rome demanded action in response to the many complaints from Jesuit and Oblate superiors about treatment of their priests by both men. Completely exonerated by their fellow bishops, the brothers sought support from their colleagues for further changes in the boundaries of their respective dioceses. Rome responded by setting the boundaries of the Nesqually diocese to match those of the newly designated Washington Territory, established in 1853. The still-born Diocese of Walla Walla was at last suppressed, and over half of its territory became part of the Oregon City archdiocese.[59]

At the return of eastern Oregon to his responsibility, Archbishop Blanchet sought the reestablishment of St. Anne's mission on the Umatilla River (the buildings had been burned during the Indian wars), and in 1852 the Oblates successfully reactivated that ministry to the Indians. Blanchet could not forget the other Indians, whom he felt he had neglected, and he sent the youthful Father Toussaint Mesplie as missionary to other eastern Oregon tribes at the recently inherited St. Peter's Mission at The Dalles. This energetic and colorful priest evangelized the Indians in the area and served various military posts, at the same time ministering to the settlers.[60]

+≈≈+

As 1849 dawned, the future seemed bright with promise for both Church and territory. Congress passed the act establishing the Territory of Oregon on August 14, 1848. Territorial Governor Joseph Lane arrived in Oregon in 1849, marking the advent of a completely new government. Mere months before, news destined to threaten not only the future of the Church but also the incipient state as well roused the population to action—gold had been discovered in California! Initially no one recognized the implications of the hasty exodus of able-bodied men, and Blanchet sent Father Brouillet, temporarily assigned to the archdiocese, to California to raise money among the miners for the Oregon mission. As gold fever spread, a large contingent of French Prairie Catholics left for California; Blanchet even delegated Father Bartholomew Delorme to accompany the men as chaplain. At least forty men died of a fever shortly after arriving at the mining sites, leaving widows and orphans at St. Paul; Father Delorme himself narrowly escaped death.[61]

Around two-thirds of the male work force departed for the gold fields, leaving the women and children to survive on their own. Father Michael Accolti of the Jesuit Mission summed up the atmosphere: "Go where you will, people speak of nothing but gold. Old and young, women and children, lay-folk and ecclesiastics, all have on their lips only the word *gold*." The numerous negative results of the gold rush included the closure of St. Joseph's College in St. Paul, since parents could no longer pay and teachers left for the mines. Shortly thereafter, the Jesuits shut down their mission and withdrew to California.[62]

Bad news continued to beset Catholics. In 1852, the Notre Dame Sisters closed their St. Paul school completely and consolidated their efforts at Oregon City. By 1853, the sisters left Oregon City and the archdiocese. Every Catholic school was locked, and every religious community departed, casualties of gold fever. Other misfortunes included the burning of the log church at The Dalles in 1855, with loss of all records. Not long after that, the Yakima Indian War erupted; mission work suffered, especially at St. Anne's, where the entire mission was once again destroyed.[63]

Fortunately for the future of Oregon, Congress passed the Donation Land Law in 1850, luring thousands of Americans to Oregon with the offer of free land. However, through manipulations of Samuel Thurston, Oregon's territorial delegate, the act deprived John McLoughlin of his land at Oregon City, giving it to the Legislature for support of a university. Oregon City's development declined because the McLoughlin claim covered so much of the town, and land sales were suspended. The territorial capital moved to Salem, and newcomers avoided Oregon City. The parish there, once the most vital in the archdiocese, was dying like the town itself.[64]

While Oregon City withered, Portland was developing briskly. Only a few Catholics lived there, but young Father James Croke, newly arrived from Ireland, served the community and others along the Willamette from his post as assistant at the cathedral in Oregon City. In the fall of 1851, he began a subscription drive for a church in Portland, though the slim budget dictated purchase of a cheap, remote tract. Portland was growing so rapidly that Blanchet decided Croke should minister specifically to that city and the area surrounding it, starting in October, 1851, and by Christmas the sacristy of a church was completed. In February, 1852, Blanchet dedicated the church at Sixth and Davis, naming it for the Immaculate Conception. Portland's Catholic Church was not only out in the woods, it was out of harmony with the growth of the city. After a good deal of agitation from irritated parishioners, tired of scraping mud off their feet every time they went to church, the building was moved to a more convenient location at Third and Stark Streets.[65]

In spite of his duties in Portland, Croke found time in the summer of 1853 to travel extensively throughout the Willamette Valley and into southern Oregon, stopping at Jacksonville, the area near Marysville (now Corvallis), and Salem, celebrating the first Masses in these areas and searching for the scattered Catholics. He continued his summer missionary trips to serve the widely dispersed Catholics of western Oregon during his years in Portland.[66]

Financial problems caused by the loss of population to California and the over-zealous building program debt continued to burden Blanchet, coloring his remaining years. The archbishop made various attempts to deal with the problem. In 1855, he left on an extended fund-raising trip to South America, visiting Chile, Bolivia, and Peru, begging for donations to free the archdiocese of its debilitating financial embarrassment. After two years in South America, Blanchet returned to Portland in December, 1857, declaring, "My collection has been a complete success; the debt of my diocese will be paid and we shall have something left over."[67]

While he was gone, the Catholic population had begun to rebound from gold fever, and Blanchet responded with conservative expansion. One of his first acts was to appoint Patrick Mackin as pastor of Portland to replace Croke, who had gone to California for his health. In anticipation of further growth, he bought land at Fifth and Market for a school, though there was no immediate hope of teachers. Father Mackin found that Timothy Sullivan had land available on the east side of the Willamette next to the public cemetery, and he bought it for St. Mary's Cemetery, now the site of Central Catholic High School.[68]

Oregon's own gold rush in southern Oregon caught Blanchet's attention. Numerous Catholics congregated in the area, and Father Croke started fund raising in several communities during his summer visits. He was realistic: "The Catholics here are so few and in general so lukewarm that it requires some time for a priest to hunt them out, and even then it is not in one day that he can inspire them with the proper dispositions." In spite of growing infirmities, Blanchet himself rode to southern Oregon in the fall of 1858 on a missionary expedition to explore the possibilities for establishing Catholic institutions. It was a wonder that he arrived at all; his two-horse buggy turned over twice throwing him roughly to the ground. In spite of his bruises, he immediately founded a mission, with no church, in Roseburg, giving it the name of St. Stephen the Martyr. Going on to Jacksonville, Blanchet authorized construction of St. Joseph's Church there.[69]

Political maneuvering in Oregon and Congress delayed the admission of Oregon to the Union for ten years. On the eve of statehood for Oregon, the Catholic Church in the territory was taking tentative steps toward recovery. Even considering the reverses of the gold rush and Indian unrest, a great deal of progress had been made—progress that no one could have foreseen when the Columbia Mission was established. No one would have predicted that the untamed Oregon country to which Blanchet and Demers came in 1838 would become the second archdiocese in the United States.

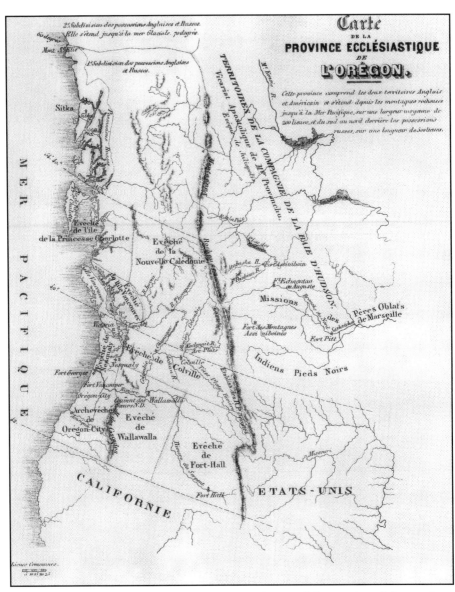

A French Canadian "Map of the Ecclesiastical Province of Oregon," showing the archdiocese of Oregon City and various dioceses in the Pacific Northwest. *Archives of the Archdiocese of Portland*

Chapter Two

The Awakening

T. VALENTINE'S DAY, February 14, 1859, was a momentous day for Oregonians. On that day Oregon finally joined the Union—after previously having voted against statehood three times. The same year proved significant in the history of Catholicism in Oregon as well, as it marked the arrival of a permanent foundation of nuns and the beginning of significant expansion in Oregon.

Seeing that his brother had rather easily secured Sisters of Providence from Canada for his diocese, Archbishop Blanchet himself departed for Montreal, just after the statehood celebrations, to search for nuns to teach in a new school planned for Portland. He went to the motherhouse of the relatively new community of Sisters of the Holy Names of Jesus and Mary, attracted by their main apostolate, the education of children. He garnered twelve intrepid volunteers to accompany him west. When they arrived in Portland on October 21, 1859, the Holy Names nuns found an unfurnished, dirty hovel, the Lownsdale House, awaiting them. Similar to their predecessors from Namur, the Holy Names sisters seemed to give cleanliness a far higher priority than did the archbishop! A pile of trunks provided an altar for their first Mass in Oregon, and Stephen J. McCormick, a prominent Portland Catholic, supplied supper.[1]

Despite the lack of preparations, on November 6 the nuns opened a new school for girls, St. Mary's Academy, starting with six students. Soon the archbishop cajoled them into accepting small boys as well. Within months, the sisters took charge of the parish school in Oregon City—again, specifically at Blanchet's request—but it closed when the cathedral was moved to Portland in 1862. Moving into the building in St. Paul left by the Sisters of Notre Dame, the Holy Names sisters also reopened that school in 1861. They were able to achieve more positive results in St. Paul than had their predecessors.[2]

Father Patrick Mackin, pastor of Immaculate Conception Church in Portland, decided that a Catholic school was needed to reach children closer to the city's population center and the parish church, since St. Mary's Academy was some distance away. He persuaded the Holy Names to rent part of a building near the church grounds, and they opened St. Joseph's Parochial School, known familiarly as the "City School." The small boys who had been attending St. Mary's transferred to the new school, and the sisters also enrolled the orphan boys who lived with them.[3]

Even with building additions and changes, St. Mary's Academy's student body outgrew its facilities. Fortuitously, Father Joseph Michaud, a Viatorian priest and architect, visited Portland and assisted in redesigning the building. Recycling parts of the original house, the builders moved one wing of the academy to a corner where it became a boys' orphanage. Two new wings, one with a chapel, were added to the original building, and the whole was topped by an octagonal tower and spire with a cross.[4]

Additional reinforcements arrived from Canada in 1863, including twelve more Holy Names nuns, accompanied by Mother Theresa, superior general. After a hasty visit to Salem, Theresa established Sacred Heart Academy there, virtually overnight. As she commented: "Though the number of Catholics is small, and some Protestants bitterly prejudiced…there is good to be done: several of the Protestants wish to confide their daughters to the Sisters' training, and the opening of a convent there will abate much of the existing prejudice against our Holy Faith." Negotiations for purchase of Masonic Hall were left to Father Leopold Dieleman, the pastor, who announced his success with a terse message, "All right, come." There were some difficulties in sweeping out the Masonic regalia, but the school was dedicated on August 22 and opened on September 7. Father Dieleman, a recent graduate of the American College in Louvain, a pastor as yet without a church, gave priority to establishing the nuns. The $300 he had gathered to build a church went instead to assist the sisters in paying their mounting debts.[5]

On the first day of school, eighty girls enrolled, only a few of them Catholics. It was far beyond the nuns' expectations; even so, they succumbed to insistent requests to open a school for small boys as well. In return for local Catholic support, the nuns' tiny chapel served the parish in Salem until a church was completed. Within a short time, the popular school was cramped for space. The Holy Names purchased six lots in Salem from Judge Reuben Boise in 1865; his sister grumbled, "If there is a fine locality in the city, the Catholics must have it." The spot became known as "Piety Hill," since the Catholic parish owned adjoining lots. However, the new building had to wait for several years, while an addition to the old Masonic Hall added more space. The new Sacred Heart Academy, destined to stand for 100 years, was built in 1871-73.[6]

Further expansion of the Holy Names' school system, motivated by the superior general's visit, took place when the nuns, persuaded by the pleas of Father Adolph Vermeersch in The Dalles, established St. Mary's Academy there in the fall of 1864. Ladies of the parish refurbished the former rectory, and provided $411.25 as an opening purse. Many eager patrons helped support the school until it was firmly established. By the end of the first year, there were 143 day students; within six years, enrollment was so large the building needed an addition.[7]

Once they saw the Holy Names school system growing, pastors vied with each other in appealing for schools. Father F.X. Blanchet's impeccable French Canadian credentials (and his status as the archbishop's nephew) may well have had priority over the realities of need when the Holy Names established St. Mary's Academy for girls in Jacksonville in 1865. The Holy Names in Jacksonville earned their place as genuine heroines in Oregon history when the town suffered a devastating smallpox epidemic in 1869. The nuns closed their school, and two sisters volunteered to nurse victims for the two months the disease raged. The sisters provided care in the homes of the victims, while Father Blanchet helped bury the dead. The grateful citizens publicly thanked the nuns for their unselfish service, which within two years claimed the life of one of them.[8]

⊹═══⊹

The Holy Names sisters incorporated in 1866, but they felt that they were losing vocations because candidates had to go to Canada for their novitiate. The archbishop requested permission from Rome to begin a novitiate in Portland. While the community waited for a response, acting on the archbishop's temporary permission, Jane Kelly, first graduate of Sacred Heart Academy in Salem, entered the congregation as the first postulant, receiving her habit from Father John Fierens on January 6, 1870. Apparently there were some technical problems with the permission. The Holy Names were getting quite anxious, in spite of Blanchet's reassurances and his nagging letters to Rome—since they already had several candidates. To everyone's relief, permission finally arrived on May 28, 1871.[9]

After eight years without opening a new school, the sisters accepted a challenge that seemed even less likely to succeed than the Jacksonville foundation when they opened Notre Dame Academy in Baker City in June, 1875. With only four students enrolled, the outlook was grim. There was already a strong anti-Catholic sentiment in eastern Oregon. But by the time the new building was ready in August, opposition from the community had turned to acceptance. As the only girls' school in a vast area, the academy flourished.[10]

For some time, Archbishop Blanchet had been worried about the education of older boys in Portland. As a result of his concern, the energetic John Fierens supervised construction of a school which rose with dizzying dispatch at Fourth and Mill in only three months in 1871. Suddenly, the problem of teachers arose. Blanchet decided that the parish at St. Paul would be least hurt without a pastor, so he appropriated Father Alphonse Glorieux to direct the school. St. Michael's College was an instant success, and it soon became necessary to add a wing and hire lay teachers. As the school grew, an old fire department building was moved to the spot to provide more space. When the old cathedral was demolished in 1878 in preparation for a new one, part of it was rebuilt at the school, becoming St. Michael's Chapel, a rather multipurpose center.[11]

Father John Francis Fierens
Pastor of Cathedral parish, 1862–1893
Oregon Catholic Press

In several towns Catholic schools sprang up in the 1870s. A Catholic elementary school opened in the Astoria Masonic Hall with a lay teacher in 1874, even before dedication of the church there. A school for boys started at Salem in 1878, again with a layman as teacher. Father Bertram Orth, unhappy at his assignment to Canyon City, seized the opportunity to start a school at that remote town, teaching it himself. In Baker City, Father Peter De Roo refused to be frustrated by lack of religious teachers for the boys of his parish and made plans to start his own community of religious brothers to teach in his intended boys' school.[12]

Although the Holy Names' rules directed that they confine their duties to education, they inevitably became custodians of the orphans of Portland; the first boarders at St. Mary's Academy were orphans. The work expanded to the point where two nuns devoted their time to this service. As soon as land was available, Mother Veronica constructed a larger home for the orphan boys in the separated and remodeled wing of the Lownsdale house. When St. Michael's College opened, the Holy Names surrendered the orphan boys to that institution and converted their empty building into St. Joseph's Orphanage for girls.[13]

The Catholic population in Portland, at least, had grown to the point that establishing lay organizations was feasible. A group of Catholic laymen established the Portland district chapter of St. Vincent De Paul Society, the first on the Pacific coast, in 1869, with Stephen McCormick as president, and Father Fierens as spiritual director. Their initial aim—to open an asylum for the poor, sick, and orphaned—was never realized. However, Blanchet had long been pleading with the Sisters of Charity of Providence, whom his brother had brought to Vancouver in 1856, to open a hospital in Portland, and he enlisted the De Paul Society in his campaign. In January, 1874, the Society opened a fund-raising drive; by July 19, officers went to Mother Joseph in Vancouver to offer land and $1,000 if the Providence Sisters would build a hospital in Portland. It is not clear if they realized they had made their offer on St. Vincent's feast day; Mother Joseph saw this as a sign of God's providence, and she could not refuse. The negotiations were completed within twenty-four hours.[14]

Unfortunately, full financing took much longer, but by the spring of 1875, the building was finished enough to permit the sisters to move in. Ironically, the first patient after officially opening (there were several patients before the dedication) was not a Catholic, but a Chinese laborer whose legs had been mangled in a barrel factory accident. After several months, he left the new hospital, minus a leg but alive and well. As virtually the only hospital in Oregon, St. Vincent's was a success from the beginning.[15]

Other Catholic societies began to flower, mainly in Portland. With so many Irish, it was not surprising that the Hibernian Benevolent Society was among the first to prosper. Then the United Irishmen of Portland sprang up, only to be supplanted by the Ancient Order of Hibernians in 1877. The Father Mathew Total Abstinence and Benevolent Society actively fought drinking. Although German Catholics in Portland were still small in number, they formed social groups similar to those of the Irish. Archbishop Blanchet personally recommended joining the Catholic Social Union. Reading was a popular activity, and organized Catholic groups provided appropriate reading materials. Among the most successful was the Catholic Library and Christian Doctrine Society, which made available reading material for catechizing children.[16]

In spite of its somewhat isolated situation, Oregon attracted Catholic visitors from other states. At Blanchet's invitation, Father James Bouchard, S.J., a Delaware Indian noted for his electrifying orations, expanded his unique apostolate from California mining camps to visit Portland in 1865. He came to preach the Jubilee proclaimed by Pope Pius IX; but Blanchet was quite likely also using him in a campaign to lure the Jesuits back to Oregon. Though the attempt to recall Jesuits failed, Father Bouchard was a resounding success. The Jesuit gave fiery sermons designed to encourage Catholics to proclaim their faith proudly. During his long career, the eloquent Father Bouchard visited Oregon at least twelve times, attracting converts on each trip.[17]

Just before his departure for the Vatican Council in 1869, Blanchet invited another noted preacher to come to Portland for a mission, Father F.X. Weninger, S.J. Austrian-born, Weninger had carved out a career as missionary to German-Americans. He had already concluded that most West Coast Catholics were Irish, so he was not surprised to find few Germans in the city. Weninger came to Oregon several more times, making memorable impressions each time, but no visit produced more long-lasting results than the first. Bouchard had already planted seeds of Catholic pride in the Portland congregation, but Weninger acted as the catalyst to bring them to bloom. During his mission, he stressed the importance of Catholic publications, and Portland Catholics suddenly felt the need not only to defend their faith but also to boast about it. What better way than through a newspaper? The archbishop was in Rome at the Vatican Council, but Father Fierens, the vicar general, felt confident that Blanchet would approve the project, so he gave it his full support. Both founding editors, H.L. Herman, a successful businessman, and J.F. Atkinson, a professional printer, had newspaper experience. They published the first issue of the *Catholic Sentinel* on February 5, 1870; Father Weninger received full credit for providing the inspiration. Defending the faith took priority in the editorial policy, but the editors featured local, national, and international news as well.[18]

While the *Catholic Sentinel* achieved great popularity with Catholics and gave them a new voice, financial problems threatened the infant publication. Within two years, Atkinson left the paper; two years later Stephen J. McCormick, Portland's Catholic renaissance man *par excellence*, took over as editor when Herman's health failed. While Herman and Atkinson had published a paper that defended the faith in the spirit of the Golden Rule, Stephen McCormick, a true fighting Irishman, defended the Church aggressively. No insult remained unanswered.[19]

After more than a year at the Vatican Council, Archbishop Blanchet returned to Oregon in December, 1870. He enthusiastically supported the

Catholic Sentinel, now almost a year old. Simultaneously with his return, the U.S. government promulgated a policy concerning treatment of the Indians; the archbishop initially greeted it eagerly. He wrote to the commissioner of Indian affairs, commenting on President Grant's new Indian policy, which was "...more liberal and more just too, in dividing the care of the Indian reservations to the various religious denominations." Religious groups already ministering to specific tribes were to administer those reservations under what became known as Grant's Peace Policy. Within days, Blanchet enthusiastically submitted the names of agents for the five Oregon agencies where priests had been ministering for years. While Catholics claimed about forty reservations in various states under the policy guidelines, they were only given eight; 80,000 Indians went from Catholic to Protestant religious influence.[20]

Archbishop Blanchet and his brother led the fight to return reservations to Catholic control, often in strident and undiplomatic tones. In Oregon, first the Grand Ronde and eventually the Umatilla reservations were placed under Catholic administration. The Blanchets believed that only a national Catholic effort would influence the government, since the Catholics had been denied the official federal representatives enjoyed by other churches. Eventually, they settled on Father J.B.A. Brouillet as their personal representative for Indian affairs in Washington, D.C. As vicar general of the Nesqually diocese, he was already in the national capital on business for his diocese. His realization of the need for a focal point for the Catholic Indian effort contributed to the establishment of a formal agency. For Archbishop Blanchet, the *Catholic Sentinel* was a mighty tool in his battle with the government over Indian problems. The editors printed anything he wanted, including some of his rather saucy letters to the commissioner of Indian affairs; the paper became a leader in the Catholic fight for Indian rights.[21]

On the Grand Ronde reservation, Father Adrien Croquet had given long and loving service since October 1860. The first Oregon missionary from the recently founded American College at Louvain, Belgium, he arrived in Oregon in 1859 on the same ship as the sisters of the Holy Names. Croquet also served the Siletz reservation, some of the north coast communities, and Catholics in St. Patrick's Mission in Yamhill and Polk counties. He built his first church, St. Patrick's, at Muddy Valley, soon followed by St. Michael the Archangel on the Grand Ronde reservation. Later the McMinnville town founder gave land for a church, and St. James Church was dedicated there in 1876, eventually replacing St. Patrick's.[22]

For ten years Archbishop Blanchet urged the Holy Names sisters to start a school on the Grand Ronde reservation, but they could not extend their forces that far. Indeed, the reservation agent opposed them, saying that all they taught were literary courses and dogma, nothing practical or intellectual. By 1874, federally supported Catholic schools operated on selected reservations under contract to the Bureau of Catholic Indian Missions. Taking advantage of one of the few good points of the Peace Policy (as well as the presence of a Catholic agent), the Holy Names established a day school on the reservation, in spite of less than ideal conditions—they had to pay for the school building through payroll deductions.[23]

Father Adolph Vermeersch, newly arrived from Belgium, reopened St. Anne's Mission of the Cayuse, destroyed during the Indian wars, at a new site on the Umatilla Reservation in 1865. When that reservation came under Catholic control in 1871, he served the Indians as both pastor and schoolteacher. Supervising just the two agencies under his control was a major problem for Archbishop Blanchet, as he continued his tilt with both the federal and Catholic Indian agencies. Politics actually played a major part in the appointment of agency employees, even if the Church nominated them. Patrick Sinnott, well known as a loyal party man, led a fairly secure existence at Grand Ronde, but Narcisse Cornoyer at Umatilla encountered problems with both church and state. In 1874, when a contentious disagreement erupted between Father Bertram Orth, missionary at the Umatilla reservation, and Cornoyer, the Catholic-appointed agent, Blanchet peremptorily transferred a surprised and disappointed Orth to Canyon City, while removing the agent. He drew Brouillet's ire when he suddenly reversed himself and requested Cornoyer's reinstatement—directly from the commissioner of Indian affairs—without telling the Catholic Indian agency, which was dutifully trying to secure the replacement's appointment. General Charles Ewing, director of the Catholic Indian agency, was offended, and Brouillet wrote from Washington, D.C., "At least you could have asked him to do it in your name, and he wouldn't have been compromised." While the temporary agent's approval languished in Congress, late in January, 1875, Father Louis Conrardy, another Belgian missionary, arrived at his new mission of St. Anne's on the Umatilla reservation. At the time his English was so poor that Blanchet despaired of giving him any parish; but Conrardy, with seemingly boundless zeal, plunged into missionary work with the Indians under his care. When Cornoyer returned, the two men worked amicably together.[24]

+≈+

The Catholic community of the new State of Oregon was markedly different from that which had welcomed Francis Blanchet as its religious leader only twenty years before. Emigration, the gold rush, and the famine in Ireland contributed to a change from a French Canadian culture to one dominated by Irish Americans. Even before the seat of the archdiocese moved to Oregon City, St. Paul itself had been transformed from a French Canadian town to a largely Irish-American community. Besides the loss of many French Canadian men from fever during the gold rush, a large contingent of French Canadians from St. Paul moved to the Walla Walla area around 1860; some of them attempted to enter the American mainstream by abandoning their culture or changing their names. After the gold rush, many successful Irish miners came to Oregon, buying farms from the French Canadians or settling in or near Portland. Typically, the Irish located near each other and close to a Catholic church.[25]

Slightly later than the Irish, German Catholics, driven from their homeland because of political conditions, militarism, and economic problems, began to arrive in Oregon. They seemed determined to establish a new Germany in the United States, adamantly demanding German language in the sacraments. With the arrival of six Dutch (German-speaking) Catholic families from Wisconsin in the Centreville area (now Verboort) in 1875, the archbishop faced the problem of finding German-speaking priests. Fortunately, in September, 1875, Father William A. Verboort, son of one of the families, came to provide spiritual leadership and a name for the colony, the first totally Catholic settlement in Oregon. Father Verboort's sudden death in 1876 forced the archbishop, grudgingly, to supply another German-speaking priest for the community.[26]

In the Tigard area, another group of Germans who had been attending services at the cathedral in Portland began to travel to Verboort for the German sermons. There was a disagreement, and the Tualatin Germans built a small church of their own, St. Mary Magdalene, in the Tigard area in 1878. Difficulties in finding a priest eventually sent them back to Verboort or Portland. However, they supported the work of St. Joseph's German Society in Portland, which began collecting funds for a German national church in 1878. While they waited, the Germans met in rooms at the cathedral and later in the chapel on the grounds of St. Michael's College.[27]

After their inoculation with Catholic spirit by Fathers Bouchard and Weninger, Catholic lay people, particularly in Portland, proudly took their place in the community. During Blanchet's time, the leading layman in Oregon after John McLoughlin, was, without doubt, Stephen J. McCormick. Brother of Father Patrick McCormick, who had come to Oregon with Blanchet in 1847, Stephen McCormick leaped into Portland's social and religious life with vigor after arriving in 1851. There was literally no Catholic event or organization in which he was not involved. His successful publishing/bookstore business produced many early Oregon books, including Blanchet's own publications. McCormick founded several newspapers, published the first Portland city directories, and originated the first monthly magazine on the West Coast, *Oregon Monthly Magazine*. He was involved in local politics, helped found the St. Vincent de Paul Society in Portland, led the campaign for a Catholic hospital and headed the fund-raising drive for a new cathedral. In his spare time he devoted himself to his large family. He is best remembered as the outspoken and aggressive editor of the *Catholic Sentinel* during its early years.[28]

Other laymen didn't necessarily have McCormick's energy or opportunities, but they, too, carried out—if more quietly—their religious and civic duties. Blanchet visited southern Oregon in the fall of 1867, spending a good deal of time in both Roseburg and Jacksonville. The visit created a statewide sensation when a number of prominent people joined the Church during his visit. In Jacksonville's St. Joseph's Church, Colonel William T'Vault made his profession of faith on October 13 and was baptized there the next day. At his home near Roseburg, General Joseph Lane, first territorial governor of Oregon, was received into the Church. Lafayette Lane, the general's adult son, along with several other well-known residents, joined the Church during the same visit. Blanchet revisited the area in 1869, again creating a small flurry of sensation when he baptized Mrs. Joseph Lane and two of her grandchildren.[29]

Perhaps no period in the Oregon church's history produced as many extraordinary priests, each spreading the gospel in his own unique way, as did Blanchet's waning years. Father Toussaint Mesplie, for example, was notoriously inept at administration and usually at odds with the archbishop; but his outgoing personality attracted many to the church. One irritation, among many, occurred when Blanchet learned that Mesplie had wangled an appointment as one of the first U.S. Army chaplains in 1872. Blanchet accused him of being tricked by the government into deserting the Indians' cause: "Don't be so simple as to let yourself be caught in this trap. To save our Indians, that is our glory and our title.... Catholic soldiers will always find priests; not so our poor Indians." Nonetheless, Mesplie continued his work, serving in the Oregon City archdiocese and as first priest in the newly founded Vicariate of Idaho, as well as ministering to the military, the Indians, and the white population of eastern Oregon and Idaho in his free-wheeling style.[30]

Priests from the American College in Louvain, Belgium, had begun arriving in 1859. The first to come, Adrien Croquet, so impressed Blanchet with his zeal and piety that he immediately sent for more Belgians. Countless tales illustrate Croquet's charity, selfless life-style, and obvious sanctity. In truth, Croquet fully merited the title of "Saint of Oregon." John Fierens, a classmate of Croquet's and the second Belgian from Louvain to come to Oregon, met the archbishop's high standards so well that Blanchet prematurely named him as his successor in 1862. After his transfer to Portland, Fierens became the archbishop's strong right arm, and eventually virtual administrator of the archdiocese in Blanchet's later years. Leopold Dieleman, another energetic Louvain alumnus who was incredibly skilled at collecting money to build churches, was rewarded by transfer to another parish each time he finished a new building. Like many of his Belgian colleagues, he had frequent misunderstandings with Blanchet; he once complained that he had never been able to please the archbishop in anything. Yet he labored tirelessly in cheerless and lonely missions all over the state.[31]

Blanchet faced many difficulties with priests throughout his administration. Possibly the most wrenching problem was the case of J.F. Jayol, the first priest ordained in Oregon, who decided to join the Oblates. The archbishop opposed his decision, threatening the young man with suspension. Their disagreement required the intervention of Rome, which reproved the archbishop for his actions, and submitted the case to the first Baltimore Plenary Council.

Interpersonal difficulties surfaced as early as 1850, when J.B.A. Brouillet of Nesqually Diocese submitted a ten-page report to the Congregation of the Propagation of the Faith, suggesting that Blanchet be removed. About the same time, all the priests in Oregon sent a similar petition asking for a replacement, citing poor administration, debt, lack of means for the clergy, poor treatment, and lack of progress for the church. They recommended that neither of his suffragan bishops should replace him, since the Church should be American not Canadian. Relations between the archbishop and his priests only grew worse as the archbishop aged.[32]

Continually through his tenure, Blanchet faced problems securing priests within his archdiocese. It was an uphill battle from the beginning, further complicated by the negative reputations garnered by both Blanchet brothers. Europe was the main source of clergy in the nineteenth century, because there were few seminaries in the United States. All Hallows College was founded in Dublin in 1842 to provide diocesan priests for English-speaking countries all over the world. Blanchet would have preferred priests from French Canada, but he recognized that his parishioners were now mainly Irish, or American, so English language skills were essential. In 1849 Blanchet wrote to All Hallows, telling of expected immigration, and his letter was published in their *Annals*. Perhaps deterred by the hard life described in De Smet's *Oregon Missions*, there was no scramble among All Hallows students to go to Oregon. Miles O'Reilly, the first All Hallows graduate to reach Oregon, told

Blanchet that few wanted to come to the wild Northwest—it vied with China in undesirability.[33]

The American College at Louvain, Belgium, was the more important source of priests for Oregon. Started in 1858 by American churchmen, the college trained European priests and seminarians to serve as missionaries in the United States. About the time that All Hallows dropped Oregon, Blanchet began to support the American College, possibly because of his intense satisfaction with his first Belgian graduates, Adrien Croquet and John Fierens. From 1859 until the late nineteenth century, a steady stream of Belgian-trained priests came to Oregon. By 1875, two-thirds of the Oregon clergy were Belgian or Belgian-educated. Multilingual, they could handle almost any language spoken in Oregon—except, all too frequently, English. The Belgians had access to financial means independent of the archbishop, and to his consternation, they frequently built facilities without his approval. Zealous, vigorous, and stubborn, they worked strenuously for the development of the Church in Oregon. Blanchet, on the other hand, remembering the dark days after the gold rush, tried to hold back expansion to avoid debt. Many of his letters to parish priests contained the standard order, "Do not make debts."[34]

The European religious came with a culture, clerical and social, far different from that of the archbishop's French Canada. Blanchet's warm, friendly relations with the French Canadian Holy Names sisters contrasted sharply with his prickly disagreements with the Belgian Notre Dame sisters, who left the archdiocese without even telling Blanchet farewell. His relations with the independent Belgian priests, often stationed far enough away from his presence that he could not readily control them, were similarly difficult. Blanchet felt at home and secure with the French Canadians, and he visited St. Paul as frequently as possible, declaring that the atmosphere reminded him of his home in Quebec. Most of the Belgian and Irish priests maintained frosty relations with the archbishop, not an unusual situation in the American church at the time.[35]

⊬══⊬

By the 1860s, everyone realized that Portland had become the state's leading city, as Oregon City continued to languish. Motivated by the 1861 Willamette River flood, which destroyed several settlements near Oregon City and caused great damage, Blanchet moved to Portland in August, 1862, before asking *Propaganda*'s permission a month later. Only in January, 1863, did he ask that Immaculate Conception church in Portland become his cathedral. Actually, Rome received the letters reasonably soon after the move; approval was quick, although Pope Pius IX objected to moving without permission. Before the decision left Rome, *Propaganda* realized that there was already a Diocese of Portland, in Maine, and asked Blanchet what he intended to do about the name. He did not plan a name change, since he thought there might be further population shifts that would require him to move *again*, perhaps to Salem, which was now the state capital. With all the misunderstanding, it was not until November, 1863, that Rome approved the move, with more acid comments that Blanchet acted incorrectly when he moved on his own judgment; the letter actually authorizing the move wasn't sent until 1864.[36]

In Portland, Blanchet appointed himself pastor of Immaculate Conception church to save money, reducing the pastor, Father Mackin, to assistant, but with the duties of pastor. Their disagreement simmered while Blanchet secretly tried to secure an Irish Jesuit. Failing that, he assigned the dissatisfied Mackin to Jacksonville, and recalled John Fierens, whose welcome was exceptionally warm. Fierens remained pastor at the cathedral for thirty years and was the driving force behind every Catholic activity in Portland. Father Mackin, however, refused to go to Jacksonville, and for a year he suffered under suspension. When he finally apologized, the archbishop rewarded him with transfer to the penitential town of Canyon City.[37]

Even after several enlargements, the cathedral was still too small for the growing parish. The congregation set up a Catholic Building Society, headed by the indefatigable Stephen McCormick, to gather funds for a new cathedral. Although the group worked hard, the campaign failed. Fierens, recognizing burnout long before the term was invented, dropped the project for six years.

The second cathedral in Portland, 1878–1893.
Archives of the Archdiocese of Portland

In March 1878, using surprise to galvanize a revived building project, Fierens startled his congregation by announcing the opening of a new drive for a cathedral. As he had hoped, his enthusiasm infected the congregation, and this crusade was on its way with a flying start. Never one to loiter, Fierens celebrated the last Mass in the old cathedral on May 19, 1878; the next day the dismantling began. During the early phases of construction, services were held in the "city

school" next door; by March 1879, the first Mass was said in the only finished part of the new cathedral: the basement. The Gothic structure was es-
timated to cost around $100,000, borrowed at high interest. Adding the sac-
risty of the old cathedral to the existing school, the building became known
as "St. Mary's Hall" and later "Bishop's House," while housing many activities and organizations—but not the archbishop, who had a separate residence
on the block.[38]

┼══╡┼

Although the California gold rush was history, Oregon and Idaho experienced mini-rushes that required spiritual ministration to miners, many of
whom were Irish. In 1861 Father John Fierens had become the first resident
pastor of the mushrooming mining town of Jacksonville, taking over St.
Joseph's Church built by Father Croke. The priest who made that community his life work was Father F.X. Blanchet, the archbishop's nephew. After his
difficulty over Father Mackin's refusal to move to Jacksonville, the archbishop
commandeered his newly arrived and still pliable nephew for the post. Obviously in his element, Father Blanchet remained for a quarter of a century.
Under his ministry St. Joseph's parish gave birth to a whole family of missions, including St. Patrick's at Allen Gulch (1864), Roseburg (1868), and
Eagle Point (1878).[39]

New churches rose as the Catholic population expanded and finances
permitted. East Portland was growing rapidly, and crossing the river by ferry
inconvenienced Catholics of the area. St. Francis of Assisi Church there was
ready for occupancy late in 1875, but lack of funds held up dedication for
almost a year. Milwaukie had a church as early as 1864, but it did not become
a parish until 1911. Almost ten years after organizing efforts started, Salem
Catholics witnessed the dedication of the church of St. John the Evangelist
in 1864. In closing the services, Blanchet disconcerted everyone by announcing Dieleman's transfer to Canyon City. The priest considered it an unde-
served and punitive reprimand for building the church. Several attempts to
build a mission at Astoria failed before the successful foundation of St.
Michael's Mission in 1874, with significant contributions from the soldiers
at Fort Stevens. When the church was built, it was named St. Mary Star of
the Sea. A growing Catholic population of English, French, and German
speakers caused division of the St. Louis parish, requiring founding of St.
Gervase and Protase in 1875 at Gervais.[40]

As the Indian reservation system developed and the Indians of eastern
Oregon gradually ceased their resistance, the long-suppressed work of

evangelizing eastern Oregon could continue. The Dalles grew into a thriving settlement, so the congregation replaced the small church, already their second church there, in 1862. Although Toussaint Mesplie had visited Canyon City as early as 1862, it was not until a shocked Leopold Dieleman found himself there in 1864 that there was a regular pastor at the mining settlement. With zeal and energy, he began construction immediately, and St. Andrew's Church was dedicated within the year. It was Mesplie who celebrated the first Mass in the Baker City area, in 1862 at Auburn; he bought a building for a church, where services were sporadic and infrequent. Again it was Dieleman who followed him as resident pastor in Baker City in 1871, quickly building St. Francis de Sales church, where the first services were held in October, 1871. The parish and its several missions encompassed almost the whole of the current Diocese of Baker, so the pastor was often on the road visiting Catholics and saying Mass in private homes, cut off from contact with fellow priests for months at a time.[41]

The Second Plenary Council of the American bishops met in Baltimore October 7–21, 1866. Both Blanchet brothers attended, for travel across the country was improving rapidly. At the opening ceremonies, Archbishop Blanchet celebrated the Requiem Mass for deceased bishops. To provide spiritual services to miners pouring into Idaho, the brothers Blanchet pleaded for establishment of a vicariate apostolic for Idaho, which the council approved.[42]

On July 18, 1869, Archbishop Blanchet celebrated the golden anniversary of his ordination with appropriate ceremonies. He had already received a call to Rome to attend the Vatican Council; and with his vicar general, Bartholomew Delorme, already in Europe, he appointed Fierens vicar general and administrator during his absence. On the whole, Blanchet played no important part in the council, but he helped shorten the proceedings by giving up his turn to speak in favor of infallibility. In spite of summer heat and the Franco-Prussian War, Blanchet stayed on until the council adjourned, sending home a pastoral letter from the Flammarian Gates. Both Blanchet and Demers were still in Rome when the temporal power of the papacy was overthrown.[43]

Once more it was a gold rush that jolted Blanchet to attention in the southern Idaho area. Originally Idaho had been part of the Walla Walla diocese, but it returned to Blanchet's administration in 1850 with the territory of the eventually suppressed Walla Walla diocese, while in 1853 all of Washington, northern Idaho and western Montana became part of the Diocese of Nesqually. Until 1860, most of Idaho's inhabitants were Indians, and the Jesuits cared for them. However, virtually no other missionary work went on until 1863, when Blanchet realized that thousands of miners, many of them

Irish Catholics from California mines, were pouring into the Boise Basin. The population swelled alarmingly, and Blanchet sent Father Mesplie from eastern Oregon in the summer of that year; in the fall, he dispatched Father Poulin from Corvallis to provide Catholic services in the vast area of southern Idaho. The priests performed incredible feats of travel and building, though they often found their churches destroyed by accidental fires almost as soon as they were built.[44]

Based on the phenomenal growth of white population in Idaho, the Blanchets had secured support for a vicariate apostolic in the Idaho area. Rome approved and, relying on the archbishop's emphatic recommendation, appointed Father Louis Lootens of the San Francisco diocese as vicar apostolic. No sooner had the poor man taken his position than the gold rush and the Idaho economy collapsed, and the population of Idaho dropped as rapidly as it had ballooned. Churches were empty, money was unavailable, and debts were crushing. In despair, Lootens asked Blanchet to take Idaho back. Blanchet responded with a letter to *Propaganda Fide* excoriating Lootens for mismanagement, and for lack of prudence, judgment, and courage. When the broken Lootens finally resigned, the Idaho region again became Francis Blanchet's burden. After unsuccessful efforts to find another vicar or suppress the vicariate, Blanchet appointed Mesplie as temporary administrator in 1876. Otherwise, Blanchet took little notice of the area except to order a collection to pay the debts.[45]

Death began claiming the hardy old missionaries who laid the foundation for the church in the Northwest. Bishop Demers of Vancouver Island, who had come to Oregon with Blanchet in 1838, died in 1871. Charles John Seghers, a young Belgian priest whose health was so poor he was almost rejected for the post, replaced Demers in 1873. Peter De Smet died in 1873, decades after his last brief visit to the Northwest. Though he was not a pioneer, Julian De Craene, the young and popular pastor at Salem, was the first priest to die in Oregon, in 1873.[46]

The strenuous life Archbishop Blanchet had lived as a missionary began to take its toll; after Demers's death, he visibly declined. A leg ailment made travel very difficult, his hearing deteriorated, his memory was undependable, his eyesight was poor. Never on friendly terms with many of his priests, he became more cranky and parsimonious as he aged. He had never really recovered from the financial crisis during the gold rush, and he had become obsessive about debt. Decision-making, never his strong point, became even more difficult, and he attempted to put the onus of administration on his council. Still, he insisted on total command, often initiating sudden, overly ambitious projects of his own, to the confusion of everyone. Yet, even in his old age he retained the rigid religious discipline of his seminary days, and he continued in the austere life-style to which he had grown accustomed.[47]

Recurring spells of poor health and limited physical mobility convinced Blanchet that he should resign, as early as 1862, naming Fierens as his replacement; but the Holy See ignored him. In 1876 he again tried to resign, but Pope Pius IX suggested that he continue in office, with the assistance of a coadjutor. Blanchet announced his recommendations for that assistant in 1877, but the appointment process went very slowly and ignored Blanchet's first candidates. *Propaganda* approved Charles John Seghers, bishop of Vancouver Island, as coadjutor in May 1878, followed within the week by official papal designation.[48]

As his long service to the Church drew to a close, Blanchet's friends and enemies saw two different men. Inflexible, difficult, and stern—devoted, pious, and humble—all described Francis Blanchet. The Holy Names sisters remembered his devotion, his fatherly counsels, and the happy times he spent with them. The French Canadians at St. Paul recalled his love of music, his saintliness, his kindness. His opponents recalled his fretful nature that dwelt on criticism and perceived injustices. Father John Roothaan, Jesuit Father General, gave his assessment of Francis Blanchet:

> He is indeed a very pious man, but one very much under the sway of imagination, who indulges a good deal in theory and weighs less the practical side of things. Hence, he is unsteady and changeful and often hesitates considerably. Of such character does this excellent man appear to be not only in my own opinion but in that of other persons here and these of the highest standing.…

Blanchet had feared coming to Oregon, to a mission he knew might be beyond his powers, but he had obeyed his superiors and heroically did the best he could. In spite of differing opinions on his personality, Blanchet's achievements were prodigious, if only for his creation of the second archdiocese in the United States from virtually nothing.[49]

Charles John Seghers (1839–1886)
Archbishop of Oregon City (1880–1884)
Oregon Catholic Press

Chapter Three
Restless Prelate

HARLES JOHN SEGHERS heartily deplored his nomination as titular bishop of Emesa, coadjutor with right of succession to the archbishop of Oregon City. He received the news on his return from a soul-stirring missionary visit to Alaska. In a letter to his uncle the young bishop lamented: "If God wishes me to become Archbishop of Oregon, I bow in submission. But, oh, what it costs me to leave this diocese, my priests, and my dear people!" Only his steely discipline and unwavering belief in obedience to superiors induced him to leave the Diocese of Vancouver Island and come, most reluctantly and with several postponements, to Portland on July 1, 1879.[1]

Born in Ghent, Belgium, December 26, 1839, Seghers came from an economically secure family cursed with tuberculosis. By the time Charles came to North America in 1863, he was the last surviving member of his immediate family, and his health was precarious. He spent most of his early years in Victoria as Bishop Demers's secretary, while he yearned to be in the field, facing the rigors and challenges of missionary work among the Indians.[2]

By the time of the Vatican Council in 1870, his health had deteriorated to the point that the doctors suggested he go with Bishop Demers to pay his relatives a final visit and enjoy the Italian climate. On their return to Victoria after the council, both men fell ill, Demers with an eventually fatal stroke and Seghers with lung hemorrhages. In his dying letter to Cardinal Barnabo, prefect of *Propaganda* in Rome, Bishop Demers begged for a special blessing from Pope Pius IX for Seghers, who was likewise thought to be on his deathbed.[3]

In fact, Seghers's infirmity almost prevented his being named successor to Demers; however, during the months while arguments about splitting the diocese dragged on, he recovered his health completely. Once installed as bishop of Vancouver Island at the age of thirty-three, Seghers simply ignored his illness; almost immediately he set off on a strenuous tour of his diocese. Although Seghers always credited Pope Pius's blessing as the source of his cure from tuberculosis, the outdoor life he pursued after becoming bishop most certainly contributed to his well being; he never suffered serious illness again. Like a freed bird, he fled from the bishop's residence in Victoria and into the long-denied missionary activity he had come to Vancouver Island to pursue. It was no wonder that he did not want to leave the people and the diocese he loved; he dreaded being trapped at a desk in Oregon.[4]

Young, charming, and outgoing, Seghers was a definite contrast to the aged Blanchet. The tall, slender Belgian was a voracious reader and classical scholar; a remarkable linguist, he spoke English gracefully, along with several European languages and Indian dialects. Blanchet assumed that Rome would quickly accept his resignation, but no word came. The old man may not have relished the thought of having his successor watch over his shoulder, for within two weeks of Seghers's arrival, Blanchet sent his coadjutor on a visit throughout the entire archdiocese.[5]

For many years, the infirm Blanchet had been physically unable to go far beyond Portland, so an episcopal visit was long overdue, especially in eastern parts of the diocese. In spite of his extensive travels in early Oregon, there were still many settlements that neither he nor any priest had ever visited, including Idaho and western Montana, inherited when Bishop Lootens of the Idaho vicariate resigned. Seghers's trip also provided a prime opportunity to meet the priests and lay people he would soon, it was hoped, be serving as archbishop.

Setting off on a steamer to The Dalles, Seghers began what would eventually extend into a sixteen-month tour. In eastern Oregon and the Vicariate of Idaho, Seghers concentrated on visiting the various Indian missions. He traveled into eastern Montana to administer the sacraments, with the permission of the vicar apostolic of Nebraska, in whose diocese this territory lay. Often celebrating the first Mass in the places he stayed, occasionally speaking to a totally Protestant audience, Seghers preached in homes, public buildings, lodges, hotels, or hovels. While he rode horseback for most of the trip, he did not refuse unusual methods of transportation—hand-operated railcars, supply wagons, stagecoaches, and shank's mare, if necessary. Sometimes alone, often with traveling companions, Seghers participated in all the chores at the daily encampments, doing the cooking or gathering firewood. He admitted to a friend: "...I have been called to do a lot of things about which I never dreamed."[6]

All along the way, Seghers won the praise of Catholics and Protestants alike. His appealing personality and his interesting and well-delivered sermons and lectures attracted entertainment-starved settlers. Not only was he getting to know the people of his new archdiocese, but they and their neighbors were also getting to know their prospective archbishop. Some of the antagonism toward Catholics, produced in part by Blanchet's abrasive style, began to dissolve in the warmth of Charles Seghers's gracious manner. Father Joseph Cataldo of the Jesuit missions accompanied Seghers on part of the lengthy trip. He marveled at Seghers's eagerness both to travel and to lecture without tiring. Seghers explained, "When I preach, I rest from horsebacking, and when on horseback, I rest from preaching."[7]

Having covered as much of the eastern area as possible, he turned his attention to settlements in the Willamette Valley, southern Oregon, and the coastal towns. Aside from Lent in 1880, Seghers was on the road until November of that year. Blanchet was so feeble by then that Seghers was somewhat precipitously forced to take over administration of the archdiocese. The next month, Pope Leo XIII finally accepted Blanchet's resignation because of age and poor health—but the papal letter did not arrive until late January 1881. A month later, Blanchet submitted his final pastoral letter, read to the cathedral congregation, and moved to St. Vincent's Hospital. With his retirement, the pioneer period of the Catholic Church in Oregon ended.[8]

✦

The first bishops in the Pacific Northwest had all been French Canadians, who, naturally, attempted to form local religious practices along familiar lines. This tended to leave the Church in Oregon somewhat out of step with the rest of the American Church. The second bishops were all Belgians; indeed, Charles Seghers replaced two of the founding bishops, first Modeste Demers, then Francis Blanchet. The Belgians tended to be more individualistic than the French Canadians, and each developed his diocese differently. Seghers was not at all sure he liked Americans at first. Americans' concept of absolute freedom disgusted him, and he believed it was incompatible with Catholicism. Yet, on his tours, he met a wide section of the western American public, and he found they were good people, even likeable. They surprised him by liking and respecting him as well. In the end, he applied for American citizenship, but he never completely trusted American values.[9]

Blanchet had devoted much time to the Indians early in his mission, but the influx of white Catholic immigrants forced him to concentrate his limited forces on their needs, resulting in neglect of the Indians. To the consternation of many white citizens, particularly in the eastern areas of the archdiocese, the new archbishop also spent what seemed inordinate amounts of time with the Indians. Seghers took pains to visit all the Indian missions, a practice he continued annually.

The Peace Policy, which Blanchet once supported, was not successful, and Seghers soon faced the problems head on. On his first visit to the Umatilla reservation, Seghers met with the Indians, who were being pressured to take their land in severalty (individual plots of land) by the Slater bill pending in Congress. Lack of provision in the proposed law for meeting the religious and educational needs of the Indians concerned Seghers, and he encouraged the Indians to request land for a church and school.[10]

The Indian commissioner closed the day school taught by the Umatilla missionary, Father Conrardy, because the Indian children were continually absent on hunting or food-gathering trips. Conrardy and Seghers, with the cooperation of Richard Fay, the Umatilla agent, immediately began a campaign to build a boarding school, which they hoped would keep the children from roaming. Certain Umatilla Indians and local white citizens complained to the commissioner of Indian affairs, demanding a secular school. Army Lt. Melvil Wilkinson was closely involved with them because of a need for students at his new Indian school at Forest Grove, and Umatilla was one of the reservations where he hoped to gather students. As plans for the Umatilla boarding school developed, Wilkinson suddenly appeared, demanding ten of the best students. Fay and Conrardy objected; they would soon have their own school ready—but away the children went, with government approval. Seghers was outraged about the incident, especially since Wilkinson's school was overtly Protestant, and Catholic children were among those taken. He could not understand why Father Brouillet, now director of the Bureau of Catholic Indian Missions, could not stop Wilkinson. In spite of this setback, slowly the boarding school at Umatilla took shape, and the search for teaching sisters became frantic.[11]

After several unsatisfactory years at the Grand Ronde Reservation, the Holy Names sisters left their school in 1880. Brouillet begged Abbot Alexius Edelbrock, O.S.B., of St. John's Abbey in Collegeville, Minnesota, to encourage the nearby Benedictine nuns to take over the Oregon school. In the spring of 1881, Mother Scholastica Kerst, O.S.B., from St. Benedict's Convent in Minnesota, accompanied four sisters to Oregon to reopen the Grand Ronde Reservation school. To honor the nuns' arrival, Seghers asked agent Patrick Sinnott to start a new church on the reservation, for which the archbishop would provide the money. The mother superior visited the Umatilla reservation as well, viewing it in the first blush of spring; she enthusiastically accepted the school planned there. She was so impressed that she encouraged Abbot Alexius to consider establishing a college in Oregon.[12]

Unaware of the primitive conditions on both reservations, Seghers optimistically counted on more Benedictines coming to staff Umatilla. He wrote Abbot Alexius again, prodding him to send priests and brothers to work with the nuns proposed for Umatilla: "Here on the West Coast there is a wide field for the activity of the Benedictine Order to accomplish much for the cause of religion. I hope you will pay us a visit to look at the country and select a place for a monastery." No answer came, so later that year he wrote again, shrewdly mentioning that another group of Benedictines was scouting the Oregon area. Almost immediately, the chapter at St. John's decided to accept the archbishop's offer, if they could work out satisfactory conditions.[13]

Abbot Alexius himself and Father Edward Ginther, O.S.B., came to Oregon in October, 1881. Alexius was recovering from a recent operation to alleviate a serious throat condition, and Oregon's winter dampness only contributed to his general grumpiness. The cold rain continued to pour down as the abbot arrived at the reservation. He was appalled by the sisters' living conditions, and he blamed Seghers for misleading Mother Scholastica and Brouillet for his method of carrying out the contract. Alexius pondered the lack of Catholic population in Oregon, the surfeit of Catholic academies, the impoverished Benedictines at Grand Ronde, and, of course, the rain. "It has rained every day we were here, in fact, it has rained here almost daily since *the beginning of September....* Everything is wet.... Besides being wet and damp, it is also *cold.*" He could not understand why Seghers wanted the Benedictines at all, and he soon concluded that it was far too early for a foundation in the state. Having once reached that decision, the abbot and his companion left so quickly that they neglected to say goodbye to Seghers. Their departure coincided with the publication of the Slater bill provisions, which promised land for an industrial school at Umatilla. The St. John's Benedictines decided against coming, and Alexius influenced Mother Scholastica to recall the unhappy nuns at Grand Ronde and to renounce her agreement to take Umatilla. Seghers and his priests scrambled frantically to find replacements, but other communities could not supply teachers.[14]

In spite of rejection by one monastery, Seghers still held the interest of the Benedictines he had used as bait to lure Abbot Alexius to Oregon. Fathers Adelhelm Odermatt, O.S.B., and Nicholas Frei, O.S.B., came from Conception Abbey near Maryville, Missouri, in the summer of 1881, at the invitation of William P. Olwell, a former Missouri parishioner, now happily settled in southern Oregon. Early in the history of Engelberg's American branch, the two founding monks, Fathers Adelhelm and Frowin Conrad, prior and later abbot at Conception, discovered that their personalities and widely different conceptions of monastic life were incompatible. Eventually, their estrangement was so complete that Engelberg's abbot, Anselm Villiger, gave Father Adelhelm permission to search for a site for another American foundation when Conception became an independent abbey. By the time that Adelhelm wrote, Seghers was already negotiating with the Minnesota Benedictines, but he was sure the state could support two communities. He urged Father Adelhelm to come and choose the best place.[15]

While the two monks looked at several other places on the trip west, Adelhelm, at least, favored Oregon. Just as they arrived in Portland, Seghers asked them to take over the Jacksonville parish temporarily. The monks enjoyed the hospitality and blandishments of the southern Oregon Catholics and seriously considered a foundation there. Seghers, however, had seen what he thought would be an ideal spot for a monastery when he visited the town of Fillmore to dedicate a church while the two Benedictines were in the south. Many of the town's residents were German-speaking families; Mathias Butsch, donor of the lumber for the church, was the natural leader and organizer. Rumors that German-speaking Benedictines were looking for a monastery site excited Butsch, and he pointed out to Seghers the old Indian sacred ground, Tapalamaho, as a perfect spot for a monastery. As soon as the two monks returned, Seghers sent them to look at the butte and urged them to become temporary pastors of Gervais and its missions at Fillmore and Sublimity. Adelhelm was as delighted with the spot as Seghers, and it took little persuasion for him to accept the archbishop's offer—just temporarily, of course. He didn't want to make a firm commitment to Oregon until he had permission from the abbot at Engelberg, although this intrepid monk wasn't always so careful to get permission for his enterprises. Adelhelm noted that the rectory in Gervais had space that could easily be adapted for use as a monastery. With this in mind, and bearing Seghers's charge to find sisters in Missouri for the Indians at Grand Ronde, Adelhelm set off for the East and Switzerland.[16]

In Missouri he persuaded the Mother Superior to send three sisters west as soon as possible, and by July 1882, they were at work on the Grand Ronde reservation. Then he set off for Switzerland to get permission for the Oregon foundation he envisioned and to recruit personnel. A most successful entrepreneur for the development of what he viewed as a New Engelberg, Adelhelm returned to Gervais in October, 1882, with a crowd of Benedictines, including priests, sisters, brothers, and students.[17]

Hard work by the people of Gervais notwithstanding, St. Scholastica's convent was not quite ready for the nuns when they arrived; some of them were housed in a leaky former saloon, and others joined the Missouri Benedictines at Grand Ronde. Mother Bernardine Wachter, the prioress, had spent some time in Adelhelm's parish in Missouri. During the various difficulties there, the two became partisans, and no doubt their friendship made securing nuns for Oregon much easier for Adelhelm. The troupe included three nuns from the St. Andrew's Convent in Sarnen, Switzerland, which was strictly enclosed; however, they found themselves drawn into all activities of the hectic missionary establishment, including service at the Grand Ronde reservation. In 1883 the temporarily consolidated Benedictine nuns opened St. Scholastica's Academy in Gervais and started a novitiate. The next year, the Sarnen sisters moved to Washington, eventually establishing their motherhouse at Cottonwood, Idaho.[18]

Both Seghers and Adelhelm worried that land speculators might inflate beyond their means the price of the butte so reminiscent of the land around Engelberg Abbey, so Adelhelm appointed Louis Schwab to take options on the land as his agent. The community began gathering money for a monastery, and before Adelhelm's departure for Switzerland, the subscription drive had netted $2,500 and a cow, calf, and steer. Still short of the necessary cash when he returned, Adelhelm borrowed heavily, speculating with the archbishop's support and approval, and bought what was then called Graves's Butte, as well as over 1,800 additional acres. At the request of the Benedictines, officials changed the name of the town to Mt. Angel, the anglicized form of Engelberg. In midsummer of 1884, the first Benedictine monastery and church in the western United States was blessed at Mt. Angel, without the presence of three men whose efforts had virtually willed it into being. Seghers was in Rome at a special meeting of American archbishops; Mathias Butsch and Louis Schwab had died. That same summer, the entire monastic community moved from Gervais to the new institution at Mt. Angel.[19]

Now that Grand Ronde's school was staffed, there was still the looming problem of teachers for Umatilla. When the Benedictines could spare no one, Brouillet finally found teachers among an informal and hastily assembled group of Sisters of Mercy who had originally applied to teach at Grand Ronde. Just when the future looked promising for Umatilla, rumors reached Seghers that the Catholic agent would soon be removed. Richard Fay, probably the most vigorous and efficient of early Umatilla Reservation agents, roused the enmity of the local populace by starting an Indian police force. Worse yet, he enforced the government regulations against encroaching on the reservation—finding, among other things, that part of the town of Pendleton was built on reservation land. Seghers urged Brouillet in

Washington to use his influence to keep Fay as agent. Just to hedge his bets, however, he suggested Bart Coffey of Salem, if the government was determined to remove Fay. Eventually, Richard Fay was removed, just after the boarding school opened, staffed by the Sisters of Mercy, hired as government employees under their secular names. Since the Peace Policy ended officially (but without public announcement) in 1882, a Protestant and loyal party man, Edward Sommerville, replaced Fay.[20]

Seghers did not realize that the Peace Policy no longer existed, and rejection of his candidate rankled. He bitterly raged to Brouillet: "It is also an act of injustice towards me: in the appointment of agents to agencies of Catholic reservations, my venerable predecessor was always consulted; I have, in this matter, been completely ignored." Actually, it was politics that decided the matter. Seghers's misunderstanding of the politics of the situation led him to unreasonable expectations of what Brouillet could accomplish. An exasperated Brouillet tried to explain the facts:

> You take a wrong view of your right in the manner of nominating Indian agents in your diocese. Even when the Peace Policy was in vogue, the right of nomination to the Secretary did not belong to the Bishop, but to their representative before the Department of the Interior—to wit: Gen. Charles Ewing, Catholic Commissioner—your right in this particular only went to recommend to him the name of a person to be by him submitted to the Secretary. But as the Peace Policy is now done away with, the Church has no right to expect to be even consulted in filling the positions of Indian Agents.[21]

Agent Sommerville and Louis Conrardy, the reservation priest, were completely incompatible. They argued over many things, especially how much land could be given for a new church; yet they did agree that the old schoolhouse/chapel was far too small for the congregation. Eventually, with Seghers's and Brouillet's intervention, the Catholic Indians received 80 acres for a mission, and Conrardy supervised building of St. Joseph's Church near the new boarding school. Conrardy's overly zealous style and outspoken support for Indian rights won him no friends with local residents, although many of the Cayuse Indians were devoted to him.[22]

Aside from the Indian schools, the Holy Names still controlled Catholic education in Oregon. In 1879 the archdiocese boasted 68 sisters, 9 academies for girls, St. Michael's College in Portland for boys, 4 parochial schools for boys, and 2 parochial schools for girls. This situation did not impress Seghers as much as it had his predecessor. Catholic education was perhaps second only to Indian missions on his agenda. Even before the American bishops began a serious campaign for Catholic schools, Seghers pressured Oregon Catholics on this point, becoming progressively more severe. However, in spite of his extensive efforts to secure teaching communities, the school system grew far more slowly than he would have liked. The Holy Names strengthened their schools, and numbers of students increased, but they did not have the resources to expand to more towns.[23]

Even the establishment of a Benedictine academy in Gervais was balanced by the closure of St. Joseph's College for boys in Baker City. De Roo's hopes of founding a teaching community of brothers died with closure of the college and departure of his novices, but his hopes for his school did not. De Roo continued his efforts, eventually securing Clerics of St. Viator from Canada. They arrived in 1883 and reopened St. Joseph's College, offering a practical, business-oriented program, rather different from the mathematics and philosophy classes at nearby Notre Dame Academy. For some years, De Roo and the Holy Names superiors had disagreed about administration of Notre Dame Academy, so when Seghers asked for suggestions to take to the upcoming Baltimore Council, De Roo composed a pamphlet airing his views on parochial schools. A copy sent to the Holy Names motherhouse in Canada created a furor, which was communicated to Seghers on his return from a pre-Council conference in Rome. Seghers devised a baroque scheme to solve the problem by closing Notre Dame Academy abruptly and devastating Father De Roo.[24]

In the summer of 1882, Seghers undertook a second visitation of the entire archdiocese, hardly a burden for a man who loved to travel. Again he went first to visit the Indian missions, then to the extreme eastern edge of the archdiocese and beyond into eastern Montana. This time, he capped his series of firsts by saying Mass in the Cleopatra Mine near Lion City, Montana. Asked to justify these excursions into remote areas with few Catholics, Seghers responded that such visits were essential to rekindle faith that could easily die without contact with a priest.[25]

On his first tour of Montana, Seghers's positive impressions of Catholics there inspired him to recommend that the whole state become a vicariate, independent from the financially shaky Idaho vicariate. Eventually, in 1883, after prolonged negotiations, Rome united the two vicariates in Montana within the state's boundaries, leaving it in the Oregon City province. The Oregon province nominated Bishop John Brondel of Vancouver Island for the post of vicar apostolic. That move still left them in a quandary: they then had to find nominees to replace Brondel in Canada. Nevertheless, John Brondel became vicar apostolic of Montana, while retaining the title of bishop of Vancouver Island; but he was required to live in Montana at a site

of his own choice. Father John Jonckau of Vancouver Island became coadjutor to Brondel, to succeed him as bishop of Vancouver Island when Brondel
formally became bishop of the city he chose as seat of his see, which proved
to be Helena. The Vicariate of Idaho was thus reduced to what became the
State of Idaho, and the Archdiocese of Oregon City at last coincided with the
State of Oregon.[26]

Against the recommendations of the Oregon province bishops, Rome
decided to appoint a new vicar apostolic for the Idaho area in 1884. Archbishop Seghers had mixed feelings about the move; he wanted to be free of
the problem, yet he was far from certain that the area could be self-supporting. The energetic director of St. Michael's College, Alphonse Glorieux, took
on what all thought would be a hopeless job as vicar apostolic of Idaho. He
proved them all wrong. Everyone, especially Seghers, heaved a sigh of relief
at this solution to the long-standing problems of Idaho and Montana. Everyone, that is, but John Jonckau, who seemed determined to upset the game of
episcopal musical chairs; he adamantly refused to accept the position as
bishop of Vancouver Island under any circumstances.[27]

Financial problems continued to grow, and the primary problem was the
overwhelming debt on the Portland cathedral, where services were still being
held in the basement. Support for that project evaporated as quickly as it had
arisen; when Seghers took over the finances, there was a formidable debt. Significant amounts due on the Astoria and McMinnville churches and subsi-
dization for some priests added to the debt. The archbishop himself went
door to door in Portland collecting money for the cathedral debt, and he donated money from lectures to alleviate the financial problems. In desperation,
he begged for more money from the Society for the Propagation of the
Faith.[28]

During one of Seghers's frequent trips to visit the Indian missions, Archbishop Blanchet, whose health had steadily declined after retirement, quietly
died on June 18, 1883. Seghers arrived in Portland just in time to escort his
body to the cathedral. At the Solemn Requiem Mass several days later,
Seghers eulogized his predecessor: "He was the first missionary, the apostle of
Oregon; he is to Oregon what St. Boniface was to Germany, what St. Augustine was to England, what St. Patrick was to Ireland!" In accord with the wish
Blanchet had expressed when he blessed the cemetery at St. Paul, the founding archbishop of Oregon was buried there.[29]

If the Belgian-educated priests, now almost two-thirds of the Oregon
clergy, had any thoughts that a fellow American College alumnus would give
them special favors, they were quickly disabused. In general, the Belgian
priests, including Seghers, shared a number of traits: zeal, piety, energy, and

perseverance. Unfortunately, Seghers's priorities for priestly virtues were the ones that he himself exhibited as a priest in Victoria: obedience (even when it made him unhappy), a spirit of submission, and prudence. Encouragement of those qualities was somewhat neglected during the Blanchet years, and many Oregon priests were proudly and happily independent.[30]

During his first visitation of the archdiocese, Seghers carefully evaluated his clergy, which resulted in a number of personnel shifts and departures. He tried to bring order to the often chaotic business affairs of missions. All priests were ordered to incur no debts, but they had heard that so often from Blanchet that it no longer registered. Seghers tried to establish good business methods and bookkeeping, but he had to be on watch constantly to put the damper on the wilder schemes of his inventive and zealous clergy.

Some of the lay people during Seghers's administration were every bit as troublesome as his priests. That arch-layman, Stephen McCormick, suddenly resigned his editorship of the *Catholic Sentinel*, and moved to San Francisco. Henry L. Herman resumed the editorship; he was more aggressive than before, but he soon sold the paper to another active Catholic, Captain J.R. Wiley, who had organized the Portland police force. The ever-present financial problems of the paper continued, and in 1884 a four-month suspension resulted. It was at this time that Father Verhaag, truant from Canyon City, joined Father Patrick Gibney and Captain Wiley to keep the paper alive.[31]

The fact that the agents at the two formerly Catholic Indian reservations were among the prominent Catholic laymen during the Seghers administration reflected the archbishop's priorities. Richard Fay had taught at St. Michael's College and worked for the *Catholic Sentinel* before becoming clerk at the Umatilla Reservation. When Narcisse Cornoyer left the post of agent there, Fay became the energetic but besieged administrator. After great success in the California mines, Patrick Sinnott, agent at the Grand Ronde agency, started his life in Oregon with his brother Nicholas by purchasing the Columbia Hotel in Portland. When the city needed the land, he managed to wangle an appointment at Grand Ronde; his nimble political actions kept him in office for sixteen years, perhaps a record for any Oregon Indian agent.[32]

Inheriting a heavy debt and a laity of generally meager means put a damper on the physical development of the Church in Seghers's era, although several Willamette Valley towns registered some progress. Blanchet, with money loaned by Father Fierens but delivered by Seghers in October, 1880, purchased the old United Brethren church at Sublimity, where the famous Wright brothers' father had once ministered. The German-speaking settlers at Fillmore Station (the post office was officially Roy, later Mt. Angel) built their own church because travel to Gervais proved difficult, and Seghers dedicated it on August 21, 1881. The archbishop had the satisfaction of blessing St. Rose of Lima mission in Monroe in the spring of 1883. Later that year Seghers dedicated the small wooden building perched on a bluff overlooking the Coquille River at Bandon to St. Mary, Refuge of Sinners. Just before his departure for meetings in Rome in September 1883, Seghers laid the cornerstone for St. Lawrence church in a new south Portland parish. In eastern Oregon, on a trip to bless the new Union County mission church at Island City, Seghers celebrated the first Solemn Pontifical Mass in eastern Oregon—significantly, not in Island City but at the Umatilla Reservation during a mission for the Indians.[33]

Several parishes required replacements for pioneer structures. St. Louis parishioners built a new church in 1880 to replace the original, lost in a fire. St. Francis, the East Portland church, still carried considerable debt in 1880 when a ferocious wind storm hit, lifting the main section into the air and smashing it to the ground in pieces moments later. Father Verhaag waded into the debris to save the Blessed Sacrament, but his beloved church was virtually destroyed. A replacement was dedicated the next year. In 1883 a new church at Verboort inspired a name change to Visitation of the Blessed Virgin Mary, while the second church on the Grand Ronde Reservation was again dedicated to St. Michael.[34]

Even while Seghers was absent, new churches and institutions received blessings. In 1884 Fierens dedicated Cedar Mill's St. Anthony's church, started in 1878. Prior Adelhelm performed similar ceremonies for the new monastery and the second church at Mt. Angel, where the Catholic population was rapidly growing. St. Lawrence Church in Portland was dedicated by Bishop Junger of Nesqually.[35]

Charitable organizations continued their quiet work during the Seghers administration, but he had more pressing interests. The Sisters of Providence expanded their successful hospital system to Astoria soon after his arrival, converting the Arragoni Hotel into St. Mary's Hospital. Shortly after that, Seghers blessed the chapel in the new wing at St. Vincent's Hospital in Portland. The St. Ann's Society, founded at St. Vincent's Hospital, possibly to replace the nearly moribund St. Vincent De Paul Society, sought to help the poor and needy; Seghers was nominal supervisor.[36]

Seghers much preferred missionary work to attending meetings, but he recognized early on that with the change of archbishops, he ought to gather his clergy together. To save expenses for his priests, he called for a trio of events: a diocesan synod, on August 10–11, 1881, followed by his reception of the pallium, August 15, and capped by the Second Oregon Provincial

Council, August 16–18. Just before his departure for Rome in September 1883, Seghers held a second synod, but its main purpose was to enable the priests to bid him farewell. Thoroughly exhausted, the priests went home to recuperate for the next council, announced for 1884. However, this was not to be. In the fall of 1883, Seghers went to Rome with other American archbishops for preliminary discussions in preparation for the Third Plenary Council of American Bishops, scheduled for Baltimore in 1884.[37]

The problem of finding a bishop for his old see, Vancouver Island, concerned Seghers urgently during his stay in Rome. His friend, Father John Jonckau, continued to refuse to take the position, vacant since Bishop Brondel moved to the new Vicariate of Montana. For some time Seghers had been considering his lot as archbishop of Oregon City. This was no longer prime missionary territory, except for the Indians; he began thinking of his days on Vancouver Island and Alaska. More and more it seemed that Charles Seghers was hearing the call of the wild. Not long after his arrival in Rome, he wrote to Cardinal Simeoni, prefect of *Propaganda Fide*, suggesting a solution to the standoff:

> Therefore, considering on the one hand that it will not be easy to find a bishop fitted for the Diocese of Vancouver Island who will also take charge of Alaska; and believing, on the other hand, that the appointment of another archbishop for Oregon City would not present any great difficulty; and moved, moreover, by the love which I have always had for Vancouver Island, I beg of Your Eminence, as a grace and a favor, that the Holy See may grant me the liberty of resigning the metropolitan church of Oregon City, and returning to the Diocese of Vancouver Island.

Pope Leo XIII recognized that not only would Seghers's offer solve the Vancouver Island problem but it would also make the volunteer himself very happy. After the meeting Seghers announced with joy, "I am going back to Alaska." Oregonians had to wait for verification until the middle of April, when the *Catholic Sentinel* officially confirmed it. Many agreed with the editor's lament: "It is a great sacrifice, the greatest sacrifice we have made for many years past."[38]

Arriving at the Baltimore Council soon after the announcement of the change of status, Seghers went beyond mere attendance. In one of a series of supplementary evening lectures he spoke about Indian missions—significantly, not Oregon's but those of Vancouver Island and Alaska. Among the bishops sharing the lectern in the series was the bishop of Savannah, William Gross, who spoke about Negro missions. There is no indication that the two men had other than formal contact, but even before Seghers returned to

Oregon, William Gross was named third archbishop of Oregon City, on February 15, 1885. By the time Seghers reached Portland after almost two years' absence, there was only time for brief good-byes before he left for Victoria. In his farewell sermon on March 29, 1885, he begged forgiveness for any offenses, pardoning his enemies at the same time. He said, "It was as a friend that I lashed and wounded." On March 31 he sailed for Victoria and his heart's desire, the missions of Alaska.[39]

So ended one of the shortest terms of an Oregon archbishop. While Seghers came to Oregon most reluctantly and returned to his first diocese at the earliest opportunity, his conscientious administrative work helped the Oregon Church to move out of the isolation of the pioneer era and paved the way for full entry into the American Church. The Seghers era had a "temporary" air, as if somehow everyone knew he would not stay, possibly because of his many long absences from the cathedral. In spite of this and the seemingly insoluble financial constraints, there was progress: the founding of the Diocese of Helena, restoration of the Idaho vicariate, the foundation of the Benedictines, the first and second diocesan synods, the second provincial council. Whatever he might have accomplished if he had traveled less, Charles John Seghers's restless missionary spirit could not be contained in such a settled climate.

Chapter Four
Man of Many Firsts

S CHARLES SEGHERS prepared to leave Oregon, discouraged by its lack of missionary challenge, William Hickley Gross was debating whether he should take on that same archdiocese, which appeared to him to be teeming with challenges: "I say that it is in reality not a promotion, but a yielding of a better for a harder and more toilsome position. It strikes me that therefore I can in all good conscience accept the position and transfer to Oregon."[1]

William Gross, who was born in Baltimore, Maryland, June 12, 1837, of an Alsatian-Irish family, aspired to be a priest from his youth. He attended St. Charles College, a minor seminary for diocesan priests, but the president dissuaded him from continuing. Only temporarily discouraged, he entered the Redemptorist novitiate in 1857. His seminary education and ordination in 1863 were accelerated by the Civil War and the fear that the seminarians would be drafted into the army. At the end of hostilities, the young priest assumed his role as part of a Redemptorist mission band, preaching to parish missions in the East and South. While serving as superior of Our Lady of Perpetual Help Mission in the Roxbury area of Boston in 1873, Gross was named bishop of Savannah. At thirty-six, he was one of the youngest bishops in the United States and the second American Redemptorist to become a bishop.[2]

With great enthusiasm, Gross took up his duties in Savannah, building schools, churches, and hospitals, somehow without developing a crushing budget deficit. Following his predecessor's plans, he completed a cathedral and dedicated it to Our Lady of Perpetual Help. The Redemptorists were entrusted with care of the ancient icon of Our Lady of Perpetual Help in 1866, and Gross probably first viewed a reproduction of the icon at the church in Roxbury. The picture made a permanent impression on Gross; for the rest of his life, he maintained a special place in his heart for this devotion to Our

William Hickley Gross, C.Ss.R. (1837–1898)
Archbishop of Oregon City (1885–1898)
Oregon Catholic Press

Lady, and frequently appealed to her for assistance. Shortly after his arrival in Oregon, he sent to Rome for a facsimile of the picture for his cathedral and introduced the devotion to Our Lady of Perpetual Help to the West Coast. Probably more churches in Oregon were named after the Virgin Mary during his administration than at any other time; when he couldn't name a parish after Our Lady, he handed out pictures of the icon.[3]

During the Third Plenary Council in Baltimore in 1884, his friend and fellow alumnus of St. Charles College, Archbishop James Gibbons of Baltimore, hinted that an opportunity for even more service to the Church might soon arise. Within months, Gross found himself named archbishop of Oregon City. Traveling across the country by train to The Dalles, then taking to the Columbia River, Gross arrived in Portland by boat, faintly reminiscent of Blanchet's arrival. Although he was the third archbishop, from the time of his appointment as the first American-born Western bishop, William Gross became the archbishop of "firsts"; during his episcopate, there may have been even more first-time events than in the Blanchet era.[4]

Immediately after his arrival, Gross wrote to Archbishop Gibbons, under whom he served as suffragen in Savannah, inviting him to invest him with his symbol of office, the pallium. Various problems, including Gibbons's elevation to cardinal, postponed the ceremony. After two years in office, Gross was anxious that this ceremony should take place, but he was determined that his friend become the first cardinal to visit the West Coast, as a means of raising Catholic morale. He explained, "Our Catholics, too, as a class, have not been a body that would inspire much respect. They have no social standing. The visit of your EMINENCE WILL GIVE A TONE TO Catholicity." Gibbons, who came from the same neighborhood as Gross, was an even closer friend of Gross's brother Mark, whose influence, rather than William's, probably induced Gibbons to undertake the long trip to Oregon.[5]

Gibbons made a triumphal public relations tour from Baltimore across the country by train, with stops at major cities along the way. Gross met the cardinal's train at The Dalles at 4:20 A.M., and Gibbons insisted on walking to St. Peter's church to celebrate Mass at 6:00; this was the first, and, quite likely, the earliest Mass by a cardinal on the West Coast. The entourage then took steamboats to Portland, where crowds waited to greet the celebrity. On October 9, 1887, Gross received the pallium in the cathedral after a Pontifical High Mass before a capacity crowd, which included such diverse personages as Father Louis Conrardy and a group of Umatilla Indians, Governor Sylvester Pennoyer, federal and state judges, and Portland's mayor. Oregon's Catholics had not had such a heady event since Blanchet's triumphant return from Rome in 1847.[6]

Making an introductory tour of Oregon similar to that of Seghers, Gross quickly fell in love with the scenery and climate of Oregon. Travelling "the back roads of Oregon," as he put it, became a regular part of his life; visitors rarely found him at home, to their exasperation. Road travel was little better than in his predecessors' time, and Gross suffered his share of accidents. His worst experience occurred when the horses jolted his carriage on a bridge and he was thrown out. After a spell of unconsciousness, he recovered and gave his scheduled lecture at Heppner.[7]

Gross had a chance to survey his clerical personnel on his travels. In spite of his genuine compassion and kindness to them, Oregon priests did not warm up to him; this caused him much pain. No doubt, some diocesan priests resented both his membership in and his encouragement of religious communities. Occasionally he cried out in distress, "Oh, that the Sacred Heart of Jesus and Mary would enkindle love and mutual forbearance in the hearts of the clergy." Gross was a private, solitary man, and few ever got to know the real person; many found him entirely too reticent. He kept his own counsel and conducted many affairs in secrecy. In spite of what many decried as snap decisions, he pondered over situations carefully. Sometimes, he forgot promises or postponed actions because of the press of business or absences. Although he had a secretary, he wrote most of his own letters, and the evidence suggests that he carried on voluminous correspondence, even sending newsy letters to absent priests. His method of handling crises frequently drew priests' ire. Gross firmly believed that his appearance during difficulties only caused greater excitement, and priests generally had to handle the situation either with written advice from their superior or with a proxy.[8]

Coming from a business-oriented family, Gross seemed more comfortable handling finances than either of his predecessors and he rarely hounded priests about spending. He understood that expansion cost money. However, as in Savannah, he kept few financial records, and critics in both dioceses suspected that his accounting ability was deficient. Somehow, new institutions rose, and the money was mysteriously paid when due. In Savannah, the supposition was that he collected funds on his speaking trips throughout the East. In Oregon, there were few such opportunities, yet he usually paid his debts promptly.[9]

Acquiring wealth, or even balancing his budget, was never one of his aims. Gross's ambition was to be a perfect Redemptorist, and he meditated daily throughout his life. He was exceptionally pious, and during his seminary years, he was responsible for introducing a number of devotional practices. During his years as bishop, he labored to bring people closer to Christ and his Blessed Mother. Like previous Oregon bishops, he was a genuine man of God, even if he frequently exhibited human flaws.[10]

If Oregon Catholics worried about whether their devout replacement for the saintly Seghers could also match his oratorical skills, they were quickly reassured. Gross's Redemptorist training prepared him to speak clearly, forcefully, and in language understandable to the uneducated. The evidence suggests that while Gross was not an orator in the classical vein, he was an above-average, fluent speaker, who gave vigorous sermons. During his first winter in Oregon, he prepared sermons for use on his tours of the archdiocese. In no time, his renown in the state was such that even Protestants asked him to speak in their churches. He found it no hardship to give four lectures a day. However, prospective listeners soon learned to specify the subject matter. When he responded to non-Catholics' insistent demands for a lecture in Baker City on the topic of his choice, Gross chose "The Existence of Hell." Totally unconcerned about the makeup of his audiences, Gross even spoke to prisoners at the state penitentiary and residents of the state mental hospital. Nothing kept him from preaching, even colds, and he once used a mustard plaster as a quick cure before giving a speech. As he wrote to Cardinal Gibbons, he really warmed up to his subject on that occasion.[11]

As the founder of an unsuccessful newspaper in Savannah, Gross immediately took notice of the *Catholic Sentinel*, in its usual financial straits; one of his first actions was to purchase part ownership of the paper. After a few false starts, Michael G. Munly became editor, and the paper again began to echo the halcyon days of Stephen McCormick's direction. Munly was another man of many talents, and he aggressively supported the archbishop and the Church, vigorously sparring with the *Oregonian* and the Protestant press about the Whitman massacre, Indian religious rights, or whatever controversy was current. After Munly returned to his law practice, the paper again fell on hard times; for a while, it even dropped the word *Catholic* from its masthead. In 1893 Gross became sole owner of the paper, with its deficit of $5,000. He assigned his assistants at the cathedral to edit it because they could do it at no cost. There is some debate about how much control he exerted over the contents; his brother Mark insisted that the archbishop did not have time to review what went into the paper. Anticatholicism, initiated by attacks of the American Protective Association, became a problem in 1894, and Gross brought in Georgia editor Charles R. Haydn to defend the church in the paper's pages. When Haydn left, Father Bertram Orth took over as general manager; at Gross's death, the paper was in relatively good condition.[12]

During the period when the *Catholic Sentinel* barely clung to life, other Catholic publications rose to fill the void. In St. Joseph's German parish, Father Alois Sommer started *St. Josephs-Blattchen*, probably the first parish bulletin in Oregon. Confident that St. Joseph himself would somehow provide financial support, Mount Angel Priory took it over, changing the name to *St. Josephs Blatt*, and issuing it until 1966. Within a short time, the Priory print shop began putting out the *Mount Angel Students' Banner*, then *Mount Angel Magazine*, which became the very popular *St. Joseph Magazine*. The

Benedictines also started a devotional magazine, *Armen Seelen Freund*, which lasted for over fifty years. Not to be left out, Father Louis Verhaag started a monthly publication covering the history of the Oregon Church, *Reminiscences and Current Topics of the Ecclesiastical Province of Oregon*, but, sadly, he discontinued it because it competed with the *Catholic Sentinel*.[13]

Like his thrifty predecessors, Gross combined a diocesan synod with the priests' retreat on August 20–21, 1891, at Mount Angel to prepare for an upcoming Provincial Council. Since the proceedings of Seghers's synods were never published, technically the 1891 synod was Oregon's first. While Gross did not promulgate many more laws, he increased the number of officials, naming two vicars general, a secretary, a chancellor, clergy examiners, tribunal officials, and school examiners—a sizable expansion of administrative structure. He also strongly encouraged priests to join the St. Joseph's Ecclesiastical Society, for a $5 fee, to prepare for retirement.[14]

Oregon's Church has the distinction of having held the first strictly provincial council in the United States (1848) as well as the last one before the American Church emerged from its mission status in 1908. With the problems of the *Catholic Sentinel* still on his mind, Gross opened the Third Oregon Provincial Council, October 18–21, 1891, by announcing that F. J. McGuire was the new *Sentinel* editor and promulgating publishing rules. The council's decrees primarily reiterated and implemented the teachings of the Third Plenary Council of Baltimore, especially in regulating the Catholic school system. Technical problems with the council's decrees postponed Rome's approval until 1895, and then the Benedictine Press published the *Acta and Decreta* of the three Oregon provincial councils in one handy volume. For four more decades, this compilation served Oregon priests as province church law, since no further councils were held until well into the twentieth century.[15]

After the government's Peace Policy for the Indians ended officially, but without fanfare, most religious groups withdrew from the reservations—except Catholics, who continued to operate as if the reservations they served were still under Catholic auspices by government order. At the Grand Ronde and Siletz reservations, Father Croquet continued his devoted ministry to the coastal tribes, and the Benedictine sisters conducted the ever-struggling school at Grand Ronde. On the other hand, the Catholic school at the Umatilla reservation was an outstanding success. The Protestant agent retained the nuns and the Catholic school, even without a contract. In fact, the Sisters of Mercy were so respected that the citizens of Pendleton urged them to open a school for their daughters. The sisters' supporters bought property rather far from the city center and started an ambitious building program. Reality forced modification of the plans, and a bond issue was floated to finish the building.[16]

Meanwhile, the agent at the reservation was relieved of his duties and re-placed by Bart Coffey, the Catholic whom Seghers had unsuccessfully nomi-nated earlier. The new agent was appointed just as Gross arrived in Oregon, and Gross gave cursory approval based on information from others. With the appointment of a Catholic agent, acceptance of the bishop's endorsement, and a Catholic school on the reservation, it is little wonder that Gross be-lieved that the Peace Policy continued at Umatilla. Unfortunately, Coffey took over just as local and national pressure was mounting to convince Indi-ans to take individual plots of land on the reservation (severalty); the remain-ing land was to be sold to eager white citizens, after approval by the Indians. Securing that approval proved to be a problem; in 1886, after several unsuc-cessful attempts, the Umatilla tribes still refused to agree to provisions of the bill. Pendletonians who coveted the Indian land tried every means to force approval. Agent Coffey had some difficulty getting Senate confirmation of his appointment, so he knew he had to hew to the government and party line in favor of severalty to keep his job.[17]

Father Conrardy continued to be the focal point of the land predators' animosity because he outspokenly advocated fair treatment for the Indians. Before the departure of the Protestant agent, Conrardy's relations with him had deteriorated to the point where the infuriated official slapped the priest openly on a Pendleton street. Petitions about Conrardy inundated Washing-ton until the government finally sent an inspector and special agent not only to make one more try at securing agreement to the Slater bill but also to check on the rumors about the priest. The two government men arrived, armed with unsubstantiated com-plaints about Conrardy and squaw men (white men married to Indian women). The officials learned that the Indians still opposed the bill and they decided that some show of government power might influence the outcome. The Catholic institutions, which they as-sumed to be under Conrardy's control, seemed most vulnerable for the pur-poses of their scheme. They perempto-rily dismissed Father Constant De Latte, principal and sisters' chaplain, and dismissed most of the nuns.[18]

The agent laid all responsibility for the conditions on Catholics and tore the

Father Louis L. Conrardy
Archives of the Archdiocese of Portland

cross off the school. In protest, the remaining sisters resigned, and the reservation Catholic school closed. This rapid and shocking turn of events had the desired effect: within days, the Indians, realizing that they were overpowered, approved the act. In the aftermath, Agent Coffey insisted that Archbishop Gross had ordered him to do something (it is not clear just what) that violated his oath of office; Gross vehemently denied doing so. Coffey no doubt made his claims to deflect charges that he allowed the problems to develop. Gross misunderstood his relationship to the agent; he failed to recognize, as Seghers had before him, that he no longer had any authority in secular Indian affairs. Nevertheless, Gross excommunicated the agent. Michael C. Munly, then editor of the *Catholic Sentinel*, carried much of the burden of a month-long, bitter battle dubbed the "Holy War" in letters about the situation in the *Oregonian* and the *Catholic Sentinel*. Eventually the government dismissed the agent, and the archbishop lifted the excommunication, but the school remained secular.[19]

The Indian Office pressured Gross to remove Conrardy from the reservation, while the secretary of the interior appointed Father George Willard, vicar general of the Vicariate of Dakota, and later secretary of the Bureau of Catholic Indian Missions, to the Umatilla Alloting Commission with the additional duty of effecting a change of missionaries. Diplomatic suggestions, possibly from Gross or Willard, convinced Conrardy that it was time to go on to a new apostolate with Father Damian and his lepers at Molokai, Hawaii.[20]

As a result of the Umatilla affair, after almost half a century of absence from Oregon, the Jesuits returned, responding to Gross's urgent pleas for temporary missionaries to replace Conrardy. The Jesuits remained, eventually assuming care of all Umatilla County Catholics. Father Urban Grassi, S.J., the first Jesuit on the Umatilla Reservation, immediately began plans for a new, privately supported Catholic school. Through Gross's influence, the Franciscan sisters took charge of this new school at St. Andrew's Mission, and it continued for almost another century. As the century drew to a close, the uneasy government-church alliance to aid the Indians ended completely; Catholics continued their private support through the Bureau of Catholic Indian Missions as the U.S. Indian Office became actively antagonistic to Catholics. Henceforth, Gross's relationship to Indian Catholics was much like that of other Catholics, although he continued contributing to the support of reservation parishes.[21]

While the government required establishment of Indian schools, it was not until after the Third Baltimore Council that the Church virtually mandated Catholic schools in each parish. Without fanfare or appearing to order them, Gross somehow managed to see that in large part the regulation was met. As if a logjam had broken, religious communities came to Oregon, mostly at Gross's personal invitation. Perhaps all of Seghers's seemingly unsuccessful efforts to develop Catholic schools prepared the way; nonetheless, Gross's influence with powerful eastern friends facilitated the opening of Catholic schools, even in the most unlikely places. Baker City was one of the first towns the archbishop visited on his original tour of the state. He saw the empty Notre Dame Academy building and within two months, thanks to his eastern connections, Sisters of the Third Order of St. Francis came from Philadelphia to make their first western foundation. By fall the school, renamed St. Francis Academy, was again open. (The nuns were so homesick that they didn't unpack their trunks for two weeks while they debated whether to stay.) Their early efforts seemed doomed to failure, but in time the school thrived. Gross found more work for the Franciscans within a short time. Just two years later, they reopened Pendleton's St. Joseph's Academy when the Sisters of Mercy foundation collapsed. Then they expanded their work to the new Catholic school on the Umatilla reservation. From there they went on to open Sacred Heart Academy in La Grande. Once planted in the state, the Franciscans took firm root, particularly in eastern Oregon.[22]

The only new religious community that came to Oregon without the archbishop's direct involvement seems to have been the Sister Adorers of the Precious Blood. Father L.A. Brosseau, pastor of Gervais, suggested inviting this cloistered community from Canada because his sister was a member. The nuns settled temporarily in Gervais, but they soon built a new convent in the Montavilla area of Portland, where Brosseau became their chaplain. Almost immediately, the sisters' chapel became the first home of the new Ascension parish.[23]

Gross himself secured Dominican sisters from California to teach at St. Anthony parish at Cedar Mill and at Verboort. Unfortunately, they left very soon afterward, but returned almost immediately to serve at St. Joseph's and Immaculate Heart parishes in Portland. Only a year before his death, Gross intervened to bring a new community to Oregon, the Sisters of the Immaculate Heart of Mary from Pennsylvania. Related to the Redemptorists, this group came to staff the new Catholic school, St. Alphonsus Academy, opened in Tillamook in 1897. The academy was immediately dubbed "The Cheese Box" because of its shape. Eventually, the Immaculate Heart sisters turned operation of the school over to the Precious Blood Sisters (later, the Sisters of St. Mary of Oregon).[24]

When the Benedictine monks opened their monastery at Mt. Angel, the Benedictine sisters remained at Gervais; but within months after establishment of the new monastery, two sisters opened a school in Mt. Angel. They lived in a small house, while a new convent was being built. The new convent in Mt. Angel was finished the next year, and in 1888 the motherhouse moved to Convent Queen of Angels. Mt. Angel Academy opened its doors, replacing St. Scholastica's Academy in Gervais. By 1897 the teacher training program became Mt. Angel Normal School, with a collegiate rating. The Benedictine sisters made a significant contribution to the development of parochial schools before the turn of the century, including service at the Indian school at Grand Ronde and parish schools at Gervais, Mount Angel, Oregon City, Eugene, Albany and Portland (Sacred Heart).[25]

The Holy Names sisters continued to dominate education in Oregon during Gross's administration, but they began to feel the competition of other communities. Nevertheless, they played a major part in the rapid expansion of the Catholic school system. Continuing to improve their own schools, the nuns built a new St. Mary's Academy in Portland in 1889, incorporating parts of the former building, notably the chapel. Gross laid the cornerstone; in his oration he affirmed his support of education for women and encouraged the sisters to continue that work. In 1893 St. Mary's charter was amended so the school could give college degrees, since so many of the graduates were becoming teachers. The school was then called St. Mary's Academy and College, the first Catholic normal school in Oregon. When Holy Names Superior General Mother John the Baptist decided Astoria might be a good spot for a health resort for her sisters, she also looked at possibilities for opening a school. No one was too surprised when Holy Names' Academy opened there in the fall of 1896.[26]

In his search for religious communities, Gross's crowning achievement was establishing an Oregon religious community from the remains of a failed religious experiment. A commune of German-speaking schismatic Catholics migrated to the Jordan area in 1884 to evade problems with Minnesota bishops. Members included young women in a quasi-sisterhood with ties to the German-founded Society of the Precious Blood. As soon as Gross landed in Portland he was greeted with stories of a strange religious group in nearby Jordan, so he visited the settlement as soon as possible. He found that the sisterhood was not canonically established, but he hoped to rectify that problem and begin a new congregation. From the moment he met the women, Gross had a vision for their future: they would staff the parochial schools he wanted to establish in every parish. The women displayed great fortitude in defying the commune's trustees, several of whom were their own fathers, and followed Gross's direction. Even putting the parish under virtual interdict, which lasted until 1895, failed to alleviate harassment of the incipient community.[27]

As he developed his plan for the new congregation, Gross arranged to remove them from the unpleasant situation; they spent several months crowded into the small house of the Benedictine nuns teaching in Mount Angel. After two months with no contact, they feared that Gross had forgotten them, while Prior Adelhelm urged them to give up the idea of a separate foundation and join the Benedictines. Actually, Gross was at Cardinal Gibbons's installation in Baltimore; as soon as he returned, he brought the community a plan that included a choice of sites for their motherhouse. They chose Sublimity, where there was already a resident Benedictine priest, and they settled in the second floor of the old United Brethren College, which at first they shared with pigeons and bats, in direst poverty.[28]

Their chaplain, Werner Ruttiman, O.S.B., named the convent Maria Zell, and for some years they were known as the Maria Zell Sisters. Their official title at the time was Sisters of the Precious Blood, and it was not until the next century that they became Sisters of St. Mary of Oregon. In 1887, after several delays, five sisters from the original community made perpetual vows, and the following year five more of the foundresses made vows. At first, the nuns required training in virtually every facet of religious life; but before long, they opened a Catholic school in Sublimity, the first parish school in Marion County. When the Dominican Sisters left Verboort in 1890, Gross commandeered the Precious Blood Sisters to staff the Catholic school. In a short time, that school became the Verboort public school, taught by the nuns, at the suggestion of the county school superintendent. Gross wholeheartedly supported this concept; in Savannah, the Catholic schools had been under control of the city school superintendent. The practice spread to other virtually all-Catholic towns in Oregon.[29]

Since his first meeting with the Precious Blood community, Gross intended that they staff an orphanage he proposed to build. In 1891 the nuns moved into St. Mary's Home near Beaverton, where the interior was still unfinished, and most rooms on the first floor had floors of bare earth. Laboring in destitution, the sisters somehow kept the home operating. They moved the novitiate from Sublimity to St. Mary's Home in 1891 so the novices could help with the orphans. For three years, the nuns endured crowded and uncomfortable conditions until they could build a motherhouse nearby, partially with proceeds from the sales from their onion patch, which also contributed to the support of the orphans. The archbishop, typically without asking the sisters, dedicated their not yet habitable convent in 1894 to his favorite, Our Lady of Perpetual Help.[30]

Gross treated all women, both lay and religious, in his usual southern gentlemanly manner and he urged their education; but he had some reservations about dealing with them. He warned his priests that the sisters were never happy unless they had a hand in school plans. In sympathizing with a priest about problems with nuns, he agreed with Artemus Ward that "Woman is a great Institution of this country," but she always imagines men as tyrants and must be handled gently. After coping with several difficult problems with nuns, he wrote in exasperation, "No wonder St. Ignatius said that he would rather govern his entire order of men than three women!"[31]

In his determination to introduce the Christian Brothers, the archbishop promised to deed them St. Michael's College. The community sent teachers even before permission from superiors in France arrived. However, with few men to spare, the superior sent as director Brother Aldrick McElroy, already very ill, with hope that the climate would help his condition. The reception of the three brothers in Portland in February 1886 was cool and indifferent; they found their housing virtually nonexistent and the food supply meager. St. Michael's College, hastily built in 1871, had not aged well. The school reopened under the Christian Brothers with 140 students stuffed into every space. In spite of limited funds, the brothers rented a house, which helped the crowding somewhat, but they never had much food. Brother Aldrick caught a bad cold that worsened because of his weakened condition, and within two months he died. The remaining brothers didn't have a dollar to their name, and a Protestant man paid for the funeral. Nevertheless the two survivors continued, although many thought that the venture was ill-fated from the start. By 1894 the building was unfit to live in, and St. Michael's College closed. At this time Gross was building a temporary cathedral in Portland, so he added a story for a Christian Brothers' school, which opened in 1895 as St. Mary's Parochial School and College. Because it was on the third floor of the building, with no such thing as an elevator, the brothers named it "The Perch."[32]

Arrival of the Christian Brothers was offset by loss of the Viatorian Brothers from St. Joseph's College in Baker City. After the sudden departure of the Holy Names, Father J.B. Manseau, the superior of the Viatorian community, lost interest in the school. His impractical schemes convinced his Canadian superiors to close the whole foundation. Offering to sell the school back to De Roo, who had donated it, Manseau's settlement offer immediately caused a fight that took both men to Archbishop Gross's side. Knowing little of the background, he declined to become involved in a private battle. De Roo secured a restraining order against the Viatorians, and after a ten-day standoff, the dispute was settled to no one's satisfaction.[33]

From his earliest days, Gross tried repeatedly to lure his own community to Oregon, especially to work with German-speaking Catholics. When they did come in 1890, eager to establish the first Redemptorist foundation in the West, their greeting was even chillier than that of the Christian Brothers. No one met them at the train; when they finally reached his residence, the archbishop was not home. Four Redemptorist priests and two brothers arrived in Portland planning to establish a parish to be called St. Alphonsus, carved out of St. Lawrence parish. They rented a building as their Northwest headquarters and tried to collect funds for a church. There were few Catholics in the area, and Gross's abrupt curtailing of the parish boundaries, his refusal to let them collect pew rent from other than residents within the parish, and his inexplicable lack of encouragement doomed the enterprise. After some vacillation by Redemptorist authorities, the archbishop's own community left for Seattle after less than a year, not to return until 1906.[34]

Another community Gross urged to come to serve the German-speaking was the Dominicans. He first appealed to them shortly after his arrival: "You may perhaps be surprised that I do not introduce the Rev. Redemptorist Fathers for this work, since I myself am a Redemptorist. My reason is, that Portland is my place of residence and were I to introduce the Redemptorists here, it might cause unpleasant consequences. I will probably at some other time offer my confreres a foundation in some part of my diocese distant from Portland." As a matter of fact, Gross had asked for Redemptorists, and they had turned him down. So did the Dominicans. However, they reconsidered when he offered them a lot in East Portland, given to Blanchet in 1873 by Ben Holladay, the railroad magnate. By summer 1893, a church and a two-story, fourteen-room residence for the friars were nearly completed. Sales contracts for Holladay's Addition included a clause that no schools, churches, or saloons were permitted—but here was a church rising, in violation of the agreement. The archdiocese had received its lot long before the development, so rather than go to court, the real estate company offered two other lots if the Dominicans would move. They agreed, and during much of August to September 1893, neighbors were entertained by the buildings' slow progress through the streets. At last the structures settled onto new foundations, and construction resumed on the monastery, which later became Holy Rosary parish and the first Dominican priory in the Northwest.[35]

The male Benedictine community in Oregon impressed Gross. However, as a member of a religious community, he thought the emphasis on parish and missionary work detracted from the order's motto—prayer and work—and he quickly set to work to remedy the condition. Writing to Abbot Anselm in Engelberg:

> I consider it to be a very great mistake to allow the Fathers to look after parishes (i.e. Benedictine Fathers). Each Father who has such a parish is left to himself. He is not able to keep the rule and is not under the supervision of a superior.… For this reason I advise you, Father Abbot,

in all politeness to send a command to Father Prior Adelhelm that he is to call all of the Fathers who are entrusted with parishes back to the monastery and not allow the same in the future.

To encourage focusing of Benedictine efforts, Gross proposed that the Benedictines open a college. On September 6, 1887, they obligingly opened Mt. Angel College, which Gross and others persisted in calling St. Joseph's College. Gross was very pleased: "They are all Swiss, and have a most excellent spirit. They, at my request, opened a college here last fall, and have had a grand success." He quickly followed up with plans for St. Anselm's Minor Seminary, the first in the West; it opened in March, 1889, on the twenty-sixth anniversary of Gross's ordination.[36]

After the monks dropped the parishes of Gervais and Sublimity, lack of priests forced Gross to modify his stance on Benedictines outside the monastery, and they took over several parishes throughout the state, notably Sacred Heart in Portland in 1893. Gross continued to encourage their educational efforts, offering them the exclusive right to provide Catholic higher education for men. He used every means to generate interest in the seminary, of which he was inordinately proud. All seemed to be going well at St. Anselm's Seminary until 1892, when within two hours, an engulfing fire destroyed all the buildings except the college. Gross immediately visited the scene of the disaster and consoled the monks. Rebuilding, somewhat delayed, took place on the top of the hill this time; by August 1898, foundations for a new monastery were ready. In 1904 the monastery gained independence and became Mount Angel Abbey.[37]

In the early 1890s three priests and a brother from the newly founded religious community, the Catholic Teaching Society, came from Rome to make their first North American foundation. When they could not accept the financial burden of Holy Angel's College in Vancouver, Gross invited them to Oregon; the priests, whose community had just changed its name to Society of the Divine Savior, known popularly as Salvatorians, took over The Dalles, briefly, then Corvallis and the Siletz Reservation.[38]

Although Gross brought new religious communities into Oregon, he expected them to support themselves or resort to begging. His policy was to let them sink or swim, whether it was his own community or a struggling group of sisters. Actually, he had few funds available to assist them. What is more difficult to understand is why he often failed to give moral support to such communities as his own Redemptorists or the Christian Brothers. Perhaps as a secure member of a religious community, he failed to realize the need for such psychological assistance.

While Gross often gave the impression that his planning was spontaneous, it actually was the result of the serendipitous mingling of carefully gathered facts, observations, and some catalytic event. The founding of St. Mary's Home was precisely such a situation. It seemed almost capricious; actually Gross put it together like a puzzle from the these circumstances: unexpected offers for the unused land near Beaverton, bought long before by Archbishop Blanchet; the establishment of the Sisters of the Precious Blood (Maria Zell Sisters); and the desperate need for an orphan home. Orphans were gathered from the various places where they had been cared for by the Holy Names and brought to the institution he built in the wilds near Beaverton, where Gross hoped to centralize their care. He envisioned not only an orphanage but also "a reformatory for the little 'hoodlums' of both sexes who fall into the clutches of the law." Within two years, the Precious Blood priest who had supervised construction was gone, and the Sisters of the Precious Blood assumed the burden of administering the orphanage, while their chaplain served as director. In fairness to the archbishop, he did organize St. Mary's Home Association in 1889, to assist in supporting the facility, although the funds collected were relatively small, with each member contributing 25 cents a month.[39]

After he launched this experiment in social work, Gross took on similar problems. Another member of the Blanchet family came to Oregon when the Sisters of Our Lady of Charity of the Refuge responded to Gross's request for sisters to open a home for "friendless young women and neglected children under twelve years of age." Sister Mary of St. Ignatius Blanchet, a niece of Francis and Augustine, arrived in 1891 with the group to open the home, by now designated as a Magdalen Asylum, on land in Portland donated by Father John Fierens. The sisters intended to help wayward girls change their lives as well as to provide a home for small children and servant girls. When Fierens died, his will specified that the land be used for an old people's home. To rescue the sisters from this situation, Mrs. Levi Anderson gave land near Park Place, and the sisters completed a new building there with mostly donated labor. At first they received some state aid, but soon they had to depend on gifts and begging to support the institution. Far from their motherhouse, the sisters struggled for ten years before they transferred to the Congregation of Our Lady of Charity of the Good Shepherd.[40]

If the original Sisters of Mercy left the archdiocese under a cloud, it did not deter Gross from inviting Sisters of Mercy from a closed Catholic Indian school in Minnesota to come to Portland in 1896 to take care of pressing problems. First they set up the Catholic Young Women's Home, a residence for young working women in Portland. Then they started a temporary Home for Aged Women, soon expanded to take in men, using the buildings vacated by the Sisters of Our Lady of the Refuge when they moved to Park Place, meeting the conditions of Fierens's will. From opening day, the institution flourished and still operates as Mount St. Joseph's Home. Within a year of their arrival, the Sisters of Mercy also began teaching in parish schools.[41]

Health care needs also caught Gross's attention, particularly in a region of the state he thought was neglected. St. Francis Academy in Baker City grew beyond its building, so the sisters bought and remodeled the old Virtue residence for use as a school. Thomas Grant, former member of Father De Roo's Missionary Brothers and now a successful Baker City contractor, remodeled the still sturdy old academy building into St. Elizabeth's Hospital. The ever-willing Franciscans took over its administration, and for many years it was the only hospital in eastern Oregon. Laboring quietly, the Sisters of Providence gained legendary success with their hospitals. The demand for trained nurses encouraged them to open a school of nursing in 1892. By the end of Gross's years, a substantial new brick and stone St. Vincent's Hospital opened in Portland; the archbishop spoke for almost an hour at the cornerstone ceremony in 1892, but somewhat less at the dedication of the new hospital in the West Hills on July 14, 1895.[42]

Many of the hard-working, dedicated, European-born priests, who still made up most of the Oregon clergy, were now aged—and still difficult to handle. Unlike his predecessors, Gross went out of his way to get along with his priests, trying to match them with posts they wanted. Gross's generous contributions helped to make rectories more comfortable, and he showed great patience with his obstreperous clergy. He encouraged incorporation of the St. Joseph's Ecclesiastical Society, a sort of local voluntary pension plan for priests, originally founded in 1882, urged a reorganization, and included it in the discussions at the Provincial Council.[43]

As the end of the century drew near, death came frequently to pioneer Oregon priests. John Fierens, who was truly the executive officer for the archdiocese and the power behind the throne, died in 1893, after thirty years as pastor of the cathedral and vicar general. The last of the three founding bishops of the Oregon Province, A.M.A. Blanchet, died in 1887. Some of the worn-out old priests such as Fathers Croquet and Delorme retired to their homeland. By far the most shocking death was that of former Archbishop Charles Seghers, who was shot by a crazed servant in the Alaskan wilderness in November 1886, at the age of 47. Gross had re-invested Seghers with the pallium as bishop of Vancouver Island less than six months before the murder, but it was well into 1887 before Oregonians learned the news of his tragic death. When the archbishop-bishop's body finally returned to Victoria in 1888 for burial, Gross celebrated the solemn requiem Mass among an ecumenical throng of mourners.[44]

In his detached fashion, Gross felt a special bond to priests of the archdiocese. He proudly added to his growing list of "firsts" in 1895 by ordaining in Portland the first Oregon-born priest, Arthur Lane, grandson of Joseph Lane, the first Oregon territorial governor. Just three years later, he ordained Bernard Murphy, O.S.B., later abbot of Mount Angel Abbey, the first native-born Portlander to become a priest. Two Gross protegés, Edward O'Dea and Charles O'Reilly, went on to become bishops. O'Dea was one of the earliest and best students of St. Michael's College, and after ordination, served both Seghers and Gross as secretary. No doubt the double influence of Gross and Cardinal Gibbons played a large part in O'Dea's selection as bishop of Nesqually in 1896. He was later bishop of Seattle, when he moved the seat of the diocese to that city. Charles O'Reilly, who had arrived in Portland with an M.A. degree at age 21, became principal of St. Michael's College, replacing Alphonsus J. Glorieux when he became bishop of Idaho. After the Christian Brothers took over the school, O'Reilly entered the seminary at Montreal. Gross ordained him in 1890, sending him out to build parishes and churches, at which he was very successful. St. Michael's College seemed to generate bishops; in 1903 O'Reilly became first bishop of Baker City. Another Gross "first" was his nomination of Father Adrien Croquet as first domestic prelate (monsignor) west of the Mississippi, during Croquet's golden jubilee year. After a glittering installation ceremony and impressive dinner in Portland, Croquet quietly put his purple robes away and became a simple missionary again.[45]

The archbishop accepted his diocesan priest-brother, Mark Gross, in Oregon in hope that the better climate would improve his health. A humble man, Mark nonetheless created many problems for his brother. Gross used his brother as a go-between in touchy situations, but kind-hearted Mark frequently added to the controversy. Mark's health continued to deteriorate and he returned to the East, dying in 1896.[46]

That there were few well-known lay people during the Gross administration was not surprising; this was the era of unparalleled expansion of religious communities in Oregon. Michael G. Munly was probably the most visible layman during the Gross era. Admitted to the Oregon Bar in 1882, he became editor of the *Catholic Sentinel* in a time of crisis, serving from 1886–1890. No doubt the need to support his family led to his return to legal work.

Eventually, he ran for Portland mayor and became a judge. A somewhat more visible, but much less model Catholic layman of the period was the colorful promoter, Ben Holladay. Although the railroad magnate generously donated to construction of the cathedral and gave money and land for church purposes, his marriages and questionable business dealings clouded his reputation. Nevertheless, he was buried in St. Mary's Cemetery after a requiem Mass at the cathedral. Quietly, but generously, Levi and Emma Anderson supported many Catholic causes. After Levi's death, his wife donated land for the Magdalen Home, and in her will she provided funds to support St. Mary's Home. Although he was no longer an Oregonian, many Catholics mourned the death of the indefatigable Stephen McCormick in 1891 in California. As successful editor of the *Catholic Sentinel* and eloquent spokesman for the Catholic community, McCormick materially helped improve the social status of Oregon Catholics.[47]

Despite McCormick's efforts, Gross continued to find Oregonians to be a challenge, sometimes a cross. After a little more than a year in the state, he wrote, "Oregon is truly a wild but little cultivated land." As he had in Georgia, Gross considered himself a simple missionary, and he traveled all over the state. After a visit to one city, he wrote: "I must say that I have seldom seen a city where religion appears to be so little, ignorance so great among Oregon Catholics, and so many Germans, French, and Irish lost to the Faith." About another town he remarked, "I never saw such an agglomera…of lukewarm, apostate Catholics, runaway husbands, and divorced women." In spite of himself, he fell in love with Oregon, and he found the climate invigorating after the heat of the South.[48]

As one of his first moves upon his arrival in Portland, Gross called a meeting of German-speaking Catholics. The Redemptorists particularly served this immigrant group, and while Gross had studied German in the seminary, he readily confessed that he spoke it poorly. He was concerned that Germans would become alienated from the Church when sacraments such as confession were not available in German, and he sympathized with their fear that they would lose their faith if they lost their language. For some years, the St. Joseph German Catholic Benevolent Society, a German-speaking social group in Portland, met in a room in St. Mary's Hall, now known as "The Bishop's House." Early in the Gross administration, the Germans bought land for a church; the archbishop made the unused chapel at St. Michael's College available until they could build it. Within two years after Gross's initial meeting, the energetic Portland Germans had built their own church, St. Joseph's, in northwest Portland, with their own German-speaking pastor.[49]

Next, Gross took up the challenge of helping the growing Italian community in Portland. Again using the old St. Michael's College chapel, recently evacuated by the Germans, he began developing a parish to serve Italians. Gross himself donated twelve pews to the chapel. This group had planned to name their new church Sacred Heart, but somehow the name of their old chapel won out, and the parish became St. Michael.[50]

Responding to the needs of Irish-born Catholics, Gross blessed the 500-pound basalt cornerstone of St. Patrick's Church in Portland in 1889 to the accompaniment of (naturally) rain, as well as colorful ceremonies, bands, flags, and lots of green. Governor Sylvester Pennoyer attended, riding with Archbishop Gross, who prided himself on providing this new parish—originally called Sacred Heart—for the Irish and Croatians who lived in the area and worked at industries along the river. Two years later, the church was dedicated in a more solemn fashion.[51]

No Oregon archbishop up to this time had witnessed such an incredible growth of parishes and missions. The increasing population of Oregon was part of the reason, but Gross also encouraged his priests to establish missions and parishes in practically any spot that contained more than two Catholics. Each time he visited a new village, he scouted the surrounding area for a suitable location for a church or other facilities. In his first survey of the archdiocese, Gross noticed the disarray in old St. Mary's Cemetery, so he bought 100 acres on the west side for a new cemetery. By 1888 Mt. Calvary Cemetery was open, and St. Mary's days were numbered.[52]

In his many travels throughout the state, he left a trail of new churches, over 30 of which he personally dedicated, many of them named in honor of the Virgin Mary. He promised Albany Catholics they would be the first new parish in his administration; true to his word, a resident priest soon arrived. The remodeled Maple School became the first church, dedicated, of course, to his patroness, Our Lady of Perpetual Help. Ironically, just months before his death in 1898, one of his last dedications was another Albany church, which incorporated the original building in the southwest corner of the new structure. After the elaborate ceremony, the archbishop consecrated the archdiocese and himself to Our Lady of Perpetual Help. Immaculate Heart of Mary Parish in Portland more than made up for initial reluctance by building two churches blessed by Gross, the original in 1887 and a new building three years later. Just months before his death, Gross consecrated the sturdy brick church at St. Paul, the first church in the Northwest to receive this honor.[53]

In eastern Oregon, Gross opened several new parishes and missions, especially St. Mary's in Pendleton, where he installed Fr. Peter De Roo as first pastor in 1886. St. Joachim's Church at Huntington was the last church dedicated by Gross before his death. At The Dalles, fire destroyed much of the town and economic problems delayed construction of a new church, but on

St Patrick's Day, 1898, Gross dedicated the magnificent Gothic St. Peter's church, still standing.[54]

Not all of Gross's relations with parishes were harmonious. At Jordan, the trustees of the commune with whom the Precious Blood Sisters came to Oregon first welcomed Gross like royalty, then stubbornly refused to cooperate with him in regularizing their status, so he just as stubbornly refused to assign a priest to serve them—a *de facto*, if not actual, interdict. They continued the communal life developed under their founder, Father Joseph Albrecht, whose body they smuggled to Oregon with them in a packing crate. Until 1897, the remaining members of the original sisterhood who had not joined Gross's new religious congregation, and the other members of the commune, had no priest, although some no doubt attended Mass at Sublimity. The Jordan parish dates its founding from 1885, when the church was built, but no priest served there until 1897. Cedar Mill parishioners suffered under a similar unpublicized experience, after a serious disagreement with Gross over Sisters of Mercy teaching in the parish school.[55]

Then there was the ever-present problem of the cathedral in Portland at Third and Stark. Before Gross arrived, Father Fierens began completing the main floor, after paying the debts up to that time; but when Gross, with misgivings, dedicated the Gothic-style building in 1885, the debt was $27,000. Services were still held in the crypt, which Gross described as "a dark, low basement." Almost at once, Gross realized that the days of the cathedral were numbered. The business district and warehouses surrounded the site; and the floods of 1890 and 1894, both of which thoroughly dampened the cathedral, convinced him to lease or sell the land to pay off archdiocesan debts.[56]

Gross knew what the building meant to the aged Fierens, and he had the sensitivity to wait until the old man was too feeble to worry about the possibility of a new cathedral; only after his death in 1893 did Gross move forcefully to remedy the situation. In 1891 he bought land bounded by 14th, 15th, D and G streets in northwest Portland from Louis Fleischner for $66,000. He obviously intended this purchase to be made public, and he seemed pleased with the excitement the news caused. By November 1891, a small frame Chapel of the Immaculate Conception was under construction on the new land. Gross, who fancied himself as being in touch with lay people, reported to friends that everyone was pleased with his plan.[57]

Actually, Catholics all over the state were outraged, and Gross handled the public relations badly. People passionately loved the old cathedral, erected at such cost and over such a long period of time. They had only used the main floor for less than a decade and were in no mood to raise more money.

From this time on, Gross became extremely unpopular. His priests initiated a petition for his removal, complaining about his real estate dealings. A Christian Brother inspector reported on his visit to Gross, "he is very authoritarian and little liked…there is much talk against him."[58]

As early as 1892, Gross confided to correspondents that very soon he planned to sell the land where the cathedral and St. Mary's Hall stood because so few attended services at the cathedral and so many at the new chapel that it already needed enlargement. Gross announced that he wanted to build the most beautiful cathedral on the Pacific Coast, but only after Fierens's death and the flood of 1894 did he disclose his full plan. By then, economic conditions, a business depression causing bank closures, and possibly congregational opposition were such that the practical Gross recognized that a magnificent cathedral was impossible. He compromised, building as quickly as possible what he termed a temporary cathedral. The first two floors comprised the pro-cathedral proper, while the third floor became St. Mary's School and College for the Christian Brothers, replacing St. Michael's College. As a salve to injured feelings, the architect, Lionel D. Deane, brought much of the not-so-old-cathedral to the new building: fourteen stained glass windows, altars, sanctuary railing, pews, gallery railing, and (of course) the picture of Our Lady of Perpetual Help. Demolishing the episcopal residence and moving into St. Mary's Hall next to the old cathedral until his new house, the remodeled St. Joseph's Church rectory, was ready, Gross became the first, and last, to live in what became known as "The Bishop's House." After less than two years there, he moved to the refurbished St. Joseph's rectory, done over to match the new temporary cathedral, with its sheathing of sheet iron covered with gray stucco. Gross celebrated the first Mass in the new cathedral, with its splendid acoustics, on December 16, 1894, at 6 A.M. By January 9, 1895, the old cathedral was in the process of demolition, and the steps were removed; by March, the never-completed building was gone.[59]

In spite of the widespread hostility, Father Bertram Orth organized priests, sisters, and lay people to collect over $10,000 to build a three-story episcopal residence for Gross in honor of his silver jubilee as a bishop in 1898. Almost half of the money came from a discreet ladies' bazaar in Portland. Many people refused to contribute, and Orth himself had had his share of disagreements with the archbishop; but perhaps he recognized that Gross would not be with them much longer.[60]

A pale complexion and slight build gave people the impression that Gross had poor health all his life; but, as his brother Mark said, he was "as strong as an ox." After the unpleasant response to the cathedral project, however, it was evident that the archbishop was slowing down and his patience growing thin.

Rarely did he complain, but in a letter to a friend he confided: "The present year has been one of the greatest crosses that I have experienced since I have been a bishop. The thought comes to me that a few devils must have been let loose in Oregon." By the time of his jubilee, Gross exhibited the signs of a serious heart condition, which he attributed to rheumatism. He did not realize how little time he had remaining.[61]

Gross had given some thought to resigning and returning to the Redemptorist community, especially when his burdens became too heavy. However, even when his health began to fail dramatically in 1898, he continued a strenuous schedule. On a trip east to a bishops' meeting and for a rest, he stopped at the Redemptorist residence at Ilchester, Maryland. He complained of weakness and memory loss, and he admitted to pangs of homesickness for Oregon. Even so, his death in a Baltimore hospital on November 14, 1898, caught many by surprise. Although Oregonians expected his body to be returned to Portland, he specifically asked for burial in Baltimore's Redemptorist Cemetery of the Most Holy Redeemer.[62]

William Gross, despite being the third archbishop of Oregon City, and without conscious effort at innovation, managed to produce more firsts in the Oregon Church than would seem possible, including: being the first American-born western bishop; introducing numerous religious communities to Oregon; ordaining the first Oregon- and Portland-born priests; founding the first Oregon religious community; and being the first Oregon archbishop to die in office. Many of his actions, though some painful at the time, paved the way for greater expansion. On his arrival, Oregon boasted 29 priests, 29 churches and chapels, 10 academies, and 2 parochial schools. At his death, there were 55 priests, 37 churches with resident pastors, 27 missions with churches, 83 stations, 13 chapels, 12 academies, 27 parochial schools, and 33,000 Catholics. It was a record of great achievement.[63]

Chapter Five
Genial Empire Builder

REGON'S FOURTH ARCHBISHOP could have been everyone's favorite, handsome, middle-aged bachelor uncle. Alexander Christie had a high, broad forehead, steely-gray eyes under bushy eyebrows, a Roman nose, a slightly cleft chin, and a dimple in one cheek. A full head of wavy dark hair, worn long, with a touch of gray, topped his rugged face. He was tall, stocky in build, and regal in bearing, and wore the episcopal robes with a distinct flair. One priest recalled, "He looked like a lion." Another remembered him as "quite a showman." Christie had a powerful, pleasing voice, and tended to drop his "r's." He enjoyed ceremony and being before the public, and apparently was aware of the impression he created. The archbishop liked making special appearances, such as at schools, where he proved popular with the students by giving them the rest of the day off after speaking to them. The archbishop also preferred to be addressed as "Your Grace," the customary salutation for English prelates, and he was partial to prefacing his remarks with "methinks"—adding a touch of Shakespearean erudition to the portrait.[1]

Yet Alexander Christie's background was neither aristocratic, scholarly, nor, for that matter, very Catholic. Born of a non-Catholic father of Scottish descent and an Irish mother in High Gate, Vermont, in May 1849, he did not even meet a Catholic priest until he was sixteen years old because the family moved to rural Wisconsin, far from any Catholic church. Nevertheless, he became interested in the priesthood and when the family moved again, this time to Minnesota, he studied at St. John's University, Collegeville, and later at the major seminary in Montreal. On December 22, 1877, he was ordained for the Archdiocese of St. Paul. Christie served as a priest of that archdiocese for twenty-one years and then, in rapid succession, was appointed bishop of Victoria, British Columbia, in June 1898, and archbishop of Oregon City in February 1899.[2]

Alexander Christie (1848–1925)
Archbishop of Oregon City (1899–1925)
Oregon Catholic Press

Despite his regal appearance and mannerisms, Christie was an approach-able man with a lively sense of humor. He loved jokes—telling them as well as playing them on others and having them played on him. His relations with his priests were informal and open, and he enjoyed their company. Christie also appreciated a well-served meal with fine silver, table linen and china, disliked the diets which poor health forced him to follow, and smoked cigars.[3]

When Alexander Christie arrived in Oregon in 1899, he found an archdiocese that was deeply in debt, similar to many other dioceses that had undergone the depression of 1893; but now that the depression was over, prosperity was returning to the state. By the beginning of the twentieth century the major railroad lines had been constructed, and Oregon was reaping the benefits of improved communications. Its population began to grow more rapidly as travel to the Northwest was simplified and its products were more easily shipped to all parts of the country, stimulating its economy; in short, Oregon was becoming more integrated into the life of the nation.

The Catholic population of the United States more than doubled between 1890 and 1916, and some of that increase found its way to Oregon, particularly during the first ten years of Christie's administration. Most Catholics in Oregon emigrated from other parts of the United States east of the Rocky Mountains, but a significant group was composed of a wave of southern and eastern European immigrants who migrated to the United States in the 1870s and 1880s. A greater proportion of these newer immigrants were Catholic than former groups; but they also seemed more "alien" than their predecessors from western and northern Europe. Increasing cultural differences posed new problems for the Church in Oregon.[4]

Theoretically, Archbishop Christie had the authority to deal with the challenges engendered by the increasing diversity of adherents to the faith, because until 1908 the United States was technically still a mission field, which allowed its bishops almost unlimited authority. Authority itself was a dominant theme in the Catholic Church in the nineteenth and early twentieth centuries. The church had adopted this theme in response to the unsettling effects of the French Revolution and subsequent events in Europe, the loss of the last of the Papal States in 1870, and, specifically in the United States, the rapid, chaotic growth of the immigrant church. The prevailing perception was that emphasizing authority was necessary to preserve the unity of the Church, and that concepts of freedom, democracy, and individualism were threats to authority. As a popular saying expressed it, Catholics were expected "to pay, pray, and obey." Yet, even when this structure seemed most rigid in the United States, it was felt lighter by Catholics in the Northwest, where clergy and laity were in the process of establishing themselves. Although the Catholic Church had the largest membership of any denomination in Oregon, only twenty-nine percent of all Oregonians considered themselves members of any church. Therefore, the authority exercised by bishops in Oregon had less to do with preserving the Church and more to do with being leaders and collaborators with their fellow Catholics in establishing their communities of worship in an indifferent or mildly hostile environment.[5]

The idea that priests should unquestioningly accept the authority of their bishop seems to have conflicted with the independence which frontier circumstances had forced on those ministering in isolated parishes and missions. Clerics in Oregon also probably were influenced by the general atmosphere in the state; the late 1800s saw Oregonians driving to reform and more directly control their government. This included passage of such measures as the initiative and referendum, direct primaries, and direct election of senators—attempts to put the governing process directly in the hands of the citizens. Oregon at the beginning of the twentieth century was regarded as the most complete democracy in the country, so its atmosphere was not conducive to the exercise of what could be regarded as arbitrary authority.

+≈≈+

A signal that difficulties in administering this Oregon region lay ahead surfaced early, one arising prior to Christie's move to Portland. While still in British Columbia, preparing to move to Oregon, Christie received a letter from Father Peter De Roo—not his predecessor's favorite priest—complaining about the archdiocesan administrator's treatment of him. A little later, in 1899, after becoming established in Portland, Christie found it necessary to deal with Father Joseph Schell, who had become estranged from his parishioners in Tillamook, by transferring him to a parish east of the Cascades.

Five years later, in Jordan, hoping to settle a dispute among parishioners over the location of their new church, the archbishop invited a group of French Trappists to assume responsibility for the parish there.[6]

The largest controversy faced by the archbishop occurred in 1903. Christie made a decision that brought a beehive of noisy protest down about his head, giving him one of the best opportunities in his early administration to show poise, administrative skills, and the authority of his office. At that time he asked Rome to divide the archdiocese at the Cascade Mountains, and erect the Diocese of Baker City in Eastern Oregon. The reasons for his request are still unclear, although size may have been a factor. The eastern diocese, however, numbered only eleven priests and 2,350 Catholics spread out over 66,826 square miles.[7] Two of the eleven priests in the new diocese were Father John Heinrich, who had resigned as director of St. Mary's Home for

Boys when Christie became archbishop, and Father Joseph Schell, formerly of Tillamook. Both men had been transferred to Eastern Oregon by Archbishop Christie.[8]

The eleven priests in this eastern area felt disenfranchised, cut off from the possibility of transfer to more settled parishes that could support them in a less rigorous lifestyle than that offered on the frontier, and from the possibility of upward mobility in a larger church structure. Their resentment quickly surfaced when the newly appointed bishop, Father Charles B. O'Reilly, former pastor of Immaculate Heart parish in Portland, tried to take possession of his new "cathedral": the small—and only—Catholic church in Baker City, and its rectory. Arriving at the church door after a long trip from Portland, O'Reilly was met at gunpoint by Father John Heinrich and Father L.B. Demarais, pastor of the church. As a result of this unusual welcome, he spent the next few days with the Sisters of St. Francis at St. Francis Academy. Eventually settled in his rectory and church, he issued two edicts threatening priests with suspension if any criticisms of him or the sisters were published. Typical of the perversity so characteristic of human conduct, exactly what he forbade occurred. First published was a lengthy circular dated May 16, 1904, addressed to the apostolic delegate, Archbishop Diomede Falconio, with a long list of complaints against Christie. The circular included a questioning of his motives for establishing the diocese, charging misuse of funds, and allowing "unworthy" itinerant priests to settle in his archdiocese. It also accused the apostolic delegate of giving his protection to all that was happening. That indictment was supported by a pamphlet supposedly signed by a large number of religious congregations, individual priests, prominent Catholic laymen and lay organizations, who all denied doing so. On June 26, 1904, a news dispatch said that formal charges had been filed in Rome against Christie— apparently the outcome of O'Reilly's attempts, after a heated discussion with Christie, to suppress the Diocese of Baker City.

Some of the tempest settled down soon after the archdiocesan newspaper, the *Catholic Sentinel,* ended its silence on the subject and printed the denials of those alleged to have signed the pamphlet, along with an editorial and numerous statements of support for Christie. Throughout the controversy the archbishop maintained public silence and, according to reports, never even spoke of it to his associates. He was ill during much of the time and was in Oakland, California, to undergo stomach surgery when news of the charges against him became public.

Two of the malcontented priests, Msgr. Alphonse Bronsgeest and Father Schell, went to Rome trying to sell church authorities their version of the affair, but the papacy (which tended to find the American Church mystifying)

stood behind the archbishop. Christie's own quiet actions may have been responsible for this favorable outcome. In addition, his ex-secretary, Father J.T.
McNally, who was in Rome on leave to study canon law, arose as an advocate
for Christie. During 1905 McNally reported extensively to Christie on the
activities of Bronsgeest and Schell, received documents from Christie relat-
ing to O'Reilly's complaints, and was in contact with church officials about
the controversy, providing them with Christie's view. The matter was brought
to an end when Rome decided in favor of Christie's decision and Bishop
O'Reilly was left in charge of his far-flung, sparsely-populated diocese.[9]

A longstanding problem in Oregon had been a shortage of priests. This
situation prompted Christie—and probably Gross before him—to welcome
any priest who came to the archdiocese, thereby adding fuel to the controversy. Itinerant priests, owing allegiance to no one, had been a problem in the
United States from the time of Bishop John Carroll. Many bishops in Europe, notably Ireland, were happy to provide one-way tickets to America to
troublemakers in their dioceses, and bishops in the United States were just as
happy to see malcontents depart from their domains. When Christie welcomed the itinerants, his opponents charged that he was willing to accommodate more "runaway or tramp priests" than those ordained for the archdiocese.

Another controversial factor—evident elsewhere in the United States as
embattled hierarchies tried to cope with waves of immigrants of various ethnic backgrounds—was the difference in ethnic composition between the
clergy and the hierarchy. Friction between Irish and French and between Irish
and German clergy already had appeared in Oregon. The earliest bishops and
clergy in Oregon had been French and Belgian, followed by German clergy
and laity, and the Benedictines from Switzerland who settled at Mount Angel. But elsewhere in the United States, the Irish had become highly visible
in the upper echelons of the hierarchy, while clergy more identified with the
newer immigrants occupied the lower ranks. Hence, cultural and ethnic differences produced additional friction and challenges to authority. Eventually,
the problem washed up on Oregon's shores, as Archbishop Christie and
Bishop O'Reilly, both of Irish descent, faced the dissent of non-Irish priests
such as Heinrich, Demarais, Schell, and Bronsgeest.

In actuality, however, Christie fared much better than his fellow bishops
farther east. Overall, Oregon was ethnically quite homogeneous, and the
newcomers at the start of the century were still primarily of Northern European descent. Just a small number of the newer migration from eastern and
southern Europe visible elsewhere in the country reached Oregon. Because
these newer immigrants tended to settle in cities—and Oregon was still a
mostly rural state—those who did come usually took up residence in the

Portland area. Without evident controversy, the Catholics among them established churches—almost always parish churches—and schools to preserve the culture and language of their homelands. St. Joseph's parish was an example of such a parish church built by and for Germans. Different ethnic groups also co-existed in the same parish without apparently too much friction. Our Lady of Sorrows parish in Portland, founded in 1917, was able to meet its early parishioners' needs with Masses in Croatian and Italian as well as English.[10]

Priest shortages were an everpresent dilemma. Because few local young men came forward with vocations, Christie, like his predecessors, had to recruit outside his archdiocese. On his many trips to the East and Middle West, Christie would promote Oregon's mild climate, hoping to attract priests having trouble with harsh winters. However, some of those who answered his invitation had problems other than with the weather, and he admitted he lived to regret some of those invitations. On the other hand, Christie did recruit some fine priests to his archdiocese; in particular, three outstanding young men who had known him in Minnesota: Edwin V. O'Hara, George Thompson, and Warren Waite. In addition, he obtained Father Charles Smith from the major seminary in Montreal and enticed several others from Baltimore. In 1910 Christie sent Father George Thompson on a recruiting mission to Ireland. The situation began to improve by the end of the first decade of his administration with twenty candidates studying for the priesthood, most of whom were sent to St. Patrick Seminary in Menlo Park, California.[11]

In order to provide a large portion of the needed ministers for Oregon's Catholics, Christie was compelled to turn to religious communities—generally a second choice for bishops since they have less control over such priests than over diocesan ones. Benedictine and Dominican religious communities were already established, and at Christie's invitation more religious congregations arrived. Many assumed or started parishes in the Portland area which are, or until recently were, associated with them.

Christie appears to be on peaceful terms with the religious communities in his archdiocese. On the occasion of the silver jubilee of his installation as archbishop he made a point of saying that he did not distinguish between them and his diocesan priests. It was indeed beneficial that he had good relations with the leaders of the religious communities, because Oregon Catholics have almost continually been served by more religious priests than diocesan ones, on a ratio of about 2:1.

In order to staff other institutions, Christie relied on communities of religious women. Among the communities already established in the state were the Sisters of Providence, the Benedictines, the Franciscans, the Dominicans, the Sisters of St. Mary of Oregon, the Sisters of the Holy Names, the Sisters of Mercy, and the Sisters of the Good Shepherd.[12]

In the years prior to World War I, Christie, whose own education had not been extensive, did his best to make Catholic education available in his diocese. Whenever possible, he encouraged new parishes to begin with a school, even if it meant worshiping in a basement or attic. At the beginning of his administration there were only twenty-six parochial schools in the entire archdiocese. By the end of his first decade the archdiocese was supporting forty schools enrolling 5,452 pupils and employing 227 teachers. At his death there were forty-eight parochial schools; twelve academies for girls; one college for girls and another, moving toward college status, for boys; three high schools and a junior college for boys; two normal (teacher training) schools; a seminary (for Benedictines); and three training schools for nurses. Some of the religious communities of women he invited to establish or take over schools were the Sisters of St. Francis of Penance and Christian Charity; the Sisters of St. Dominic, Congregation of St. Catherine of Siena; the Sisters of Charity of the Blessed Virgin Mary; and a group from England, the Sisters of the Society of the Holy Child. The Christian Brothers continued, through most of Christie's administration, to conduct a school for boys. With Christie's encouragement and promise of financial aid, they went heavily into debt to acquire property and build a business school in Portland in 1907. Unfortunately, the school never prospered, the promised financial aid was never given, and finally, after several warnings and attempts to resolve problems, the school closed in 1922—much to the archbishop's not very logical disappointment.[13]

Christie's vision included establishing higher education for Catholics in Oregon. In 1901, as a result of negotiations with the University Land Company, he acquired property and a building on the Willamette River in North Portland, formerly belonging to the Methodists. He named his new acquisition Columbia University (in complete disregard of the one in New York City) and invited Holy Cross priests and brothers from the University of Notre Dame to operate the university. Taking charge in 1902, they gradually developed the school into the University of Portland.[14]

Young Catholic women had the benefit of already having higher education available to them in Oregon, provided by the Sisters of the Holy Names of Jesus and Mary. In 1893 St. Mary's Academy in Portland was authorized to grant bachelor's degrees and became known as St. Mary's Academy and

College. This was the first four-year liberal arts college for women in the state and one of the first Catholic women's colleges in the United States. The Holy Names' educational activities began to expand during Christie's administration, until by 1930 they had moved both college and provincial house to a site on the Willamette River just south of Lake Oswego. Then St. Mary's College took the name Marylhurst College (now University).[15]

⊹══⊹

At the turn of the century, Catholic laity was for the most part still struggling to establish itself and advance economically. Families tended to do much of their entertainment and socializing in the parish, so many of the lay organizations supported were parish ones; but by 1920 lay organizations with archdiocesan-wide ties were becoming more visible. Lay organizations listed in the *Catholic Sentinel* as being active beyond the parish level in the archdiocese as of 1920 were the Knights of Columbus, the Daughters of Isabella, the Ancient Order of Hibernians and its Ladies Auxiliary, St. Joseph's Verein, Men's and Women's Catholic Orders of Foresters, Catholic Knights of America, and the Holy Name Society, which was organized on an archdiocesan-wide basis by Christie in 1917.

Three women's groups were active in charitable work. Prior to 1900, St. Ann's Society met regularly with non-Catholic charitable groups in Portland to coordinate their efforts on behalf of the "worthy poor." In 1900 three socially prominent Catholic women started the Ladies Aid Society to assist poor families referred to them by pastors. One organization that was outstanding for its activities in the community was the Catholic Women's League of Portland. It was organized in 1909 by Father Edwin V. O'Hara and Caroline Gleason to help "self-supporting girls and women" and those "adrift" by establishing a small center in the downtown Portland area with a lunchroom, rest rooms, and classrooms for lectures for working women. In 1913 the Catholic Women's League helped pass a landmark law in Oregon to provide minimum wages for women.[16]

A more controverial lay organization, the Knights of Columbus, was welcomed early in the 20th century into Christie's archdiocese. The Knights had been established in 1882 in the eastern United States for insurance purposes and to provide a Catholic response to the popularity of secret societies in the late nineteenth century. However, its secret ritual aroused suspicion and hostility in some bishops, who regarded it as too similar to the Masons. This sentiment still lingered when Archbishop Christie encouraged the establishment of the first Council, No. 678, in Portland on June 15, 1902. The tension apparently did not trouble Christie, who may have shrewdly regarded the Knights of Columbus as potentially good spokesmen for the Church. Membership grew to the extent that when the Knights conducted a nation-wide campaign to make Columbus Day a holiday, its Oregon contingent wielded sufficient clout to get the legislation passed and signed by Governor Oswald West in February 1911.

The Knights of Columbus also encouraged a distaff counterpart, the Daughters of Isabella, which in Oregon changed its name to the Catholic Daughters of America in 1921. Begun in Eugene in 1909 with Court Oregon 118 in St. Mary's parish, the society quickly took on a life of its own, aiding destitute families.

A more subtle lay contribution to the well-being of the archdiocese was effected through the *Catholic Sentinel,* which, while it announced itself to be the official organ of the archdiocese soon after Christie arrived, was lay-owned throughout his administration. Nonetheless, Christie apparently had a great deal of influence over it. Early in his administration he twice changed its editor, finally settling on John O'Hara, who became at least part owner of The Sentinel Publishing Company. O'Hara was a brother of Father Edwin V. O'Hara, who was already a prominent personality in the community and church. Not surprisingly, under John O'Hara the *Sentinel* was a very pro-Irish voice, and also provided extensive coverage to the three local active Irish organizations: the Ancient Order of Hibernians, the United Irish League, and the Gael's League of Portland. The paper also gave publicity to candidates with Irish names running for political office.[17]

America's entry into World War I provided an opportunity for Catholics to be drawn further into the mainstream of national events. For Catholics nationwide, it was a chance to prove their loyalty and patriotism. The American hierarchy proclaimed its support for President Woodrow Wilson and the war effort, and Catholics engaged in a wide variety of home-front activities. Catholics in Oregon responded as well, many individually taking part in war-related activities in their communities.[18]

The United States' declaration of war against the German Empire in April 1917 had an immediate impact on Columbia University (University of Portland), then a high school for boys. Students, some of them as young as sixteen, rushed to enlist; eventually 178 students, alumni, faculty and former faculty members served in the American armed forces.[19]

The War Department gave the Knights of Columbus official status as a social service agency for the armed forces. Twelve Oregon Knights served in its Overseas Service, including three chaplains: Father Edwin V. O'Hara, Father John A. Moran, and Father E.P. Murphy. These men ministered to soldiers at Knights of Columbus service centers rather than as members of the armed forces. The Portland Council also collected funds for a War Bond Drive, and had a center for servicemen in the Portland area with Frank Lonergan as the secretary.[20]

Christie gave wholehearted support to the war effort. In spite of the continuing priest shortage, he encouraged priests to enlist as chaplains. In 1917 he called on Catholics to revere the flag and he urged the purchase of war bonds. The following year he joined other American archbishops in Washington, D.C., to plan an extension of American Catholic war work in France and Italy. The *Sentinel* contributed its bit by publishing numerous accounts of Catholic war heroes. Interestingly, while Archbishop Christie was busy promoting Catholic patriotism, his name appeared briefly on a Justice Department list of possible subversives engaged in activities on behalf of the Irish Republican Army; but then it was quickly removed. The Catholic community was apparently never aware of this information.[21]

The church received less attractive publicity when a German-language newspaper for German Catholics, *St. Josephs Blatt*, published by the Benedictines at Mount Angel Abbey, was suppressed by the government as being too pro-German. Anti-Catholic prejudice had become more visible as early as 1914 when fundamentalist Protestant preachers had begun voicing such sentiments, and it was stimulated by the influx of shipyard workers to Portland during the war, many of them Catholics from Southern Europe. In addition, the war increased general anti-foreign feelings, and the Catholic church was perceived as having international ties, thus being less than wholly "American."[22]

Before World War I, a combination of prevailing anti-Catholic sentiments and the fact that most Catholics as new arrivals were still struggling to establish themselves, resulted in the average Catholic keeping a low profile. However, a number of Catholics were beginning to have an impact on the wider community, including a handful of men in public office, such as Henry E. McGinn, Daniel J. Malarkey, Andrew C. Smith, John Driscoll, Michael Murnane, and G. Heitkemper—all of whom served in the state legislature—and John M. Gearin in the United States Senate. Others beginning to emerge on the Portland social and economic scene included Joseph Jacobberger, architect, Lansing Stout, banker, General D.W. Burke and Colonel John Murphy, United States Army, Colonel David M. Dunne, who also served as a leader in the Republican Party's conservative wing and as northwest collector of internal revenue from 1898–1913, Joseph Albers, flour mill owner, and families such as the Sheas, Malarkeys, Tongues, Dalys, and Sinnotts. Also during this pre-war period, Father George Thompson began a long career as a mediator in labor-management disputes, and served on a number of arbitration boards in the Northwest.[23]

In particular, two Catholics had a decided impact in Oregon and far beyond its borders: Father Edwin V. O'Hara and Caroline Gleason. Father O'Hara, especially interested in education, served as the first superintendent of Catholic schools and president of the Catholic Education Association of Oregon. He also was concerned about social welfare and the labor problems and acquired fame as a speaker on those topics throughout Oregon. In 1914 the Oregon branch of the National Consumers' League asked him to become chairman of a special committee to study the minimum wage question, and in that capacity he began an investigation of the wages and conditions experienced by working women. He and Judge Henry E. McGinn, a prominent Catholic judge and ex-legislator, recruited Caroline Gleason, a professional social worker who had graduated from the University of Minnesota, done graduate work in Chicago, and lived at a settlement house there. She was commissioned to conduct a social survey for the Consumers' League, and she and her committee accumulated the factual information on the mistreatment of working women that formed the basis for reform legislation sponsored by the Consumers' League and the Catholic Women's League, which she and O'Hara had founded in 1908. Working with Oregon Governor Oswald West and two Catholic legislators, Dan J. Malarkey, president of the state senate, and Michael Murnane in the state house of representatives, O'Hara and Gleason helped to secure passage in 1913 of the first effective minimum wage law for women in the nation. Both then served on the Industrial Welfare Commission set up by the governor to implement it, and Gleason was the commission secretary from 1913 to 1916.[24]

In 1917 O'Hara persuaded Christie to found the Catholic Children's Bureau to coordinate all cases involving Catholic children in the Portland courts and to represent the various Catholic institutions serving children. He moved into new fields when he was assigned in 1920 to St. Mary Parish in Eugene after he had asked for a rural parish. There he took charge of the work among the poor being done by the Daughters of Isabella and turned it over to the men of the parish, establishing the St. Vincent de Paul Society of Eugene. He also developed *A Program of Catholic Rural Action,* which included proposals for religious vacation schools and religious correspondence courses, launched the Rural Life Bureau of the National Catholic Welfare Council (Conference), and began a catechetical program that became the Confraternity of Christian Doctrine. He rounded out a career of national importance by becoming bishop of Great Falls and then archbishop of Kansas City.[25]

Caroline Gleason, after her contribution to passage of the minimum wage law, conducted a survey of living conditions of working women in Portland at the request of the Oregon Consumers' League. This survey resulted in a new city housing code. She joined the Sisters of the Holy Names in 1916, the year before the United States Supreme Court upheld Oregon's minimum wage law in *Stettler v. O'Hara*. As Sister Miriam Theresa, S.N.J.M., she was the first woman to get a Ph.D. from Catholic University of America's School of Social Work, and became director of the Department of Social Work at Marylhurst College. She received a number of tributes during her lifetime and was eulogized at her death in 1962.[26]

The positive contributions made to social justice by O'Hara and Gleason were not credited to Catholic ideals or inspiration, but tended instead to be included by Oregonians within the parameters of a statewide progressive movement, through which Oregon was emerging as a national leader. Prevailing prejudice against Catholicism made it much more acceptable to broadcast negative images of the institution to the public. There was a flurry of escapades involving religious personnel that brought negative publicity to the Church during the pre-World War I years. For example, in 1910, Abbot Thomas Meienhofer, O.S.B., resigned his post at the Mount Angel Abbey and then left religious life, all in a burst of embarrassing publicity. His story was followed by an emotionally disturbed Sister of Providence, Sister Lucretia, who in 1912 represented herself as an "escaped nun" and spoke to groups of Portland women on the horrors of convent life. In 1913 another woman, claiming to be a nun who had escaped from the Benedictine convent at Mount Angel, enjoyed a brief summer of notoriety; and an ex-priest and his wife, an ex-nun, came to Oregon in 1917 to titillate the public.[27]

The ease with which these episodes could be exploited and the hypersensitivity of Catholics during World War I give some indication of the prevalence of antipathy toward Catholicism in Oregon. A tradition of anti-Catholicism had been brought to Oregon in the nineteenth century by immigrants from the Upper South—evangelical, Bible-belt country—and it was still strong. There was a tremendous veneration of those Oregon Trail pioneers by Oregonians, many of whom were their descendants. Many residents of the state, because of their heritage, felt that immigrants from elsewhere—particularly Catholics—were somehow a corrupting influence.[28]

During the first decade of the twentieth century, Catholics often found themselves socially excluded, and reminders of their status were frequent.

Advertisements for maids and cooks in Portland newspapers often added that a "Catholic need not apply." Frank L. Smith and his family were unable to sublet a farm near Scappoose because of their religion. Later, when the Smith girls became teachers and sought positions in the public schools, they could only find employment in communities that were mostly Catholic or by describing themselves as "Christian" where religious affiliation was indicated. Older Catholics who attended parochial schools remembered exchanging taunts with their public school counterparts, calling each other "Catlickers" and "publickers," accompanied by occasional fistfights. One remembered playing baseball on a Holy Name team that was in the City League. If they struck out someone would shout, "The Pope wouldn't like that!" or "Put some holy water on it!" The players were admonished: "Don't have rabbit ears, just make out you don't hear them."[29]

The end of World War I was accompanied by a new swell of intolerance, stimulated by the hatred which had been encouraged against the now-defeated Central Powers, and further fed by economic uncertainties following the war. It first found expression in a "Red Scare" as Americans, shaken by the outcome of the Russian Revolution, sought out feared communists. As one historian noted: "the backfire of intolerance swept out of control and began to sear the country. Not only radicals, but labor organizers, aliens, Catholics, Jews, and blacks became its victims." Oregon was ready fuel for the flames of intolerance.[30]

In 1921 Columbia University, which at the time was still a high school, was forced out of the Portland Interscholastic League, and was not allowed to play sports with any public high schools. Although Michael Murnane and Dan J. Malarkey, who helped pass the minimum wage bill, and other Catholics served in the state legislature, Oregonians now became so reluctant to elect Catholics to public office that Judge John P. Kavanaugh resigned because he believed he had no hope of being reelected. He was probably right, because in the 1922 election every circuit incumbent judge endorsed by the Ku Klux Klan won reelection; the only incumbent to lose, W.N. Gaten, was a Catholic. Frank Lonergan, a prominent Portland trial lawyer (later to become an influential member of the state house of representatives), regularly informed clients who came to him to defend them in a jury trial that if they felt his being a Catholic might be detrimental to their case they were to feel free to engage another lawyer.[31]

Intolerance in the nation found its noisiest advocate in the neo-Ku Klux Klan which became prominent after World War I. Although only 8½ percent of Oregonians were Catholics and, with the possible exception of Utah, Oregon was the most homogeneous state west of the Rocky Mountains, the Klan found it easier to focus on Catholics than on even smaller minorities of blacks or Jews. Soon after the end of World War I, the Klan appeared in Oregon, spread rapidly through the Willamette Valley, and out to the coast. It built an enthusiastic organization in Portland and in July 1922 an initiative petition began to circulate, supported most prominently by Masons and the Klan, entitled "Compulsory School Bill." Although compulsory education already existed in Oregon, this bill required compulsory attendance at public schools. While it would have suppressed all private schools, its primary target was Catholic schools. Christie tried unsuccessfully to combat it by hiring a lawyer with experience fighting the Klan and, in cooperation with Bishop Joseph McGrath of Baker City, attempted to mobilize public opinion. Similar attempts to close parochial schools occurred elsewhere in the country, but the most successful campaign took place in Oregon. On a wave of anti-Catholicism, the initiative passed in the fall election. Walter M. Pierce, who supported the measure, was elected governor, and other Klan sympathizers won election to the legislature and to local offices. For a brief period Oregonians seemed to be overwhelmed by a wave of emotional bigotry.[32]

With Christie's active support and funds provided by the Knights of Columbus and the National Catholic Welfare Conference, the Sisters of the Holy Names challenged the constitutionality of the new law. The case was argued jointly, with one brought by Hill Military Academy, by John P. Kavanaugh, the archdiocese's attorney, with assistance from Hall Lusk, Dan Malarkey, Frank Lonergan, and the tireless Father Edwin O'Hara, who was still superintendent of Catholic schools. The court decided for the sisters and the academy, so the State of Oregon appealed all the way to the United States Supreme Court, which in 1925 upheld the decision, declaring the law unconstitutional because it violated the Fourteenth Amendment. By that time Christie was dead, but this last and biggest challenge of his administration to the church he served, and the Church's victory over it, had the lasting positive effect of giving Oregon Catholics greater confidence in dealing with the communities in which they resided.[33]

In November of 1922, just after Oregon voters approved the Compulsory School initiative, Christie founded the Catholic Truth Society of Oregon. He appointed Father Charles Smith to be its director, and, at least once, contrary to his usual policy, directed that a special collection be taken up for its support. Its purpose was to provide—through publicity, such as newspaper releases, pamphlets and lectures—non-Catholics with information about the

Church and the activities of its educational and charitable institutions. Off to a fast start, within two years the society had distributed 250,000 pamphlets to twenty-five states, the Philippine Islands, and parts of Canada; instituted a lecture program to provide speakers in Portland and elsewhere in the state; began sponsorship of a weekly half-hour radio broadcast in 1925; and provided an auto chapel car to bring the church to isolated areas.[34]

One of Christie's dreams, which was painfully slow to be realized, was to build a new cathedral to replace the building on N.W. 15th Avenue and Davis Street (which one historian described as a "huge wooden crate"). The cathedral building fund grew slowly and by the time it was large enough to start construction Christie was terminally ill. However, he retained a lively interest in the project and the cathedral was built as he and his architect Joseph Jacobberger had envisioned it.[35]

In spite of recurring spells of poor health, Christie grew to know his archdiocese thoroughly, and believed that he could best serve Oregon Catholics by establishing many small parishes accessible to as many Catholics as possible, scattered as they were throughout the western portion of the state. In Portland alone, he established over twenty new parishes, eight of them between 1911 and 1913. Statewide, between 1910 and 1919 he dedicated more than fifty churches and chapels.

Characteristically, once he had selected a site for a new parish and named its pastor, he gave the priest the autonomy to solve the problems of financing, building, and organizing his new parish. Religious communities that started parishes, unlike diocesan-owned parishes, were expected to acquire the land in their own names and retain ownership, along with responsibility for ensuing expenses. In the early days of his administration Christie was extraordinarily active, visiting established parishes and looking for sites for new ones. After the automobile came into general use he apparently never learned to drive, but he enjoyed being taken on drives through the countryside to scout out potential sites for new parishes to buy when the price was right. He was a shrewd land speculator and his real estate deals were an integral part of the remarkable growth of the church during and after his administration.[36]

Providing facilities for religious services where there were no parishes was sometimes a challenge. After the newly founded Catholic Church Extension Society built its first chapel railroad car in 1907, through Christie's efforts it was sent to Oregon in 1909 to provide accommodations for religious services in remote areas. The railroad companies transported it and allowed it to park on their sidings for worship services free of charge. Named the St. Anthony Chapel Car, it contained an altar, pews, and accommodations for a chaplain and superintendent of the car. Christie placed the program under the direction of Father Charles Smith, with George Hennessey as car superintendent. Its visits brought Catholics together and often stimulated them to build churches in such areas as the Lower Columbia River and remote spots in the Willamette Valley. Christie became a member of the Board of Governors of the Catholic Extension Society, whereby he kept the society interested in providing financial assistance to Oregon missions and for the construction of churches. The increased railroad activity of World War I sidetracked the chapel cars and, though they resumed activities for a few years afterwards, by the end of 1924 the automobile, with its greater ease of transportation, permanently ended their function as mobile chapels.[37]

Although the Extension Society provided Christie with some aid, a shortage of finances continued to plague the Oregon archdiocese. When Christie arrived, he sold some of the Church's property to liquidate a large portion of debts owed by the archdiocese. Nevertheless, debts continued to mount, and his successor encountered the same problem. Throughout Christie's administration the archdiocese was very poor. Neither bishops nor priests drew regular salaries. At one point, Christie wrote a letter appealing to the laity in all the parishes to contribute directly to the support of the archbishop. He noted that the custom had been to impose a tax on parish or mission revenue, "but, owing to the condition of the diocese, this method of supporting the archbishop has proven a failure."[38]

Though Christie lived very frugally, he had a casual attitude toward money and other facets of administration. It was rumored that when he was short of money he supported himself from the offerings of the votive lights at the cathedral. He conducted business from a makeshift chancery office upstairs in the rectory of the temporary cathedral. He must have kept most records in his head, because he seldom wrote anything down (what he did write was not very legible) and his priests claimed that he "had the chancery office in his vest pocket." Most financial transactions took place through verbal agreements—often over the telephone—with few, if any, records kept. An anecdote claims that when his successor, Archbishop Edward Howard, inquired where the church records were, he was referred to a suitcase in Christie's bedroom closet.[39]

However haphazard his methods may have been, on his death Christie left an impressive legacy of new parishes, schools, and other Catholic institutions. This legacy also included pieces of property around the Portland area, a residence on SW Myrtle Street in Portland, and a large parcel of property in Beaverton. Later on, this land became a tremendous asset for the archdiocese. After contributing materially to the church structure in his archdiocese and working with and leading his fellow Catholics into the twentieth century, Christie died in St. Vincent's Hospital in Portland on April 6, 1925; he was a month short of seventy-seven.[40]

+⟩═══⟨+

Bishops in the United States were required to be administrators, unlike their counterparts in Europe. They had to be builders of schools, churches, and other institutions needed to meet the needs of an immigrant church in a non-Catholic environment. Unlike their fellow prelates in many countries, they did not inherit longstanding infrastructures. They were appointed to their positions without any prior business administration training and had to learn on the job.[41]

In many dimensions, Archbishop Christie admirably fulfilled the expectations of an American bishop. He helped further establish the Church in Oregon and carried the archdiocese to a new level. Christie took the lead in the struggle to provide institutional structures for the growing Catholic population in Oregon, was active in recruiting priests, seeking funds, and acquiring land. He showed himself an effective leader in times of crises, through World War I, and during the fight to retain parochial schools in Oregon.

Concerning local administration, Christie preferred to allow individual parishes to take action for themselves. Despite Christie's directive of December 1899, reminding all pastors of a provincial decree that any debt exceeding $50 had to have the written permission of the bishop, little attempt was made by the archdiocese to monitor parish finances; and parishes, largely ignoring the directive, generally borrowed whenever and whatever they could. The poverty of most Oregon Catholics, combined with Christie's casual approach to record keeping and the scattered nature of Catholic enclaves, led to a continuing burden of indebtedness during his tenure.

Christie's 1899 directive also informed his priests that when they bought property for the archdiocese all deeds had to be made in the name of "Roman Catholic archbishop of the diocese of Oregon," and he had to inspect them before they were recorded. This part of his directive was honored, an indication of respect for Christie's authority and his recognized talent for making shrewd land purchases.[42]

Christie landed on a very successful pattern for governing Oregon's Catholics. The parcels of property, and the parish churches and schools built on them—so important to the future growth of the Church in Oregon—were firmly in archdiocesan hands; but the development and growth of the individual Catholic communities was allowed to remain within the control of parish priests and their congregations. Christie's overreaching contribution was to permit Oregon's Catholics to work out their own manifestations of faith locally—with his encouragement but not his encroachment—and he reaped the benefit of seeing them planted more firmly than ever in their state's soil.

Edward Daniel Howard (1877–1983)
Archbishop of Portland in Oregon (1926–1966)
Oregon Catholic Press

Chapter Six
Iowa Schoolmaster

N INTERREGNUM of just over a year followed Archbishop Christie's death while church authorities conducted a search for a new archbishop. Reportedly, more than one cleric turned the position down. Then, once again, the Middle West provided a prelate, Edward Daniel Howard. The new archbishop was born in Cresco, Iowa, on November 5, 1877, to Irish parents who owned a small horse farm. Edward's father died when he was thirteen years old. His mother, who had had a strong influence on him, accompanied her son to Portland and lived with him until her death six years later.[1]

Howard came to his position with a much more extensive educational background than Alexander Christie. He attended St. Joseph's College in Dubuque, Iowa, followed by St. Paul's Seminary in Minnesota, and was ordained by Archbishop John Ireland in St. Paul on June 12, 1906. Ireland immediately assigned him to teach at St. Joseph's High School, where he rose to become principal. After several years in that position, promotions suddenly rained on him: he became president of St. Joseph's College in 1921, auxiliary bishop of Davenport in 1924, and archbishop of Oregon City in 1926. In appearance he was less impressive than Christie—smaller in stature and not as regal—but he possessed a dignity of bearing that complemented his office. Gray-haired, stocky, and of medium height, Howard was a well-kept man who carried himself erectly. One of his priests claimed that he "looked like an archbishop in every sense of the word." He wore thick, dark-rimmed glasses, had a hearty laugh, and, by his own admission, did not know what it was like to be ill. A man who enjoyed life, Howard was at ease with himself and with others—school children, priests, seminarians, parishioners—even the pope. Though clergy and laity found him to be very approachable and pleasant, he always maintained the reserve of a schoolmaster, retaining a certain space between him and those who approached him. He took the dignity of his office

seriously, particularly on ceremonial occasions, and insisted on proper deference to him as archbishop. In his contacts with others, like Christie, he desired to be addressed as "Your Grace." One person remembered him as "an
interesting combination of intimacy and retention of dignity."[2]

The new archbishop did not have the easy, genial relationship with priests
that Christie had maintained. Though he was approachable up to a point,
they sensed a line beyond which they were not to step, even in casual conversation and joking. "Woe betide you if you overstepped that invisible ring."
Or as another priest phrased it, "You darn soon knew if you went too far."[3]

Archbishop Howard was fair with his priests and if he gave one a job to
do, he also gave him the authority to do it and fully supported him. However,
because he had spent all of his previous clerical career in education, he did not
have the pastoral experience that might have made him more understanding
of the problems some of his priests faced. Sometimes he permitted or asked
them to take on more assignments than they could handle reasonably. He did
not believe priests at the chancery office should be full-time officials, so almost everyone also had a parish to attend to. He did not postpone action in
dealing with problems and, though he could get angry to the point of losing
his temper, he did not let such outbursts destroy a good relationship. He
thoroughly enjoyed having priests drop in on him at his home in the evening
for a visit, often appearing to be reluctant to see them leave; but he was still
more their superior than their confidante; as one expressed it, he was "at a
crozier's distance."[4]

The portrait that emerges is that of a plain but attractive man, with a
good sense of humor, simple life-style and frugal personal needs, who was
very much in charge. His temperament was such that he never took his problems home with him to trouble his sleep. As one of his priests remarked, he
lived a long time because he liked his position and he never worried about it.
If he encountered a problem, he handed it on to one of his priests to cope
with. He moved through life with little stress, comfortable with God, himself, and the world, doing what he believed needed to be done, breasting the
waves of change that washed around him without worrying too much about
what stirred beneath. His clothing was immaculately clean, but sometimes
patched, and his black coat frequently did not exactly match his black pants.
Howard soon found that his simple life-style fitted well in his new diocese,
since the Catholic community in Portland was small and its archbishop not
particularly notable. He soon encountered Oregonians' lack of recognition
for his status: the day after he arrived he had trouble cashing a check, even
though he was wearing a black suit with a Roman collar that included the
touch of red that bishops wore at that time.[5]

Cathedral of the Immaculate Conception, 1927. *Oregon Catholic Press*

Howard introduced a new era by setting up a chancery in the Cathedral rectory, and in 1931 started construction of a building at 2051 S.W. 6th Avenue in which were housed such diocesan offices as existed, the Catholic Truth Society, and the *Sentinel*. Eventually the *Sentinel* moved its presses across the street and the diocesan offices expanded to include the Office of the Superintendent of Catholic Schools; but as late as 1940, the chancery still employed only two secretaries and the offices tended to be closed by 12:30 each day.[6]

When Howard took control of his archdiocese, he discovered, as had his predecessor, that it was almost bankrupt. He rectified Christie's informal financial practices by hiring an accounting firm to make a survey of archdiocesan assets and liabilities—which had an immediately beneficial effect on its credit rating. Finding that each parish was negotiating its own debt, he streamlined the process so that parishes would be required to borrow from the chancery office, thereby giving him greater control and influence over parish borrowing. If the borrowing were approved by Howard, the chancery would in turn borrow from banks on the parish's behalf.[7]

After setting up the chancery office in the cathedral Howard began to deal with some of the archdiocese's other problems. He abolished the custom of pew rents in churches, began to provide the *National Catholic Directory* with more accurate statistics on his archdiocese, and dealt with the itinerant priests Christie had tolerated. Howard insisted that they be incardinated, swearing obedience to him, or leave. "So," exaggerated one priest, "every freight train going out of Portland was loaded with them."[8]

In 1929 Howard took another effective step when he took over owner-ship of the *Catholic Sentinel*, which had from the outset been lay-owned and financially unprofitable. By 1929 its owners, John O'Hara and Patrick Sullivan, were deeply in debt and anxious to sell the paper to the archdiocese. Howard, delighted with the success of the Catholic Truth Society, encouraged it to incorporate, so it could borrow money to purchase the *Sentinel*. It did so in April 1929. After the *Sentinel* came under his control, Howard did not micromanage it, but the editorial staff was well aware of what was or was not acceptable to the archbishop.[9]

The Catholic Truth Society further expanded its activities by producing radio broadcasts from about 1925 into the early 1930s, and sponsoring guest speakers, among the most notable being Gilbert Keith Chesterton in 1931. In 1934 the society moved on another opportunity by beginning to publish the *Sunday Missal*. These were pamphlet missals, each one for a specific Sunday, that were mailed out weekly to subscribers and in bulk to parishes. Growing lay participation in the Mass, the switch to the vernacular, and new music for congregational singing have since given the Catholic Truth Society (now Oregon Catholic Press) an expanding field for its publications. Still, its most visible product is the *Sentinel*, which the press subsidizes through its more profitable publications, since the *Sentinel* does not generate enough revenue to pay for its publication.

Believing that the archdiocese should be more correctly identified, in 1929 Howard requested that Rome recognize the longstanding fact that its headquarters were in Portland, not Oregon City. Rome changed its name to Archdiocese of Portland in Oregon, adding "in Oregon" to distinguish it from the Diocese of Portland, Maine. Howard continued to be Metropolitan of the Oregon Province, which included Alaska, Washington, Idaho, and Montana—geographically the largest province in the world at that time. Provinces in the early 1930s were supposed to hold yearly meetings, and Edwin O'Hara, then bishop of Great Falls, encouraged Howard to convene the Fourth Provincial Council in 1932. Howard entrusted O'Hara with the preparations and, influenced by Howard's interest in education and O'Hara's background in Confraternity of Christian Doctrine (CCD) programs, the council enacted a number of decrees emphasizing catechetical programs—particularly vacation schools, study clubs for adults, and Sunday schools for children in public schools. In fact, the Council's meetings under Howard issued so many decrees that Pope Pius XI allegedly remarked that God had only given ten; but then added that, of course, Howard was not "il Signore."[10]

One of the primary demands of the archdiocese is that its archbishop draw together its scattered parishes, which means constant travel from the Columbia River to the California border and from the Cascades to the coast. Though automobiles had become common by the time of Howard's arrival, he never drove, and there is speculation as to whether or not he knew how to drive. Oregon roads in the 1920s were still poor, most were unpaved, and many small communities, especially in southern Oregon, were difficult to reach. Yet somehow Howard always reached even the most remote churches for confirmation and other important occasions, and he apparently enjoyed visiting with priests and laity in each parish.[11]

It was vital for Howard to know the priests and people of his archdiocese in 1926, because the Church and society were starting to change profoundly. Society would be shaken out of the pseudo-prosperity and complacency of the 1920s by the stockmarket crash of 1929 and the ensuing Great Depression. In the Church the parishes would also be awakened from the defensiveness forced upon them by the bigotry of the early and mid-1920s. Catholics' defensive posture began to change nationally by the end of the decade, as the effects of the National Catholic Welfare Conference's endorsement of the Social Gospel, a liberal Protestant protest against the abuses of the Industrial Revolution, began to feed the movement known as Catholic Action.[12]

Catholic Action was a world-wide movement, encouraged by Pope Pius XI who saw it as a way in which the laity, working in the world, would become an extension of the priestly hierarchy, with a special mandate from their bishop. In Oregon, as elsewhere in the United States, the action was more likely to originate with the laity or lower clergy and be supported by the archbishop, whose support was more likely to be moral than material.[13]

Still, Howard set the tone soon after his installation in 1929 when, with the aid of John Leinweber, he revived the St. Vincent de Paul Society. He summoned the existing parish conferences, about fifteen in Portland, to form a council and appointed Father Lucien Lauerman, who was already interested in social work, as its first director. The Society had been founded in Portland in 1869, and one of its early notable actions had been to attract the Sisters of Charity of Providence from across the river in Vancouver, Washington, by giving them $1,000 to start St. Vincent's Hospital. After World War I, the Society became moribund until Howard acted to draw Catholic men into charitable work. The response from men to Howard's appeal to revive the St. Vincent de Paul Society was immediate and generous. Because of its interest in general aid to needy families, it became associated with Catholic Charities when that agency was organized, and under its supervision the Society became responsible for the Family Welfare Program of the archdiocese.[14]

In 1930 the Great Depression settled over the land. In 1932, as Howard began to interest laymen in charitable works, Cardinal Patrick J. Hayes of New York visited Portland. He spoke of his special interest in New York's Catholic Charities and the importance of all Catholics giving for charity. The following year he offered to take a priest from Portland to study at the New York School of Social Work and train in Catholic Charities there. The same year that Cardinal Hayes made his offer, a citizens' committee in Portland conducted a survey of Catholic charitable agencies and concluded that a need for "remedial and progressive programs" existed. The committee's report may have increased Howard's willingness to accept Hayes' invitation, and Lauerman, active in the revival of the Society of St. Vincent de Paul, eagerly accepted the assignment. When Lauerman returned from the East in 1933, he made a detailed study of all charitable activities in the archdiocese, both religious and lay. Then he set to work to consolidate the institutions that served children, the Catholic Children's Bureau, and to some extent the other religious and lay charitable efforts, into a single organization: Catholic Charities. Catholic Charities also served to legally represent all Catholic institutions involved in caring for children in the courts. In 1933 Lauerman organized the Board of Catholic Charities, the first significant lay board in the archdiocese, composed mostly of prominent businessmen. Charles Wentworth of Wentworth Chevrolet was its first president. Archbishop Howard faithfully attended its meetings at the Benson Hotel in Portland and had a major role in selecting its members. The Board of Catholic Charities was incorporated as a nonprofit corporation in 1936, with Father Valentine L. Moffenbeier as its second director.[15]

Welfare efforts by the state were also expanding at this time, encouraged by appropriations from the federal government through New Deal programs. In 1941, to meet the standards and requirements of new state welfare laws passed in 1939, Catholic Charities formalized its relations with member institutions by drawing up contracts under which it undertook responsibility for all children under Catholic auspices; it also began to employ trained caseworkers. While the primary concern of Catholic Charities was the welfare of children, after its incorporation it began to broaden its scope. It embraced the Catholic Youth Organization as a subsidiary, after its formation in 1934, and worked with the Society of St. Vincent de Paul, which had among its interests the interracial Chapel of the Little Flower and the Blessed Martin Day Nursery.[16]

Howard was supportive of lay initiatives in the area of Catholic charities. One such initiative was providing spiritual and material help to the unemployed men on lower West Burnside Street, Portland's skid row. With financial support from his mother, Estelle Kraft Larkin, and verbal encouragement from Howard, in the fall of 1935, Father John Larkin rented a building at S.W. 3rd and Ankeny and revived what had been an earlier, short-lived downtown mission. It included a chapel and a reading room for idle men on the streets in the area, as well as for people in downtown offices and those waiting at a nearby streetcar transfer point.[17]

Another initiative in Catholic Action was born in the spring of 1937. A handful of Marylhurst College students who belonged to a Catholic Action group started a Saturday afternoon nursery school for Japanese children, which they dedicated to a Japanese martyr, St. Paul Miki. The following fall, the Sisters of the Holy Names, who conducted Marylhurst College, took it over, and expanded it into a full day school for Japanese children from pre-nursery through second grade. It targeted the children of poor Japanese living in the lower West Burnside area and ostensibly was a missionary work, although it emphasized care, education, and, surprisingly for that time, preservation of Japanese language and culture. It failed as a missionary effort but provided loving day-care and good rudimentary education for a handful of Japanese children.

Howard was especially supportive of the St. Paul Miki School, often stopping in on his walks to visit when it was on N.W. 17th Street and attending many of its functions. But after the attack on Pearl Harbor he distanced himself from it and warned the sisters they would probably have to close the school, which they did after the Japanese evacuation order was issued.[18]

The Japanese were not the only racial minority of interest to the church. In 1929 Father Lucien Lauerman, at that time an assistant pastor at the Cathedral, started a Catholic Society for Filipino Boys, and later Father Francis Schaefers served as chaplain for a Filipino Club at the cathedral. He saw as part of his duties checking out communist meetings in Portland and scolding Filipinos he found there. Oregon law forbade interracial marriages, so Filipinos who wanted to marry American girls went across the river to Vancouver, Washington. It often took them a while to validate their marriages in the Catholic Church; Father Schaefers remembered more than one such wedding with a baby in the bride's arms.[19]

An apostolate among African-Americans also began during the 1930s. Apparently a few blacks were already Catholic and at least one black child attended Cathedral parish school before 1924. However, a 1926 editorial in the *Advocate*, a Portland black newspaper, criticized the parochial schools for their segregation, charging that two attempts to enroll black children in Catholic schools in Vancouver and Portland had failed because of discrimination. In 1930 two schools, St. Mary's Academy and St. Andrew's parochial school, began to admit black students. In a further move to serve the needs of black Catholics in Portland, the St. Vincent de Paul Society aided in the formation of the Blessed Martin League of Oregon in 1939. Howard gave the League permission to establish a chapel, the Chapel of the Little Flower, at 21 N.E. Broadway. Apparently this was not an attempt to segregate blacks, because, although it was intended chiefly for them, they were still expected to support their own parishes while the Blessed Martin League maintained the chapel.

Father Jerome Schmitz
Archives of the Archdiocese of Portland

In 1940 the St. Vincent de Paul Society, under the leadership of Father Jerome H. Schmitz, its spiritual director, and Charles E. Royer, its executive secretary, started an interracial day nursery. It was variously staffed by Holy Names Sisters, Sisters of St. Mary of Oregon, Benedictine Sisters and Sisters of Providence. Later it moved to N. Williams Avenue and Graham Street, and in 1973 to what had originally been Immaculata Academy. It was renamed St. Martin DePorres Day Nursery and finally became known as the St. Vincent Day Nursery until it closed its doors in 1990.[20]

Aiming at the adult sector, in the fall of 1937 two priests stationed at the Cathedral, one of them directly influenced by lay Catholic activist Frank Sheed, decided it was time to do some aggressive evangelizing by street preaching—such as was occurring on the East Coast and in England. They used Father Larkin's Downtown Chapel as their base of operations and set up their soapbox (literally) in front of it. Encouraged by what they saw as an interest in their presentation of Catholic dogma, they tried to extend their operations into "enemy territory"— Lonsdale Square, where communists were reputed to gather. Their debut resulted in a near riot when the young and impulsive speaker, Father Frank Foster, reacted violently to a heckler who made a nasty remark about priests and nuns. That evening Howard, whose flexibility and acquiescence had limits, telephoned the leader of the band, Father Francis Schaefers, and told him to discontinue their activity. Subsequently, they confined their preaching to the front of the Downtown Chapel until American involvement in World War II put an end to the endeavor.[21]

Individual lay members also carried their ideals into the secular world. In the 1920s, long before Catholic Action became a recognized movement, Caroline Gleason, later Sister Miriam Theresa, S.N.J.M., and the Catholic Women's League had been active on behalf of working women. During that same period, Elizabeth Jane Keegan Williams, a cathedral parishioner when Father Edwin V. O'Hara was pastor, involved herself in the women's rights movement, becoming secretary of the Portland local of the International Ladies Garment Workers Union and later of the State Federation of Labor. Governor I.L. Patterson appointed her to the State Women and Children's Welfare Commission, on which she served until 1930. In the 1930s Mrs. J.T. Temple, described as being "an eccentric lady," had charge of the reading room at the Downtown Chapel and actively supported the St. Paul Miki School.[22]

Without necessarily being a part of Catholic Action in a formal sense, clergy and laity struggled to help others during the Great Depression in uncoordinated activities, ranging from distributing and sharing food from gardens and farms to the opening of a soup kitchen and Salvage Bureau by the St. Vincent de Paul Society. Many pastors found employment for parishioners and provided Christmas food baskets for needy church members.[23]

<hr/>

Despite the prominence of a few Catholics in the larger community, into the 1930s many Oregon Catholics continued to suffer from a "siege mentality." Vivid memories of anti-Catholic sentiments were revived during the 1928 presidential campaign of Catholic Democrat Alfred E. Smith, a campaign in which Oregon Catholics took a lively interest. Although there was widespread support for Smith among Catholics, most of those who were politically active registered as Republicans because of the near-invisibility of the Democratic Party in Oregon. One example of the bigotry stirred by the campaign occurred in 1930 when the Portland City Council attempted to deny permission for construction of a parochial school at All Saints Church.[24]

However, as the 1930s advanced, Catholics became more open in expressing opinions on a number of current concerns. Earlier, in 1929, Father Edwin O'Hara had visited Mexico and subsequently had written a series of articles for the *Sentinel* about the persecution of Catholics there. After the Spanish Civil War broke out in 1936, the *Sentinel*'s editor, Father Charles M. Smith, was a vocal defender of General Francisco Franco and the nationalists. A couple of young, activist priests also made sure the Portland community knew where the Church stood. Father Francis Schaefers disrupted a pro-republic rally at Reed College to defend Franco, and Father Martin Thielen got into an altercation when he attended a similar rally at the Civic Auditorium—an action that broke up the meeting and earned him first-page publicity in the *Oregonian.* Howard's only reaction was to remark to him later,

"My, they gave you a rather hot time, didn't they?" The archdiocese allowed an advocate of the nationalist cause to speak at several parishes, but if Oregon Catholics were similar to their co-religionists elsewhere in the country, their views were probably spread over a spectrum from support to opposition. The conflict was far away and the cruelty on both sides was equally repulsive. Far more relevant was the related issue of opposition to communism, a topic of concern in the schools and in talks to church groups. In the *Sentinel,* admiration for Franco was linked to hatred of communism, and Smith kept up a vigorous crusade against it into the post-World War II years.[25]

In terms of national politics and events, the *Sentinel* and most Oregon Catholics, Republicans as well as Democrats, supported Alfred E. Smith when he ran for president in 1928. James Robinson, a prominent Astoria Catholic active in the local Republican party, was enthusiastic about President Franklin D. Roosevelt. On Oregon's south coast in 1935–36, Father L.A. Le Miller, who served missions from Star of the Sea Church in Brookings, drove around his extensive territory in his Model-T Ford to speak on behalf of the Townsend Plan, which advocated special benefits for retired people. On the other hand, while the *Sentinel* supported popular radio preacher Father Charles E. Coughlin until he ran into trouble with his superiors, he seems to have had little impact on the Oregon Catholic community; his appeal and support were strongest among working-class Irish and Germans in the upper Middle West and New England. Although Oregon was one of only five states to give William Lemke, Coughlin's protegé as presidential candidate of the Union Party in 1936, over five percent of its vote, Catholics did not appear to have contributed to this outcome. The *Sentinel* most likely generated more interest among its readers by regularly publishing Bishop Fulton Sheen's sermons and featuring him in its news columns.[26]

⊹⇤⇥⊹

Of the Catholic clergy in Oregon at this time, Father Thomas Tobin was probably the most visible member. Just six days after his installation, Howard appointed Tobin, who had been ordained only the year before, as his secretary. It was the beginning of a harmonious and complementary relationship between the two men that lasted until Howard's retirement. Howard disliked attending meetings, such as those of the National Conference of Catholic Bishops or Vatican II, so Tobin, who seemed to enjoy them, represented him and kept him informed. With Howard's encouragement—or at least acquiescence—Tobin became active on behalf of labor unions in Portland in the

Father Thomas Tobin
Archives of the Archdiocese of Portland

1930s, was involved in the organization of pension plans, advocated women's rights, and was instrumental in getting banks to remain open until 5:00 P.M. to accommodate working people.[27]

As a forerunner in liturgical matters, Tobin was the first priest in the archdiocese to use English in the Mass. Long before Vatican II, he advocated saying Mass facing the people, and when he rebuilt St. Francis Church he insisted that it have a detached altar. A man of many interests, Tobin also encouraged Leo Smith, a prominent Catholic attorney, to run for election to the state legislature, and Tobin became one of his advisors after he was elected. He loved Rome so much he bought an apartment there and spoke Italian to his dog. During World War II, he substituted as a weight-lifting instructor at the Multnomah Athletic Club, where he was a member, when the regular instructor went into military service. Despite his gifts, however, Tobin was not universally popular. He was a bright, impatient man who, according to one observer, "did not suffer fools gladly," and had a way of irritating people; but as chancellor and then vicar general, he was a major influence in bringing about changes in the archdiocese, under the auspices of the archbishop. Tobin and Howard, according to an observer, formed a nice combination of loyalty to Rome and an understanding, particularly on Tobin's part, of where the Church was headed.[28]

Indications of major changes to come were not very apparent during the late 1920s and1930s. However, growth was steady and Oregon Catholics were beginning to assimilate more into mainstream American life and culture.

Most lay organizations were the same ones that had been active in earlier decades. Catholic Germans continued into the early 1930s to belong to the Catholic Central Verein; parish altar societies pursued their traditional pattern of service; and the Knights of Columbus, which had figured prominently in the Compulsory School Bill controversy, settled into a less visible but still active pattern. One newcomer to the lay organization scene was the National Council of Catholic Women, whose purpose was to coordinate the work of all Catholic women's organizations. It established a branch in Portland in 1925.[29]

Howard took a special interest in the Holy Name Society and urged each parish to have one. Beyond their commitment not to take God's name in vain, they were often the lay group a pastor relied upon most for volunteer activities—from building booths for the parish fair to ushering at Sunday

Masses. Organizations like the Holy Name Society and the Knights of Columbus were composed primarily of blue-collar and middle-class Catholics.

In an effort to interest Catholics in learning more about their faith, in 1935 Howard began to promote Study Clubs. This was after receiving a report from O'Hara, bishop of Great Falls, Montana, on how and why in 1931 he established "Religious Study Clubs." The Portland Provincial Council in 1932 had recommended establishing them, especially for Catholics who had not continued their education after high school. Following O'Hara's format, Howard encouraged their formation at the parish level with lay discussion leaders and texts based on the Gospels. He appointed Father Joseph E. Vanderbeck as their Director, and the *Sentinel* reported regularly on their progress and devoted a special section to them.[30]

Organizations for Catholic youth were also important, and at the parish level Young People's Clubs sponsored sports events, dances, and picnics. Boys' and girls' sodalities continued to be popular, and in Immaculate Heart parish Father Arthur Sullivan started St. Mary's Club (using the original name of Immaculate Heart) for youths out of high school who were unable to get jobs because of the Depression. In order to keep young people out of mischief, the club offered athletic activities and sponsored basketball, softball, and touch football teams that played in a number of city-wide leagues. One of the leagues included teams from the Multnomah Athletic Club and the Portland Police Bureau, and another had teams from Protestant churches.[31]

The idea for an area-wide Catholic athletic organization came to Portland in 1934 when Chicago Auxiliary Bishop Bernard J. Sheil brought his Chicago Championship Boxing Team to the Civic Auditorium to take on all comers. This event introduced Oregon to the concept of a Catholic Youth Organization (CYO), which was formally started in January 1935 by a group of laymen as a subsidiary of Catholic Charities, with Father Michael E. Fleming as director. It emphasized sports at all levels through high school and was limited to boys in Portland-area parishes, though gradually and reluctantly it allowed girls' teams to join. The organization quickly grew in popularity; within a year or two almost every parish in Portland and surrounding areas, such as Beaverton and Milwaukie, had teams. They competed against each other in basketball, culminating in a tournament at the University of Portland. After Father John Larkin succeeded Fleming as director, the organization began to broaden its scope. When Catholic Boy and Girl Scout units were organized they were placed under the legal jurisdiction of the CYO, and were often sponsored by schools and lay organizations such as the Knights of Columbus. They participated in regional and national activities, giving

Catholics a chance to express their patriotism, while avoiding emphasis on their religion.[32]

One of Howard's goals for the Portland area was to provide a diocesan high school for boys that could supply candidates for the diocesan priesthood. The Holy Cross Congregation already conducted Columbia Prep and the Jesuits desired to start a high school, but Howard temporized with the Jesuits because he wanted a high school for boys in which diocesan priests would be the role models. Due to the Depression, funds were slow in accumulating, but the laity and organizations like the Knights of Columbus staged fund-raising affairs, such as bazaars. At Howard's urging, the *Sentinel* kept its readers constantly aware of the drive for money. Finally a $20,000 bequest by Susan Kratz enabled Howard to start construction on the grounds of what had been St. Mary's Cemetery, property already owned by the archdiocese and in an excellent location for a high school. Still, the land's previous function provided embarrassing moments when, during ongoing construction, students found skulls and bones, which they enthusiastically brought to the attention of the principal. Central Catholic High School's dedication on May 9, 1939, by the apostolic delegate, Archbishop Ameleto Cicognani, was a prominent part of the archdiocesan observance of the centenary of the first Mass celebrated within its present-day boundaries. The school opened with about 125 freshmen and sophomores. In addition to their other duties, Principal Schaefers and Prefect of Discipline Thielen also taught classes, along with five sisters, each from a different community—an unusual arrangement in those days. A dress code was enforced, punctuality required, and, what is almost unbelievable, absolute silence prevailed in the lunchroom until after grace was said.[33]

One remarkable aspect of Central Catholic High School was that it was debt-free. No money was borrowed to get it started and through vigorous fund-raising, with most of the support coming from middle- and lower-class Catholics who hoped to send their sons there, the continuing construction of the early years was performed on a "pay as you go" basis. Originally, tuition was $50.00 a year. Overhead was kept low since the priests and sisters who taught at the school were paid just $50.00 a month. Many of the priests did not even take their salaries, maintaining themselves as chaplains at institutions or as "in residence" priests in parishes. The one fully paid employee was a janitor who lived on the premises. The principal's secretary, who took care of correspondence and bookkeeping, was a volunteer. Howard watched over, cared for, and enjoyed Central Catholic for a long time. He actively recruited teachers for it from his meager reservoir of priests, encouraged its students to visit him, and attended as many of its events as he could.[34]

No diocesan institution existed to serve as a seminary. Training to become a priest of the archdiocese sent aspirants out of state. In the early days of Howard's administration some candidates still went to the Seminary at St. Paul, Minnesota, but increasingly they were sent to St. Patrick's Seminary in Menlo Park, California. For a while in the 1920s, Mount Angel tried to fill the need for the Northwest Province, but a fire and financial troubles forced it to concentrate on its own candidates. Rome then ordered the Northwest Province to provide its own seminary, so in 1931 the Sulpicians opened St. Edward's Seminary near Seattle. They established a strict discipline that older priests in the archdiocese remembered vividly, if not always fondly.

Howard's policy was to require candidates to pay for their first year at the seminary, and if they stayed beyond that, the archdiocese paid their tuition. The need to provide funds for the training of seminarians produced the most important yearly event on the Portland Catholic community's social calendar, the Seminary Tea. The first tea took place May 25, 1935, on the State Steamship Company's *General Lee* at Terminal No. 1. The sandwiches were made in the garden of sponsor Gladys Dunne's home, and it was a "silver tea," meaning that donations of silver coins were expected. The sponsors collected $350.00, encouraging them to start a tradition. Wealthy Catholic families, beginning with the Sheas, lent their spacious homes for the event. After Howard acquired his residence at N.W. 20th and Johnson it was held there from 1939 until his retirement in 1966. Continuing the custom, Archbishop Robert Dwyer hosted it at his residence between 1969 and 1973.[35]

In the meantime, and with less fanfare, the Holy Names Sisters continued to enlarge educational opportunities for women. In 1930 St. Mary's College, which had occupied the same facilities as St. Mary's Academy, moved to the land the sisters were developing near Lake Oswego and was renamed Marylhurst College. The following year it earned accreditation from the Northwest Association of Secondary and Higher Schools. It encountered a certain amount of competition from the University of Portland, which began to offer summer school courses to both men and women, introducing desegregation of the sexes in Catholic higher education in Oregon. But neither competition nor the Great Depression deterred the sisters at Marylhurst College. Somehow they managed to keep operating and building during those years, under the exceptionally able presidency of Sister Margarita Miller, S.N.J.M, who had been a successful businesswoman before she joined the Holy Names Sisters. To help finance their college, the sisters secured funds from the National Youth Administration, a New Deal agency which provided work-study opportunities for poor students, and conducted "buy-a-brick" campaigns in the Washington and Oregon Province grade schools in which they taught.[36]

By 1941 and World War II, Oregon's Catholics had emerged from their ghetto. They were providing extensive charitable, social, and educational services for themselves and others, and were ready to participate as fully accepted members of their communities in the war effort. Like their peers, Catholic young people felt the impact of the war in their daily lives in many ways. Before the war began, the government set up a Civil Pilot Training Program at the University of Portland, which in September 1942 became a full-fledged officer training program directly under university control. In conjunction with the University's already-established four-year degree nursing program, the government also established a Cadet Nurse Corps to replace nurses who entered the military services. Providence Hospital likewise participated in the Cadet Nursing Program through its School of Nursing. At Central Catholic High, where most students went directly from graduation into the armed forces, the government asked for a senior course on aeronautics to be taught, to interest young men in the Air Corps. The school obliged and Fathers Richard Fall and Francis Schaefers—neither of them experts on the subject—struggled to teach the class. The reality of the war touched students even more intimately when former classmates, who had returned to visit in their new uniforms, were later reported killed or missing. At the University of Portland the student newspaper, the *Beacon*, kept students up to date on reports of former classmates who had been wounded, killed or were missing.[37]

Individual priests in Oregon directly experienced the impact of war in their own lives. Father Thomas Tobin, who was known for his work in labor relations, was appointed to the War Labor Board. Apparently he was the only one recommended by both labor and management to be on the board that decided whether or not a worker in a war industry could change jobs. The priest at All Saints Church scheduled a 5:00 A.M. Mass to accommodate shipyard workers and others who had to work on Sunday mornings. Oregon priests said Mass in nondenominational military chapels at such installations as the Portland Air Base and Camp Adair. More priests were willing to enlist as chaplains than Howard, always concerned about having enough priests for parish work, would allow to do so. Father Alfred Williams got around Howard by enlisting in the National Guard, assuring Howard he would never be called up; but he managed to get himself called to active duty, and wrote letters to the *Sentinel* about his experiences in the Aleutians. Howard was so angry with him that he refused to give him a parish when he returned, but Father Williams created St. Elizabeth's Parish in Portland on his own by using the GI Bill to build his rectory and getting a job as a part-time chaplain at the nearby Veterans' Hospital. Howard, always practical, accepted the *fait accompli* and incorporated his parish into the archdiocese. Other priests who served during World War II were William Walsh, John Reedy, Alexander A. Williams, and Bernard McDonnell, who died in service in Guam after the war. Richard Carberry, the only war casualty among priests from the Portland archdiocese, was captured in the Philippine Islands, survived the Bataan Death March, prison camp, the bombing of two prison ships, and died of exposure, neglect, and starvation on a third prison ship.[38]

Parishes and individual Catholics on the home front also contributed to the war effort. They bought war bonds, gave blood, collected various kinds of scrap, and knitted socks for servicemen. The Catholic Daughters of America, in addition to their activities, contributed one member to the Women's Land Army, "Mrs. Oswald, who was a platoon leader in helping to harvest the crops." A much-reduced University of Portland Glee Club and band played for war bond drives. St. Joseph's in Salem converted its parish hall into a recreation center for servicemen from Camp Adair, and St. Mary's Church in Albany, across the river from the Camp, had to add Masses on Sunday to accommodate all those who wanted to attend. St. Mary Star of the Sea, Astoria, also had problems coping with increased attendance because of a Navy base at Tongue Point and Army units at Fort Stevens. In Portland, St. Stephen's and St. Clare's parishes took advantage of the booming wartime economy and an influx of new parishioners to pay off their debts. Howard urged all parishes to do the same.[39]

Many Catholics were among those who came to the Portland area to work in the shipyards. For his workers Henry J. Kaiser built Vanport, a housing project which was the largest such wartime development in the world. Soon after it began to accept inhabitants in February 1943, Father Michael Raleigh started a mission there, named St. Catherine, to minister to Catholic newcomers, with Franciscan sisters to teach catechism to the children. No provision was made in the housing project for the construction of churches, so Raleigh rented one of the largest units available, a three-room apartment at 2701 N. Victory Boulevard, and started to celebrate Mass in the empty living room. His parishioners, many of them refugees from the dust bowl, stood until chairs could be found. Attendance grew so much that by the fall of that year Raleigh had to increase the number of Masses offered each Sunday from four to six. Howard conferred confirmation in the presence of over one thousand persons in the project's social hall that fall, and eventually Raleigh had to rent the local theater for Mass. The only problem with that arrangement was that the service had to be over promptly by noon so departing worshippers would not collide with incoming children carrying popcorn and candy for the first showing of the movie.

The flood that destroyed Vanport after the war in 1949 also washed away an entire parish, but not a church building. Aware of the community's wartime nature and shifting population, Howard had wisely refused to allow the construction of any permanent structures.[40]

By the end of World War II, Oregon's Catholics had become so much a part of the state's mainstream population that they were fully caught up in the changes that the war brought to the state and the nation. Whatever might have been unique or delayed in Oregon Catholics' experiences, as compared to those elsewhere in the nation, was wiped out by their wartime participation. Oregon Catholics would have to cope, along with Catholics elsewhere, with the tremendous changes in the Church brought about during the postwar years.

Chapter Seven

Winds of Change

 S OREGON CATHOLICS resumed normal living after World War II, they began to realize how extensively the conflict had changed the world around them. The changes in the nation and the world would effect far-reaching consequences in their church and their lives. Reshaping Catholics' worldviews were a new threat of nuclear destruction, a pervasive fear of Communism, and profound changes in the social system, particularly in attitudes toward moral values. The resulting uncertainties caused a great increase in religious commitment and participation in the life of institutional religions in the 1950s. Oregon Catholics could not escape sharing in the turmoil all this would bring to their corner of the globe. Dissent, diversity, and change would come to all levels of an institution Catholics had come to think of as unchangeable.[1]

Increases in Oregon's Catholic population and its distribution resulted in the establishment of seventeen new parishes between the end of World War II and 1960. This was an average of more than one parish a year, eight of them in the Portland area, where Catholics joined the rush to the suburbs. Elsewhere in the state, communities such as Myrtle Creek, Waldport, and Eugene started new parishes. St. Wenceslaus in Scappoose and St. Paul in Silverton took advantage of military postwar surplus sales to acquire chapels that they moved and renovated into new or larger churches. Interestingly, during that period of expansion only a small increase took place in the number of officials listed as part of the church bureaucracy. That increase was to come later when the structure, rather than the population, of the Church began to change.[2]

The postwar increase in Catholic population included an increase in vocations to the priesthood, but it was still insufficient to meet the enlarged need. However, additional religious communities of women moved to

Oregon, including the Sisters of Social Service; the Franciscan Missionary Sisters from Santa Cruz, who had fled from China; the Sisters of Mercy from Merion, Pennsylvania; and the Sisters of Notre Dame de Namur, who had left Oregon for California 100 years earlier during the gold rush. Two contemplative orders also arrived, one male and one female: the Trappists, who returned to Oregon, and the Discalced Carmelite Sisters, who established the Carmel of Maria Regina near Eugene.[3]

Particularly visible to the average Catholic was the growth and emergence of the Archdiocesan Office of Education, whose impact on parish schools became increasingly evident. It had been instituted in 1912 when Archbishop Christie decided the various, mostly autonomous, Catholic schools throughout his realm should be organized into an archdiocesan system. Howard appointed Father Edwin V. O'Hara, who had been president of the Oregon Catholic Education Association, to be superintendent of schools, along with an archdiocesan school board composed of priests. Through these steps an archdiocesan school system was created, including a uniform course of study, textbooks, and standards for promotion. Though there was some opposition to centralization, schools and parishes eventually submitted to authority—"in those days archbishops usually got what they wanted…"[4]

✛⚊⚊⚌✛

In 1951 newly appointed superintendent Father Martin Thielen found himself facing some of the challenges of the post-war years. The decade of the 1950s was the decade of the Catholic school, and the Archdiocesan Office of Education was well aware of it. The number of parochial schools increased by sixteen, and increased enrollment led to a shortage of sisters to teach them. Catholic parents were determined to enroll their children in Catholic schools, to the extent of sometimes sitting on the school steps and refusing to leave until their children were accepted. They also resisted having their children taught by lay teachers. This sent Thielen, during the first summer of his ad-

Father Martin Thielen
Archives of the Archdiocese of Portland

ministration, on a frantic search for teaching nuns throughout the United States—as he phrased it, "sister-hunting." Extolling the beauties of Oregon and the potential for vocations in the state, he succeeded in getting enough sisters to staff about five schools, but the victory was short-lived; as the teacher shortage worsened nationwide, many religious communities recalled their members. So, despite parental opposition, by the time of Thielen's administration, every parish school included at least one lay teacher.[5]

Parochial schools generally had not paid much attention to children who were not enrolled. The reasoning seems to have been that if parents wanted them to receive Catholic instructions they would send them to parochial schools. The post-war years witnessed a change in this attitude. The Confraternity of Christian Doctrine (CCD), originally started by Father Edwin V. O'Hara, was active in eastern Oregon, but had not received support where parochial schools existed in the western part of the state. With a newly perceived need to reach out to children in the public schools, Thielen and Father Edmund J. Murnane sought advice from the Baker Diocese on how to develop CCD courses in western Oregon. Catechism classes and vacation schools began to appear in western Oregon parishes, and with the addition of a program for CCD in his office, Thielen's title was changed from superintendent of schools to director of education, and the Office of Education began to broaden its scope.[6]

On a more significant level, the archdiocese became embroiled in a minefield of church-state relations over the issues of bus transportation for parochial school children and the use of state-issued textbooks. It had started in 1939 with a law passed by the Oregon legislature that provided busing for parochial school children. The archdiocese escaped challenge on church-state grounds because it provided only for transportation for parochial school children to the public school they would otherwise have attended, and thereby avoided the controversies generated by busing laws elsewhere in the country.

Two years later, the legislature passed a bill to provide parochial school children with textbooks, but Governor Sprague vetoed it. He was only persuaded to let it become law without his signature after Father Alcuin Heibel, O.S.B., of Mount Angel, who was active in lobbying for church interests, asked his friend, U.S. Senator Charles McNary, who controlled the Republican Party in Oregon, to pressure Sprague to change his mind.[7]

After that, the potential for controversy lay dormant until 1953, when many parochial schools lost their full accreditation because of overcrowded classrooms. The loss of accreditation also meant losing the right to free textbooks. To deal with this, in 1957 the legislature added an amendment to an unrelated bill that changed the conditions for distributing textbooks so private schools could receive them. This action sparked a lawsuit in Oregon City challenging the textbook law, *Dickman v. Oregon City School District*. The case became a tangle of church-state constitutional issues, with differences between the state and federal constitutions further complicating the case. The controversy was resolved in 1962 when the State Supreme Court declared the law unconstitutional and the U.S. Supreme Court refused to review the decision.[8]

While the archdiocesan Office of Education was mainly concerned with primary education, changes were occurring in secondary Catholic education during those postwar years. After the war, enrollment at Columbia Preparatory School began to decline again, and the school closed in 1955, after Howard refused to allow a fund drive. Waiting in the wings were the Jesuits with their long-expressed desire to start a high school for boys in the Portland area, and now the archbishop finally agreed. They bought property outside the city limits, and Jesuit High School opened in the fall of 1956. Howard allowed the Jesuits to conduct a fund drive and even contributed himself. In 1959 Catholic high school co-education made its appearance—without archdiocesan opposition—when John F. Kennedy High School in Mount Angel opened its doors. It was followed in 1967 by La Salle High School in Milwaukie.[9]

Higher education in the archdiocese also reflected a changing world. At the University of Portland the flood of veterans studying under the GI Bill ebbed after a few years, forcing the university to retrench. In 1962 it acquired a new, dynamic president in Father Paul E. Waldschmidt, C.S.C. Under Waldschmidt, the university became technically laicized in 1967 without changing its essential character as a Holy Cross institution, staffed and run by the Holy Cross Congregation. Marylhurst College did not experience the immediate postwar fluctuations that the University of Portland did, but its enrollment increased as the Catholic population of Oregon grew. Under the pressure of requirements from the State Department of Education, it began the process of integrating the Normal (Teacher Training) School with the College of Arts and Sciences. Throughout his many years, Howard and the Holy Names Sisters enjoyed an especially close, warm relationship.[10]

The postwar years brought an increase in vocations, as well as changes in their training. Mount Angel Seminary, where diocesan aspirants to the priesthood were now sent, became one of the largest seminaries in the country. Discipline was not as strict as in seminaries run by the Sulpicians; studies were more community-oriented, with emphasis on social issues and liturgy; and the faculty included outstanding teachers, some of them laymen. Still, as long as the Sulpicians' St. Edward's Seminary continued, archdiocesan seminarians were sent there to complete their training. Howard apparently wanted something of both tradition and innovation to shape his priests; however, neither seminary encouraged independent thinking or taught the latest interpretations in theology or Scripture that were enabling European seminaries to prepare their students for the changes Vatican II would introduce. Also, both seminaries encouraged them to find their friends among other priests, and neither supplied them with practical, hands-on experience as parish priests. That experience was expected to be gained after ordination, under the supervision of their first pastors, along with periodic exams for junior clergy.[11]

During that same period another part of the church structure had to reshape itself to deal with legal and societal changes. In 1939, Catholic Charities began managing the various child-caring agencies. To more effectively meet state requirements, they standardized procedures. The consolidation had worked well during the war years and the period of immediate readjustments afterwards, but by the end of the 1940s it became apparent that the individual agencies needed to become more independent in their activities. In 1951 and 1952, under its director, Father Jerome N. Schmitz, Catholic Charities reorganized, dissolving the management contracts it had signed with individual agencies. This enabled the agencies to incorporate separately, employ their own caseworkers, apply directly to the state for certification, and make their own appeals for funds. This period also saw the beginning of Catholic Charities of Lane County by Msgr. Edmund J. Murnane in Eugene in 1952, and the establishment of Camp Howard as a summer camp for boys.[12]

Among activities among students, a group from the Sigma Pi Upsilon fraternity at the University of Portland decided to turn their club into a service organization. They invited a diocesan priestwho was drawn to missionary work, Father Frank Kennard, to be their chaplain, and he challenged them to start a hospitality house like those identified with Dorothy Day, a well-known Catholic social activist. Consequently, in 1952 the boys started Blanchet House, which has continued to operate according to Day's philosophy, without asking its patrons about religious affiliation or requiring attendance at a religious service, and without government funds. Along the same lines, another charitable effort took place to provide a refuge for street people in the basement of the reestablished Downtown Chapel, where formerly the Archdiocesan War Relief Services had set up a post-war Catholic Maritime Club with a reading room and showers for sailors from around the world.[13]

After the war, when other nurseries which had provided services for war workers closed, the Portland Council of Social Agencies asked Catholic Charities to expand Blessed Martin Day Nursery. In 1946 the St. Vincent de Paul Society moved it to a lot on N. Williams Avenue, and opened an enlarged interracial nursery, dedicated by Archbishop Howard. The archbishop's role in the promotion of the nursery may have been more morally than financially supportive; however, when he was awarded the B'nai B'rith's Brotherhood Award in 1959, he was cited for having founded the nursery. The award also credited him with making it possible for African-American girls to be accepted without discrimination for hospital training in Portland—presumably in Catholic hospitals. Earlier, in a 1946 Lenten Pastoral

Letter, Howard referenced blacks when he pointed out that all men belong to the same family. In 1951 the Fifth Portland Provincial Council, perhaps sensing the need for change, added a paragraph on racial equality to its Decree on Professing the Faith.

Despite some official changes in attitude, postwar Oregon Catholics were generally as reluctant as most other Americans to accept African-American demands for an end to discrimination; but as those demands became more strident toward the end of the 1950s, the Church began to respond. Father Emmet Harrington, a member of the Human Rights Commision of the Oregon Education Association, became involved in efforts to prevent forcing low-income housing into the Albina area. When Martin Luther King Jr. was assassinated, a few black students who were attending Mount Angel College arranged for a Mass in the gymnasium at Kennedy High School. In 1950 Howard provided for the ordination of a black priest for the Portland archdiocese, Father James Edward Mosley. Mosley was born in Natchez, Mississippi, and was trained and ordained for the Portland archdiocese in St. Paul, Minnesota. After a reception at the Blessed Martin Social Center upon his arrival, Mosley ministered in a number of parishes, including Portland, Lincoln City, and Sherwood—none of which possessed any sizeable number of blacks.[14]

The post-World War II climate that brought about changes in racial tolerance also benefited Catholics as well. Anti-Catholic prejudice declined. Because of widespread prosperity following the war, Oregon Catholics were able to achieve rough social and economic parity with other citizens of the state and nation by the 1960s. This in turn had an impact on parish life. As one observant pastor noted, a pattern developed in which the more rigid parish organizations—the "overchaperoned Sodality and Altar Society"—now took on broader, more adaptive forms. The parish became less essential as a center for Catholic lay activity and therefore had to become more flexible in adapting to meet parishioners' desires. Ultimately, however, other forms of entertainment, especially television, drew the attention of many Catholics elsewhere, outside the Catholic parish sphere.[15]

The postwar years gave Father Thomas Tobin a renewed chance to reach out to the marketplace with the Social Gospel message. In 1944, with Howard's blessing, he instituted the Catholic Conference on Industrial Relations. Co-sponsored with the National Conference of Catholic Bishops, it became an annual event during the late 1940s and the 1950s. The conferences featured a very diverse group of speakers, for example, E.B. MacNaughton, president of the First National Bank; Sister Miriam Theresa Gleason, S.N.J.M., head of the Social Sciences Department at Marylhurst College; Roger D. Lapham, Mayor of San Francisco; Cesar Chavez of the United Farm Workers; Msgr. George Higgins; and Senator Richard L. Neuberger. The conferences, usually held at the Neighbors of Woodcraft Hall in Portland, did not attract a large attendance, but they gave publicity to the church's position regarding the Social Gospel. The Discussion Club, which had no connection to the conferences, confined itself to Catholic issues, such as allowing priests to marry, birth control, the magisterium, etc. The Discussion Club proved to be very durable, outlasting both the conferences and Tobin.[16]

Slower to change during those postwar years were the ways in which Catholics communally expressed their relationship with God. Throughout the country, nonliturgical devotions reached their peak in the 1950s. These included practices such as Benediction of the Blessed Sacrament; First Friday and First Saturday observances; novenas to popular saints; and seasonal practices such as devoting May to Mary, June to the Sacred Heart, and October to the rosary. The period from the late 1940s into the early 1960s has often been dubbed the "Age of Mary" because of the widespread devotions to her, with 1954–55 being designated a "Marian Year." Praying the rosary in groups and the Rosary Crusade were popular, as were observances related to the apparitions at Fatima, with their subtle anti-Communist overtone in the requests for prayers for the conversion of Russia. Other devotions included May processions, to which Mexicans in the country added the Feast of Our Lady of Guadalupe.

The trials and suffering of the Great Depression and World War II reinforced the popularity of the novena in honor of Our Sorrowful Mother, and devotion to it continued into the postwar years. In Oregon, however, the most popular novena was that to Our Lady of Perpetual Help. Pietistic practices at the cathedral were typical of many parishes. Besides the Novena to Our Lady of Perpetual Help held on Tuesday afternoons and evenings, a chapter of the Third Order of St. Francis met regularly at the cathedral. Parishioners gathered for weekly Exposition of the Blessed Sacrament, featuring the rosary followed by a Holy Hour. At times, there was a program of Forty Hours Devotion. Much of this seemed to confirm the following observation by one parish historian about the 1950s: "In popular theology there was a prevailing opinion that this was the way things had always been, that nothing in the Church had ever changed and that nothing would ever change."[17]

However, winds of change were stirring. The resurgence of pietistic practices may have been simply a conservative reaction against an undercurrent of change. Young people, who tended to move into the newer parishes, particularly those started after World War II, did not tend to possess the same commitment to non-liturgical devotions that older Catholics did. By the mid-1960s most parishes in Portland had discontinued evening services, except for an occasional mission, and were placing more emphasis on lay retreats. Retreats were not a new idea: in 1914 the Knights of Columbus sponsored the first laymen's retreat at St. Mary's Academy in Portland; in 1920 they began holding annual retreats for their members at Mount Angel Abbey during the summer when the seminary building was vacant. But after World War II retreats took on new popularity. In 1946 Howard persuaded the Jesuits, in lieu of a high school, to establish a retreat house, which they did at St. Ignatius parish. By 1959 retreats had become so popular the Benedictines constructed a year-round retreat house at Mount Angel Abbey.[18]

The heart of Catholic religious practice, the liturgy, was also undergoing a shift. Throughout the Christian world—not only among Catholics—the concept of corporate worship was being rethought; part of that rethinking involved the active participation of the laity. In the United States, most Catholics by the mid-1950s—perhaps because of improved economic status and better education—had an intelligent grasp of the true nature of acts of worship in their church. This awareness caused them to become increasingly desirous of active participation, which prompted a movement for changes in the liturgy.[19]

The Oregon archdiocese was in the forefront in this move. When Father Thomas Tobin became pastor at All Saints parish he began experimenting by saying the Mass while facing the congregation. With a reputation for his advanced position on the liturgy, and as chancellor and vicar general, Tobin was probably the catalyst responsible for Howard's support for liturgical change. Demonstration Masses with the priest facing the people were celebrated in the cathedral in Portland in 1944; but still, meaningful participation by the laity required prayers in English. The National Liturgical Conference, meeting in Portland in 1947, recognized this. Howard was present when its members passed a resolution calling for study of the possibility of having some rites in English. Responding to the portent of these changes, the Catholic Truth Society began to publish Mass leaflets in English. Howard supported, with two pastoral letters, the Liturgical Conference's recommendations that English be permitted in some parts of the Mass. By 1955 he was urging priests to use English in administering sacraments, and in prayers and blessings.[20]

Thus, Howard and his progressive archdiocese were more than ready for the pronouncements of Vatican II. He attended the first session in 1963, well into his eighties, with Tobin as his *peritus,* and was introduced to Pope John XXIII as the oldest archbishop in the United States. Due to his age, he received permission not to attend the succeeding sessions, but he kept in close touch with what was happening through Tobin. Regardless of his personal feelings regarding the drastic changes introduced by the council, Howard made certain they were authoritatively implemented in his archdiocese, and most parishes inaugurated the changes when they became official.[21]

The Oregon laity's reaction to the many changes resulting from Vatican II was mixed. For some, who envisioned new possibilities for spiritual growth and involvement opportunities, the changes could not come fast enough. Others accepted some of the changes, but found the rest hard to swallow. Perhaps a majority, however, begrudged the reforms. They were pained when the altar rail was removed and the organ brought down from the loft to the front of the church. Some churches resisted the modernizers' efforts to rearrange their interiors. For example, St. Patrick's and St. Michael's in Portland retained much of their pre-Vatican II atmosphere, and St. Boniface in Sublimity is one of the few churches in the archdiocese to still have a *reredos,* the ornate screen above an old-fashioned altar.[22]

More in the spirit of continuity than change was the archdiocese's contribution to the American missionary effort in Latin America. An archdiocesan priest, Father Francis Kennard, had persuaded Archbishop Howard in 1954 to let him go to Peru. As such, he became the first American diocesan priest in that country. After several years in Peru, Kennard sent out an appeal for help to several American bishops. Cardinal Richard Cushing of Boston responded, so Kennard traveled to Boston where he and the Cardinal set up the St. James Society in 1959 to recruit and train diocesan priests for service in Latin America. Disagreement arose over where the first group of priests should be assigned; Kennard thought they should be sent to poor, rural parishes; but the priest heading the St. James Society decided to send them to more prosperous parishes where they could enjoy a more customary standard of living. The result was that Kennard received little public credit for his part in starting the Society.[23]

Father Francis Kennard
Archives of the Archdiocese of Portland

Religious communities in the archdiocese also contributed to the missionary effort. The Sisters of St. Mary of Oregon sent four sisters to Tamshiyacu in the jungles of Peru from 1966 to 1975, and a nurse, Barbara Whilford and Sister Joan Marie Littlejohn, S.P., from St. Vincent's Hospital, joined them in 1969. In 1962 the Holy Names Sisters sent missionaries, some from their Oregon Province, to Arequipa, Peru, and Sao Paolo, Brazil.[24]

Meanwhile, activities continued to expand at home. In 1965 at the start of Lent, Howard directed that a pastoral letter be read at all Masses. Entitled "The Ecumenical Movement," he defined ecumenism to mean striving for Christian unity and urged Catholics to "acknowledge and esteem the truly Christian endowments" of their "separated brethren." He also mentioned that he was gratified to note that participation by the faithful in ecumenical work was growing daily. Catholic parishes responded by joining with their religious counterparts to form Community Action Programs (CAP) to combat poverty. In another venue, Father Edmond Bliven represented Catholics for eleven years on a television inter-faith program called "Perspectives 3," on Channel 8.[25]

In the area of social work, of course, Catholic lay organizations and social agencies had been working with their religious and government counterparts for many years; now individual members of the laity were encouraged to get involved. Howard himself set an example of sorts on his way to collecting a surprising number of awards. In 1959 he was awarded a B'nai B'rith plaque "in recognition of his outstanding leadership for work with the blacks and underprivileged"; and in 1968 he received the Brotherhood Plaque from the Oregon Regional Council of Christians and Jews. In 1975, after his retirement, he was granted a certificate of honor for ecumenism from Lewis and Clark College; and the following year Governor Robert Straub gave him the Oregon Distinguished Citizen Award.

Less ecumenical was the Church's interest in politics. While Leo Smith was in the Oregon House of Representatives, 1939–43, he met often with Howard, especially before and during the legislature's sessions. Archbishop Howard was not knowledgeable about politics, but "he was smart enough to listen to those who were and he knew how to solicit the help of good (mostly Catholic) laymen." Howard, as one person phrased it, "was not a crusader by any means." His efforts were low-key but effective. Representative Smith met with him, with Tobin, and with Father Alcuin Heibel, O.S.B. Heibel loved politics and was a sort of unofficial lobbyist in Salem. During every session of the legislature Heibel would invite the legislators and lobbyists to Mount

Angel for a sausage feed with free drinks—"a good fellowship meeting"—for which free transportation was also provided. Specific issues were not discussed at the sausage feed. Occasionally, Howard, with Smith's help, hosted a dinner at his residence for legislators who were considered friends of the archdiocese. Among the state legislators remembered for being helpful to the archdiocese were Grace Peck in the House of Representatives and L.B. Day in the Senate. Before a legislative session began, Howard would meet with Bishop McGrath of Baker Diocese, Heibel, Tobin, Smith, and some of the lobbyists to discuss potential issues of concern to Catholics and how to keep in contact to deal with them.[26]

Howard's relationship with his archdiocesan attorney could be a two-way street. When Smith was appointed Multnomah County District Attorney in 1957 to complete the term of William L. Langley, who had been accused of corruption, Smith discovered that bingo games—many of them in parishes—were being conducted throughout the county in violation of the state constitution. Smith warned the archbishop about the potential for legal problems. Howard, who never was a bingo enthusiast, arranged for Smith to meet with the priests involved and inform them about the law. Then Howard instructed the parishes to stop holding bingo games. Priests who were upset about losing this source of revenue tended to blame Smith, rather than Howard, for putting an end to the activity. Eventually, however, the state constitution was changed and bingo games returned to parish halls.[27]

The bingo controversy brought a small flash of publicity, but generally Howard enjoyed a low-key but favorable image. Because of his office he was considered a community leader and he was highly respected by such groups as the United Way and ecumenical organizations. If asked, he would take forthright positions in accord with church doctrine on moral issues. On the whole, though, he was not one to make sweeping pronouncements, and seemed content to let others be in the limelight. He did not belong to any prestigious clubs or develop a special relationship with any important political personality. Not a showy person, Archbishop Howard was probably best and most fondly known by ordinary people in Portland's northwest district, where he lived. He had been quite athletic in his younger days; in his later years, he enjoyed riding horseback at the Vancouver Barracks. Walking was his usual exercise in Portland, to the chancery office and around the neighborhood in the evening, saying his rosary. Even after his office moved across the Willamette River to 28th and E. Burnside, he would walk part way, then take the bus on Burnside, conversing with everyone he met—an easy, genial figure, somewhat of a local character.[28]

Catholics as an identifiable group continued to grow in visibility and acceptance in the larger community. Leo Smith campaigned for Richard

Neuberger when he ran successfully for the U.S. Senate in 1954. During the challenge to the textbook law, Catholics formed the Catholic Committee on Religious Rights in 1962 to question legislative candidates on their position regarding aid to parochial schools, then disseminate the information to voters. When anti-Catholic literature surfaced in Oregon during the 1960 presidential campaign of John F. Kennedy, Howard, who rarely got involved in political matters, publicly denounced inflammatory statements and urged Catholics to vote as "free, patriotic citizens." When President Kennedy was assassinated, many parishes, as well as the cathedral, offered special Masses for the repose of his soul. The 1968 assassination of his brother, Senator Robert F. Kennedy, was marked by ecumenical services in the cathedral and St. Andrew's Church in Portland.[29]

Catholic response to the perceived threat of Communism after World War II was similar to that of their fellow Americans. The Fifth Portland Provincial Council in 1951 added Communist groups to its list of forbidden societies. Some Catholics saw an imminent threat. A Mindszenty Society, named for Hungarian Cardinal Josef Mindszenty who was imprisoned by the Communists, was formed and sponsored talks warning about Communist threats to American society. But, unlike many of their counterparts in the Midwest and New England, most Oregon Catholics did not show fervent support for Catholic Senator Joseph McCarthy.[30]

Another instrument of Catholic visibility in the community was the archdiocesan newspaper, the *Catholic Sentinel*. Father Charles N. Smith, director of the Catholic Truth Society in 1928, also became editor of the *Sentinel,* and occupied that position until 1958. Smith was a small, unprepossessing man, and a workaholic. He was usually pastor of a sizeable parish, as well as directing the Catholic Truth Society and almost single-handedly writing and publishing the *Sentinel*. Besides shaping each edition, which usually contained a good many items he rewrote from the *New York Times* and the National Catholic News Service, he also began changing the nature of the Catholic Truth Society. It evolved from being primarily an organization to defend and explain the faith to non-Catholics, to one that met Catholic worship needs, starting with the publication of Sunday missals in pamphlet form in the 1930s. When Smith's health began to fail, Tobin organized a group of Catholic laymen who were prominent in the local radio, television, advertising and public relations fields to recommend a replacement. They named two of their members, one of whom was a layman, Gorman Hogan, of the staff of Associated Press in Portland. Accepting Hogan, Howard appointed him in 1966 to be editor and general manager and selected Father Edmund Bliven to take charge of the editorial page. Howard did not interfere with its content, and Bliven was able to write his editorials without having to first consult with the archbishop. The *Sentinel* covered Vatican II so enthusiastically that "sometimes it seemed there was little else in the paper while the Council was in session."[31]

━━━━━

In the 1960s, as Howard's long tenure in office approached its end, additional changes took place. The building housing the chancery office stood in the way of a ramp for the new Stadium Freeway built on the west side of the Willamette River. At Tobin's suggestion, the archdiocese bought a former streetcar barn at 28th and E. Burnside and renovated it to provide quarters for a much-expanded chancery office and the complete facilities of the *Sentinel.* The newspaper began publication in its new location on April 19, and the other offices moved in on June 6, 1963.[32]

Financial demands, a seemingly ongoing problem, worsened during Howard's final years as archbishop. Although the chancery office tried to control parish debts by requiring pastors to borrow from the archdiocese, a revolving fund had never been set up to help absorb the costs of needed construction. The fund that did exist—the D-Note Fund, in which parishes and individuals were encouraged to deposit money for future construction projects—proved inadequate. The archdiocese's only income came from assessments on the parishes—and because of changing needs and other factors, many parishes often resisted paying their full assessments. The financial problems compounded for the archdiocese with the construction costs of new, larger parish churches and sometimes schools, like La Salle and Marist high schools, which were to have been paid for by the parishes they served, although the schools were owned by the archdiocese. Consequently, the archdiocese's outflow exceeded its income, and it was forced to keep borrowing from banks without being able to service its growing debt. By the middle of the 1960s, the archdiocese was in deep trouble, owing about $7,000,000 to three banks: U.S. National Bank, First National (now Wells Fargo) Bank, and the Bank of California. Robert McQuarry, later to become business manager at the chancery, noted: "If the archdiocese had been a private corporation, it would have been bankrupt."

Howard, with Tobin's help, had always directly managed the archdiocese prior to World War II and had done so quite successfully. However, after the war, the archdiocese grew in both complexity and size to the point that by the mid-1960s its administration was beyond the capabilities of two aging men who had not been trained in finance. Howard seemed to believe he could handle the problem, but his Administrative Council on Finances, itself newly created and composed of clergy and laymen, persuaded him to appoint a

Council of Temporalities. to be composed of financially astute, successful businessmen. Among the prominent men who served on this council were John Eloriaga, later president of U.S. National Bank; Harry Kane of Georgia Pacific Corporation; Dudley Jones, a prominent real estate broker; Paul Murray, a developer; and Charles Duffy, an attorney. After the banks, patiently watching the archdiocese's debt grow by some $600,000 a year, finally warned Howard that the debt was getting out of hand, the Council urged an archdiocesan-wide fund drive. Called the Action Campaign, most of its funds were dedicated to debt retirement and it was moderately successful. After Archbishop Robert Dwyer succeeded Howard, it was followed by the Stewardship Campaign.[33]

In 1966, at the age of 89, Howard resigned his position, responding to the suggestion of Pope Paul VI that all bishops over 70 years old retire. In his last year in office he was as active as ever, still walking around the neighborhood, blessing churches, bestowing confirmations, and traveling throughout the archdiocese at his usual rate. Looking to the future, he appointed four laymen to the Archdiocesan School Board and named a committee to plan for a Senate of Priests. Still very much in the center of the action, in May 1966 he celebrated his sixtieth year as a priest and his fortieth as archbishop.

Howard's style of administration wore well through those busy forty years. When he arrived, there were 81 parishes, 174 priests and approximately 61,000 Catholics in Oregon; when he retired, 440 priests were serving 197,856 Catholics in 108 parishes. At the beginning of the 20th century, American bishops often had to fight to gain authority in their dioceses, to bring parishes, agencies, and finances under their control. Christie had begun that process in the archdiocese, and Howard continued the pattern—perhaps with a firmer grip on the reins—but still with something of Christie's permissiveness. He would put a priest in charge, allow him great flexibility in performing his job, and would support him all the way, although not necessarily with funding. If a priest acted unwisely, Howard would support him publicly, but see to it in private that he changed. He also was willing to allow innovations, such as street preaching and Tobin's experiments with liturgical change. Perhaps he never lost some of the characteristics of a teacher: encouraging his students to reach out, receptive to their ideas, permissive in the latitude he allowed them—but always in charge.[34]

Archbishop Howard's willingness to permit innovation may have produced a legacy more complex than generally perceived. On the surface, many Oregon Catholics appeared to accept the changes that some of his priests—with Tobin in the forefront—enthusiastically promoted. However, not all laity or clergy were very happy with the reforms. Howard may have let changes proceed too swiftly for many in his flock, for a hairline crack was beginning to appear in the solid front that persecution-sensitive Oregon Catholics had always maintained. Howard, perhaps by not deliberately slowing the process of change, handed on to his successor a more complicated inheritance than he intended.

After retirement, Archbishop Howard moved to Beaverton to live in a small home on the property of the Sisters of St. Mary of Oregon, near Maryville Nursing Home. He enjoyed a close and cordial relationship with the Sisters of St. Mary, and with their care he continued to enjoy excellent health and to attend functions around the archdiocese. One acquaintance recalled Howard claiming that he had a long life because he never smoked, never drank, never drove a car, and never crossed the street against a red light. The same person recollected, "Nobody—even at half his age—had a clearer memory than Archbishop Howard, and no one could tell a story or recount an anecdote with as much accurate detail, or in more picturesque language and with greater enjoyment."

Howard probably gained more public notice after his retirement, as the oldest living archbishop in the world, than prior to it. In recognition of his ninety-sixth birthday, November 5, 1973, Howard received greetings from a long list of well-known members of the American hierarchy, including Cardinal John Carberry of St. Louis; Cardinal Terence Cooke of New York; Cardinal John Dearden of Detroit; Cardinal Timothy Manning and retired Cardinal James F. McIntyre, both of Los Angeles; Cardinal Patrick O'Boyle of Washington, D.C.; Cardinal John Kroll of Philadelphia; and a brief but eloquent note from Bishop Fulton J. Sheen. Howard was quoted on his 100th birthday as saying that he enjoyed life, had had exceptionally good health, and considered his greatest contribution to have been the encouragement of education. His standing in the community had become such that a Portland television channel covered his 100th birthday Mass live in Memorial Coliseum. (His funeral Mass was televised also.)

When Howard had been in Rome attending Vatican II, Pope John XXIII wished him many more years, which one historian believes might be the reason he lived long enough to witness the installation of two successors. Edward Howard died on Sunday, January 25, 1983, at age 105, after witnessing over a century of profound change in the world and in the Church he had served.[35]

Robert Joseph Dwyer (1908–1976)
Archbishop of Portland in Oregon (1966–1974)
Oregon Catholic Press

Chapter Eight
The Throes of Transition

Y THE TIME ROBERT JOSEPH DWYER was installed as the sixth
archbishop of the archdiocese, the Catholic community in
Oregon was somewhat like an adolescent youth: parts of the
body (a progressive and nontraditionalist minority) had developed in advance of other parts (the majority of more traditional Catholics, in
various stages of accepting changes in the Church). And, typical of adoles-
cence, confusion and inconsistency surfaced at times, as some headily
pursued new opportunities and liberties, while others hung on to tradition,
preferring the familiar. It was this body, in the throes of such transition, that
Robert Dwyer was appointed to shepherd and try to bring together into
unity of purpose.

Born August 1, 1908, in Salt Lake City, Robert Dwyer was the only child
of Irish immigrant parents who were prominent in Catholic lay activities in
a predominantly Mormon community. Their environment no doubt called
for a particularly strong affirmation of traditional Catholicism.

As a boy, Dwyer attended a Salt Lake City public school for the first six
grades, then finished his secondary education at Catholic schools. Showing
no taste for sports, Dwyer was an avid reader (a fellow seminarian claimed
that by the time Dwyer graduated from high school he had read every book
in the Salt Lake City Library). For his seminary education, Dwyer first studied at St. Mary's Manor in South Langhorne, Pennsylvania, and then pro-
ceeded to St. Patrick's Seminary in Menlo Park, California. He was ordained
in 1932 at the cathedral in Salt Lake City at the precocious age of twenty-
three, the first Utah native to become a priest. In that capacity he became a
chaplain and instructor at the College of St. Mary-of-the-Wasatch, served as
editor of the *Intermountain Catholic Register,* earned a doctorate in American
history at Catholic University of America, and became superintendent of
education for the diocese. His only experience as a parish priest came when

he served as vice rector and later rector of the cathedral in Salt Lake City. In 1952 Dwyer was consecrated bishop of Reno, and in 1967 he was installed as archbishop of the archdiocese of Portland in Oregon.[1]

Contrasts between Dwyer and his predecessor were immediately apparent. Even as Howard was introducing Dwyer to personnel at the chancery office, many were struck by a sense that the still-vigorous, lively Howard seemed the younger of the two. While Dwyer was a bigger man than Howard—measuring five feet, nine and a half inches and weighing 170 pounds—his bearing was not as erect, his demeanor not as energetic or imposing. He was a short, stout man with a receding chin, round face, heavy jowls, and small eyes accentuated by rimless glasses and embedded in puffy cheeks. Unlike Howard, Dwyer was not comfortable striking up conversations or exchanging pleasantries and anecdotes with acquaintances and parishioners. One contemporary described Dwyer as "always quite formal." Another remarked that "he did not have the common touch." A third described him as "an aristocratic gentleman."

It is probable that some of Dwyer's public formality stemmed from his ingrained regard for the office of archbishop. The man did have a more personable side. Especially to those who were privileged to know him more intimately, he was a warm, understanding, approachable man, and, perhaps because of his bouts with illness, compassionate. A priest who had served with him in the chancery office described him as "too big-hearted"—willing to help anyone, worthy or unworthy. For those who were intellectually compatible, he was a delightful conversationalist. He could discuss a wide range of topics, and his vocabulary was so extensive it must have kept the less well-read reaching for a dictionary.

A dictionary would also have come in handy for those who read his columns. He was an elegant wordsmith—outspoken and opinionated, with touches of ironic, self-deprecating humor. To the annoyance of his critics, Dwyer tended to use the royal "we" in much of his writing. Moreover, he was sure of himself, having been an editorial writer and accustomed to stating controversial positions. He did not mind giving interviews to reporters from secular and religious newspapers, so everyone knew exactly where he stood on many issues. He possessed a temper that could explode into an intensive but transitory torrent of words. One historian claims: "Howard had roared at his priests, so loudly, they say you could hear him in the next county. Dwyer roared and also snapped, in a language so elevated some of his people could not understand him."[2]

Dwyer had a particular perception of his position and the image he should project as archbishop. Like his predecessors he upheld church protocol, insisting that ceremonies be performed properly and requesting due deference to his rank (preferring to be addressed as "Your Excellency" or "Your Grace"). However, parting with the simpler life-styles of former Oregon archbishops, Dwyer retained an Old World notion that a prelate should live in a princely fashion. This concept probably stemmed from the historical European model for the upper hierarchy as well as from 19th-century reasoning that it would benefit the image of the Catholic Church in America if its prelates lived well, thereby raising Catholic pride and confidence, impressing businessmen whose aid was desired for financing Church projects, and displaying to the world a highly visible, triumphal leadership. Unfortunately for Dwyer's reputation among his flock, Oregon Catholics were not accustomed to archbishops who had either the finances or the predilection to implement princely life-styles. Dwyer had both. He had inherited considerable wealth and he had definite ideas about the manner in which an archbishop should live.[3]

His installation, on February 6, 1967, provided the first indication of his affluent style. Georgia-Pacific Corporation flew him from Reno to Portland in a private jet, and eight archbishops and twenty-seven bishops attended, the largest gathering of Catholic prelates in the archdiocese's history. Afterwards the archdiocese hosted a banquet for 600 guests, among them retired Archbishop Edward D. Howard, who received a standing ovation; Oregon Governor Tom McCall; Portland Mayor Terry Shrunk; and Oregon Supreme Court Justice Hall S. Lusk. In his address Dwyer indicated he would work for ecumenism and noted some of the difficulties the Church faced, such as theological speculation, "discipline adjustment," and problems of disloyalty and disobedience.[4]

The banquet had been a lavish affair, and a sense of that opulence lingered when soon afterwards Dwyer sold Howard's residence on N.W. 20th Avenue and Johnson Street in Portland and bought a more expensive home in the fashionable Council Crest area, at 2728 S.W. Greenway Street. Howard's home would have required expensive repairs to its antique plumbing system, it had no garage, and its garden area lacked the privacy needed for entertaining. Dwyer's new home, which was purchased and maintained for him by the archdiocese, included extensive, landscaped grounds with a pond and a view of the city below. The house itself had quarters for a housekeeper, a basement apartment, and several bedrooms for visitors, as well as a master bedroom. Ultimately, the archdiocese probably gained on the real estate deal, but at the time Dwyer's move precipitated open criticism and led to the first of several incidents of picketing in front of his new home. Neither did it help his image that he drove a long, limousine-type car—in contrast to Howard who, living modestly in semi-commercial northwest Portland, had walked and ridden the streetcar or bus to work.[5]

Dwyer's obvious affinity for luxury was not only a jarring contrast with his predecessors in Oregon; it also seemed out of step with the general movement of the Church. The changes inspired by Vatican II, for instance, were in the direction of producing a more collegial, lay-oriented paradigm. To his credit, Dwyer—though evidently not overly sensitive to the social climate of the Oregon Church—was not a grasping man. He happened to have the personal means to enjoy the refinements he thought befitted a man of his office and to which he was accustomed. The prelate expected to live in a comfortable home, a place where he could display to best advantage the art he enjoyed and the books he loved to collect and read. In his own home, he was reputed to be a gracious host, setting a gourmet table and engaging his guests in wide-ranging discussions.[6]

Unfortunately, the ideas he championed in his articulate, erudite weekly column only seemed to confirm the opinion his critics formed of him as a conservative churchman more comfortable in the nineteenth century than the second half of the twentieth. The views represented in his articles, speeches, and interviews reflect a complex man, highly intelligent, and totally loyal to the pope. He possessed a fascination with Church history and saw an attractive stability in its traditions and dogma. In contrast, he found the changes in the postwar American Church and society very disquieting. He was a staunch defender of church doctrine inculcated since his childhood.

Dwyer's views on Vatican II are illuminating. He attended all four sessions and believed they deepened his understanding of the Church. In an address, given sometime soon after the last session ended, he described Vatican II as "a middle-of-the-road Council always veering slightly to the left...." He opined that the document *Church in the Modern World* revealed too great a fascination with the sociology of change and too little sensitivity for the compensating balance of the whole history of the Church and the forces that formed it. In 1967 Dwyer admitted that his voting at Vatican "showed a liberal tendency," but became more conservative toward the end. A few years later, he saw a threat in what he felt was a growing distinction between the Church, "Catholic and Roman in its obedience and loyalties, in its full faith in matters doctrinal and its full conformity in matters moral and disciplinary, and the American Church, Catholic all right insofar as that note is necessary and useful, but far more concerned to conform to the 'American spirit' than to be tied to Rome's apron strings."[7]

That "American spirit" showed itself in an articulate opposition that had appeared in a minority of the religious. They were mostly younger priests and sisters not as strongly immersed in the traditional view of church structure—although it was the elderly retired sacristan at the cathedral, Romeo Lamire, who may have best articulated the essence of the independent American spirit: "I didn't like it when he [Dwyer] went into the pulpit with mitre and staff: 'I am your archbishop!'"[8]

Probably the majority of Oregon Catholics—especially in rural areas—and older clerics, had no trouble with Dwyer's conventional views. His conflict was largely with the younger generation of priests and religious who, in his view, had wandered too far afield of tradition and history. In an effort to remind his flock of their history, Dwyer named retired Bishop Francis Leipzig to head an Archdiocesan Historical Commission, and encouraged him and Fathers John Laidlaw and John Larkin to go on speaking tours to acquaint people with the history of the archdiocese. He appointed Father Willy Price, who had followed him from Reno to Portland, as the first archdiocesan director of archives. Both Price and Laidlaw were also active in the leadership of the early Historical Commission.[9]

Relationships within the church structure were in a state of change, and the structure itself was being modified. Before Vatican II, an archbishop was "an episcopal monarch" who was able to make practically all important decisions himself, because he was generally well-informed on everything going on in his archdiocese. After Vatican II, the great increase in the number of diocesan programs made a bishop's direct control more difficult, if not impossible. The Portland archdiocese was no exception. The anticipation of, and response to, Vatican II in Oregon under Howard's benign administration had brought about an increase in lay and clerical participation in church administration and in church programs and activities. This increase only accelerated during Dwyer's tenure. In 1970, about midway through Dwyer's administration, the *Catholic Directory* listed eleven new agencies or positions in his administrative structure, including a vice chancellor, apostolate to the deaf, and committees on priestly training, promotion of vocations, and religious unity.

In some ways, Dwyer continued traveling the permissive course Howard had mapped out. For example, he permitted the implementation of the Priests' Senate (he had been one of the first bishops in the United States to establish one, in Reno, soon after his return from Rome) and the issuance of guidelines for parish councils, and he allowed commissions and boards more latitude than Howard had.[10]

A certain *laissez-faire* effect may have stemmed more from Dwyer's reluctance as an administrator than from his willingness to depart from tradition. His interests focused particularly on doctrine, rather than on the details of running an archdiocese. He rarely attended meetings dealing with archdiocese affairs, so Father Bertram Griffin, who became chancellor, administrated the archdiocese. Dwyer also appointed the archdiocese's first full-time business manager, Robert McQuarry, who took the necessary steps to place its operations on a more businesslike basis. He set up the archdiocese's first formal budget, installed uniform accounting practices in all the parishes, introduced a self-insurance plan, and began the process of selling some of the unused parcels of real estate earlier archbishops had accumulated. The budget, with its rigid allocation of monies and expectations that parishes would meet their debt obligations, caused some resentment, but McQuarry's actions brought the archdiocese into the modern world of corporate responsibility. McQuarry had quite a free reign to manage these business affairs as he wished, with little interference from the archbishop.[11]

The publication of the archdiocesan newspaper, the *Catholic Sentinel*, was one element of administration in which Dwyer was directly involved, perhaps because of his newspaper experience. Even preceding his arrival, the *Sentinel* had begun publishing his weekly column. The archbishop held frequent meetings with the paper's publisher, Gorman Hogan, and its editors, Fritz Meagher and Father Edmond Bliven. Meetings were usually harmonious, but sometimes his famous temper flared. He took a direct interest in, and control of, material that was printed in its columns. Although he himself did not appear to oppose the United States Vietnam policy, he allowed Bliven to publish editorials criticizing the Vietnam War, provided he made clear the opinions expressed were his, not those of the archdiocese.[12]

Though Dwyer disliked the day-to-day details of administration required in a modern chancery office, he was reluctant to delegate authority. Therefore subordinates often felt like they were operating in something of a vacuum, unsure of their boundaries. If Dwyer disapproved of their actions, he could intervene summarily. His abrupt dismissal of Bob Gregor, without consulting the department heads involved, was a case in point. Director of adult education, Gregor disagreed with the manner in which adult education was being encouraged.

Until the Personnel Board was established, Dwyer had direct responsibility for the appointment of priests to parishes and offices; but, particularly early on, he seemed at a loss on how to make selections, often asking for opinions openly in groups of priests. He neither drew on Howard's exhaustive knowledge nor employed his predecessor's method of confidential consultations.[13]

In defense of Archbishop Dwyer, the state of his health may have greatly affected his performance as an administrator. While still bishop of Reno he had developed heart trouble and had suffered a serious heart attack. This circumstance was not widely known. In Portland he usually worked in the chancery office just for three hours in the morning and rested in the afternoon, as much as his schedule permitted. He had been an active administrator in Reno, despite his health problems; but the size, complexity, and problems of the Portland archdiocese put additional strain on him. In early January 1972, he suffered a severe heart attack, which further limited his ability to deal with challenging situations and people.[14]

Health problems notwithstanding, Dwyer enjoyed traveling throughout the archdiocese. Unlike Howard, he enjoyed driving himself, and was a pleasant companion to Father John Larkin who accompanied him on most of his travels and acted as his master of ceremonies. Dwyer seemed to endure well the inconveniences and discomforts of "one-night stands" in a variety of rectories throughout Oregon. He had an additional traveling companion as well: a poodle named Minnie (short for Minnette). She always sat quietly between Dwyer and his companion during the trips, and once at their destination, she stayed in his room at the rectory. Pastors did not always feel like welcoming this additional guest, but Minnie was Dwyer's closest companion and he kept her at his side, often on his lap, even when he was in his office at the chancery. In his column in the *Sentinel*, a year or so after he took office, he wryly commented:

> It has come to our ears (as such things do) that a gross calumny filters through clerical ranks of the archdiocese which presently groans under the writer's tyrannical lash, to the effect that all policies are made and decisions dictated by a small salt and pepper poodle…there is contained here under thick layers of exaggeration, a microscopic kernel of truth… it is an incontestable fact that when once you make a pet of a poodle, thereafter you build your life around her. There is no other way.[15]

In his travels around the archdiocese, Dwyer tended to be formal and reserved in his relationships with parishioners, but more relaxed with parish priests. Some found him more sensitive than Howard had been to their concerns, because Dwyer had had experience in pastoral care. One priest described Dwyer to the *Oregonian* as "warm, compassionate, understanding and easy to know," one of the kindest men he had ever known. He also exhibited concern about their welfare; worked with priests in trouble; gave second chances to some who had experienced difficulties elsewhere; and set up a Commission on Counseling, with two psychologists among its members, Sister Marian Dolores Robinson, S.H.J.M., and Dr. Frank Strange.[16]

⊹⟞═⋰═⟝⊹

Early in his command, it became apparent that Dwyer intended to slow the pace of change, pull in the vanguard, and try to unite the body of the Oregon Church within a more historical framework. Dwyer's traditional views were manifested early when he ordered Father Leo Remington to shave off his beard and wrote a letter to his priests telling them not to wear blue shirts, only black ones, and not to try innovations in the vestments they wore for Church ceremonies. Soon after Archbishop Howard's retirement, the progressive Msgr. Thomas Tobin began stepping back from some of his former involvements. For years Tobin had been in the vanguard of change, but advancing age was affecting him. He resigned his position as vicar general to devote full time to serving as pastor of All Saints parish. Dwyer's administration also coincided with a marked drop in the number of priests serving the archdiocese. This attrition corresponded with a national trend—particularly in the 1960s and '70s—of men leaving the active priesthood. (One priest, responsible to help some of these Oregon priests prepare the papers for their dispensations, found the process "very, very painful.")[17]

Eventually, it became apparent that regardless of Dwyer's views, disposition, abilities, or efforts, the church was continuing to undergo transformation. And not always was he opposed to change. He summarized his outlook in the following statement: "I'm called a conservative, but I run as liberal an establishment as any bishop. I've consulted, but when you finish consulting, someone has to make the decisions and that happens to be what I'm here for."[18]

⊹⟞═⋰═⟝⊹

One change agent within the liberal establishment that enjoyed Dwyer's wholehearted support was Catholic Charities. As a result of World War II and subsequent wars, a new wave of people requiring help appeared—refugees. In 1945, right after the end of World War II, Catholic Charities became responsible for Catholic refugees in Oregon. These largely were people of German ethnic origin, former inmates of refugee or displaced person camps. Catholic Charities responded with activities such as helping prepare immigration papers, arranging transportation, and aiding with job and language instruction. Next, it helped a wave of immigrants fleeing the Hungarian Revolution of October 1956, and later that same year, a small group of Dutch Catholic refugees after Indonesian independence was declared.[19]

Heightening the challenge to the organization, Hispanics began to arrive, just after Father Morton E. Park became director of Catholic Charities in 1960. In 1959 Fidel Castro came to power in Cuba, which caused an influx of middle-class Cubans to the United States. By 1969 Catholic Charities had settled about 700 Cubans, aided by federal funds available for housing and food, its initial experience working with the federal government.[20]

Father Morton E. Park
Archives of the Archdiocese of Portland

Those early Cuban refugees assimilated into middle-class America with comparative ease. Hispanic immigrants from south of the American border, however, presented a much greater challenge to the Catholic community. As early as the 1920s there were Mexican immigrants in the Pacific Northwest, particularly in eastern Oregon communities like Nyssa and Ontario. World War II and the signing of a labor agreement between the United States and Mexico in 1942, which initiated the Bracero Program, was a turning point for Hispanics. Mexican labor played a significant part in winning the war, and Governor Earl Snell expressed the gratitude of Oregonians in a letter to the Mexican government. After the war, as the Bracero Program was phased out, farmers recruited Mexican-Americans from Colorado, Wyoming, Texas, and California. Some of these laborers who migrated to Oregon became permanent residents, but found themselves alienated from the "Anglo" Catholic community. Their expression of the faith was quite different from American Catholicism. It was family-centered, and domestic rituals and the celebration of saints' days were more important to Mexican believers than regular attendance at Mass. The institutional Church did not play a major role in their lives, except for the essential ceremonies of baptism, marriage, and funerals. As a result, Anglo religious and laity regarded them as ignorant of their religion and in need of evangelization, a perception that alienated the two Catholic communities from each other.[21]

Still, Oregon was a magnet for Mexicans. Young Mexicans who had been involved in the Bracero Program returned with their families, joining Mexican-Americans, and increasing numbers of Mexicans crossed the border to work in Oregon agriculture. Many were seasonal workers who left in the fall, but many settled in such areas as Hood River, Woodburn and elsewhere in the Willamette Valley, as well as in Eastern Oregon. They began to become more visible with their traditional cultural practices, such as family celebrations of baptisms and marriages, the preparation of special foods, folk healing, dances, and fiestas.[22]

As a result, the institutional Church in Oregon began to reach out to them. In Woodburn in the mid-1950s the pastor of St. Luke parish, Father John Larkin, started a summer school for the children of Mexican workers, and the Woodburn public schools cooperated by making their school buses and drivers available to transport the children. By 1966 over two hundred children were attending the summer school, which was taught at various times by Benedictine Sisters from Mount Angel and lay instructors, Spanish-speaking seminarians from Mount Angel, Franciscans, Jesuits, Jesuit scholastics, and, for more than ten years, a priest from Mexico, Father Ernesto Bravo. Larkin joined the newly formed Valley Migrant League, took its leaders around to inspect some of the labor camps, and worked with the league to alleviate poor conditions. St. Mary's parish in Mount Angel became aware of Hispanic families in its midst in 1960, when the first non-Germanic surnames appeared on the parish rolls. In Woodburn, it took some time to overcome hostility between the Anglo- and Mexican-American communities, but gradually resentment diminished and St. Luke became a bicultural parish, as many others have since, with Masses celebrated in both English and Spanish.[23]

In 1971 the archdiocese established the Vicariate San Salvador, covering six missions for Hispanics between Medford and Portland under Father Francis Kennard who had recently returned from missionary work in Peru. He started to work with Mexican farm workers in their camps, and soon had an opportunity to show what pastoral concern could mean to illegal migrant workers. A large corporation gave them work in a mushroom-growing plant in Salem, and—coincidentally or otherwise—just before payday the Immigration Service raided the plant and started to take away the workers without papers. As they were about to board the buses, Spanish-speaking Kennard and his brother, Mark, who was a lawyer, worked their way down the lines obtaining powers of attorney and vital information, such as names and addresses. After running out of paper, they used anything they could write on, including paper towels. Armed with the legal documentation to represent the deported workers, the Kennard brothers were able to obtain their pay and forward it to them in Mexico. The incident helped Catholic Charities, which worked closely with the vicariate, to recognize the needs and vulnerability of illegal migrants, and to start an immigration counseling service for them.[24]

Throughout the United States in the 1960s the Catholic Church was experiencing an awakening on the issues of race and ethnicity, and painfully beginning to move toward becoming truly "Catholic." Dwyer accepted the growing cultural pluralism introduced by the various refugee groups, was kindly disposed toward them, and readily agreed to help Hispanics, the most highly visible group during his term of administration. Whatever his opinion of African-Americans, he showed a concern with the inner city and the tiny black Catholic community which lived mostly in it. In 1970 he appointed three young priests to inner city parishes: Father Don Durand to St. Francis, Father Carl Flack to Immaculate Heart, and Father Bertram Griffin to St. Andrew's. He wanted those parishes to relate to the community in terms of social justice issues, and supported them with money to keep their schools open and with public statements promising that the Catholic Church would not leave the inner city. Griffin joined the Albina Ministerial Alliance, and as part of it sponsored a health clinic and a free legal clinic, as well as making available St. Andrew's Center for community activities. When the Alliance wanted to hold a rally to raise funds for the defense of Angela Davis, a black activist involved with the Black Panthers and an avowed Communist, Griffin provided the hall at St. Andrew because it was the largest in the area. Catholics, lay and cleric, accused him of being a heretic and Communist; Dwyer, however, invited him to dinner at his home and told him that anyone who did not have enemies was not doing good work.[25]

Other groups within the Catholic community also implemented social apostolates during Dwyer's administration. A potentially more radical approach to those in need was the opening of a Catholic Worker House of Hospitality in 1972, by Pat and Mufti McNassar. This led to the establishment of an urban commune consisting of several houses on the city block in Portland between S.E. 19th and 20th, and Alder and Washington Streets. A small group of Catholic families lived there, took in homeless people, and ran a soup kitchen—first at Centenary Wilbur Methodist Church and then at St. Francis Church, until the St. Vincent de Paul Society took it over in 1985. The celebration of Mass by an archdiocesan priest in one of the communal homes once a week indicated that Dwyer at least tolerated their presence in his archdiocese.[26]

He also permitted an increase in lay participation in church functions. His directive in 1969 encouraged the establishment of parish councils to help the pastor. Like all human institutions, parish councils brought mixed blessings. Some, like the one started at All Saints parish, helped its pastor, Father Willis Whalen, extricate the parish from a difficult financial situation. Others were, as one observer noted, "great on ideas but short on execution."

Nevertheless, the growth in lay participation at the parish level continued. St. Charles parish in Portland started a parish council in 1973, and in addition was one of the first parishes to hire a pastoral associate, Sister Florence Peterson, S.N.J.M. In 1976 St. Anthony's in Tigard invested its first lay ministers, and in 1980 inaugurated Family Offertory Processions.[27]

A dynamic lay movement that began sprouting in Oregon in 1970–71 was the Charismatic Movement, to which the American Catholic hierarchy had given cautious approval in 1969. Dwyer was suspicious of the movement; in his column of December 15, 1974, he criticized it as "an extremely dangerous phenomenon, pregnant with many errors, the seedbed of dissensions and divisiveness among the faithful and the fomenter of a false spirituality." Still, the movement took root and in 1976, two years after Dwyer's resignation, a Mass celebrated at the Sanctuary of Our Sorrowful Mother in Portland attracted more than 1,200 Charismatics.[28]

To meet the needs of another group of Catholics, Archbishop Dwyer and Father Bertram F. Griffin encouraged a survey of Maronite Catholics living in the Northwest, particularly in Portland, conducted by Father Paul Mouawad. In 1971 Mouawad began offering Mass in the Maronite Rite and in 1974 a church was established as part of the Maronite Exarchy in the United States. It was dedicated to Blessed, later Saint, Sharbel.

Anticipating another need within the Church, in 1974 Dwyer took advantage of Vatican approval of a petition by American bishops to reinstitute the permanent diaconate. He ordained Loris Buccola in a quiet ceremony at St. Paul's Church in Silverton, making him the archdiocese's first permanent deacon.[29]

+≈+

Regarding liturgical changes, Dwyer did not keep his conservative opinions to himself. He was wary of embracing many of the transformations in the liturgy, although in 1965 he had admitted that much good could come from the liturgical movement, and he was not opposed to the use of English "if it has quality." But over time, he grew more critical of liturgical reform. In 1973 Dwyer stated his belief that Vatican II, in voting for *The Constitution on the Sacred Liturgy,* had tampered with the cultural lifelines of the Catholic Church. Though in public Dwyer was loyal to Rome and the liturgical reforms it had instituted, in private he was thoroughly traditional. When he offered Mass at home in his private chapel, adorned with the modern art he loved, he spoke in Latin at an altar facing the wall.[30]

Dwyer was upset about what was happening with nuns in the archdiocese in the 1960s and '70s. He was angry that many were leaving the schools and was concerned about what was happening in the convent. Shortly before his retirement he was quoted by the *Oregonian* as saying, referring to the sisters, that "Their ability generally to maintain a true religious life is not evident, although there are shining exceptions." The Sisters of St. Mary of Oregon may have been one of those "shining exceptions." Though they decided to change their habit, as did most nuns, they did so slowly over two decades, and kept the use of a veil. His relations with them continued to be cordial and when they renovated their motherhouse chapel in Beaverton, he gave them new Stations of the Cross and other religious artifacts. In contrast, the Holy Names Sisters were not on his list of "shining exceptions"; they had been in the process of changing rapidly to secular clothing about the time he came to Portland. Dwyer was not happy about this; seeing sisters without their veils rankled him. Sister Marian Dolores Robinson, S.N.J.M., who served on two commissions and had other contacts with him, was always careful to wear a veil when she met with him, a gesture he seemed to appreciate.

Sister Robinson's tact notwithstanding, Dwyer's relations with the Holy Names Sisters remained strained, reaching a climax of sorts in March 1973, at a banquet the sisters gave in an abortive attempt to launch a fund-raising drive for Marylhurst College. His ire aroused, he gave a highly critical speech summing up much of what he believed was wrong with their congregation. The following year the Holy Names Sisters—as if to emphasize the unconventionality that rankled Dwyer—took Marylhurst College on an innovative course to cope with a changing world. The board of trustees closed Marylhurst College in spring 1974, and reopened it the following fall as the Marylhurst Educational Center, with the same charter, renewed accreditation, and an orientation toward adults seeking a college education offered in a nontraditional manner.[31]

Dwyer's relations with the University of Portland also cooled after he gave a speech there to the students in May 1967, and found himself in an altercation with them during the question and answer period. The university was recovering during that time from the financial problems which had also threatened many other institutions of higher education toward the end of the 1960s. By the 1971–72 academic year, the university was balancing its budget, beginning to eliminate its debt, and preparing itself for growth.[32]

Of all the Catholic institutions, Mt. Angel College was the greatest thorn in Dwyer's side. No institute of higher education gave Dwyer more fuel to complain about the decline of obedience and tradition than that one. The college had been a small institution for women conducted by the Benedictine

Sisters until 1958 when it started to admit men. However, enrollment declined, and the college went from one crisis to another: the sisters withdrew from its administration; it defaulted on a government loan; the administration engaged in a theological dispute with Dwyer; and they became involved in controversial issues like the Vietnam War and the table grape boycott, which alienated more conservative Willamette Valley Catholics. It looked hopeful that the tide was turning by December 1973, when Ernesto Lopez, who had been the college's and Oregon's first Mexican-American academic dean, took over as president of a revamped school. He had support from Dwyer, who was sensitive to the needs of Hispanics and approved of its new direction as an institution dedicated to preparing Mexican-American students to enter regular institutions of higher education. Unfortunately it still failed to achieve viability in what one critic was quoted as calling "the longest running death scene in history." The school finally ceased functioning in 1982.[33]

Concerning the education of aspirants to the priesthood, one of Dwyer's most innovative efforts was to institute a House of Studies near Portland State University. He requested Father Bertram Griffin to start the house for young men who wanted to be priests but who, in the restless environment of the 1960s, rebelled against the discipline and structure of the seminary at Mount Angel. The House of Studies was a place where they could live together while obtaining a college education, have access to priest advisors, and continue to explore their vocations. Along the way they would learn such priestly practicalities as the absolute necessity for rules to ward off chaos in human society and how to have healthy human relations without sexuality, in preparation for celibacy. The concept of a house of studies had been discussed for several years, but it was Dwyer who permitted implementation of the idea.[34]

Father Francis Leipzig, pastor of St. Mary's Church, Eugene. Later, Bishop of Baker Diocese, 1950–1971.
Oregon Catholic Press

Unlike Howard, who believed that Catholic students should go to Catholic institutions of higher education, Dwyer, who had been a chaplain at a state college in Utah, believed in ministering to students at secular institutions. Thus, he was willing to spend money to support Newman centers. Father Edwin V. O'Hara and his brother, John, had been active in the Newman Center at the University of Oregon, and Bishop Francis P. Leipzig supported the center at Oregon State University when he was pastor at St. Mary's Church in Corvallis and later at the University of Oregon when he was at St. Mary's in Eugene. During Dwyer's administration Newman centers were started at state institutions of higher education at Monmouth and Ashland, and one was active at Lewis and Clark College for a time.[35]

In the area of formal seminary training, Mount Angel Seminary continued an orthodox curriculum. Dwyer's relations with the Benedictine monks and the seminary officials at Mount Angel were warm and sympathetic. Abbot Damian Jentges, O.S.B., shared the archbishop's distress over the changes occurring in the Church and especially in his monastic community, and the archbishop became a good friend of the monastery and seminary. Upon his retirement he felt that one of his greatest accomplishments as archbishop of Portland had been the improvement of Mount Angel Seminary to make it a strong, orthodox school for training young men for the priesthood. As a further indication of his regard for Mount Angel Abbey, Dwyer willed his extensive collection of books to the Aalto Library there, which had been dedicated in 1970 during his tenure.[36]

As Catholic institutions of higher education were adapting and preparing to flourish in a changed environment, schools at lower levels were not faring as well. Serra High School in Salem closed in 1969 because of declining enrollment and financial troubles, as well as some indication of disagreement between the archbishop and the Franciscans over its coeducational status. Father Martin Thielen, who was superintendent of education during part of that time, commented, "Looking back, neither side was overly diplomatic." The declining number of religious groups, particularly sisters, greatly affected Catholic elementary and secondary education, and led to greater dependence on lay teachers. As late as 1960 the average ratio of religious to lay teachers in all parochial schools had been 5 to 2. By 1980 lay teachers outnumbered religious by 2 to 1, and many schools had closed. As if in anticipation of change, in 1971 at St. Mary's parish in Albany, Dwyer broke ground on the site of the old school for a multipurpose building that would serve the religious instruction needs for all parishioners, from kindergartners to adults.[37]

<hr/>

Increased emphasis on religious instruction for all Catholics, similar to the Confraternity of Christian Doctrine programs instituted by O'Hara, indicated the archbishop's interest in education. In Salt Lake, Dwyer had been

superintendent of education for the diocese and in Portland he faithfully attended the meetings of the Commission on Religious Education, because he
was actively interested in their activities. But Dwyer's strict views on orthodoxy and how properly to teach the faith brought about estrangement between him and some of the priests in his archdiocese. In 1969 he removed
Father Daniel Fuesz from his position as Associate Pastor of Sacred Heart
Parish in Medford, charging that he had been teaching "inexact dogma."
About the same time he also disciplined Father Joseph Biltz for publicly dis-
senting from the Church's teaching on birth control and a married clergy.
These problems with a handful of priests, though significant, paled in contrast to the controversy surrounding his controversy with his Superintendent
of Education, Father Emmet Harrington, in 1972.[38]

Dwyer had acquired the energetic and highly visible Harrington in 1968.
In addition to other educational duties, Harrington's office also provided a
variety of in-service programs for parochial school principals. In the summer
of 1972 the Adult Education Office prepared booklets dealing with four of
the sacraments: baptism, penance, eucharist and confirmation, to help families studying together. Dwyer had expressed some concern about the contents
of the booklets, but staff members in Harrington's office ascertained that they
contained the points required by the U.S. Bishops' *General Catechetical Directory.* During summer 1972, while the archbishop was away from the chancery office, partly because of his health, the Education Office had the booklets reproduced and set up a series of workshops at which they planned to
distribute them. Plans were well under way in September when the archbishop returned, read, and disapproved of the dogma contained in the booklets—only to be told that it was too late to change them. Consequently,
Dwyer fired Superintendent of Education Harrington. Secure in the right-
ness of his action, Dwyer obviously had no idea of the repercussions that
would result from it. Harrington was popular with the religious and lay personnel in the archdiocesan schools and was well known in the community at
large. He was on good terms with the superintendent of the Portland Public
Schools and with the state education system and he had been active on the
Human Rights Commission of the Oregon Education Association. Therefore the *Oregonian* and *The Oregon Journal* provided unusually wide coverage
of the archbishop's action.

In the wake of the furor that arose, the Archdiocesan Board of Education
held an open and well-publicized meeting in downtown Portland in the auditorium of St. Mary's Academy for public debate over the archbishop's decision. According to one newspaper account, Harrington's supporters were
mostly religious and clergy, while Dwyer's were mostly laity and parents. In

the meantime, the Board of Education and the Priests' Senate were quietly working on negotiations between the two protagonists. Late the following Tuesday, September 26, an agreement was reached whereby Harrington agreed to withdraw the booklets and to submit all future materials to the archbishop for his approval. In return, Harrington was reinstated as superintendent of education and the archbishop denied that he had ever strayed from Catholic doctrine. This situation appears to have well illustrated Reese's comment that the paradigm of the archbishop as "an episcopal monarch" no longer functioned in most archdioceses. The field was becoming too broad for an archbishop to maintain direct control over everything.[39]

Other than the controversy generated by his dispute with Harrington, Dwyer's publicity within Oregon's wider community seems to have been minimal, except for his occasional informative and articulate interviews with newspaper reporters. He was not as likely as Howard to frequent the banquet circuit and was not active in any community organizations. It is likely that his health was a factor in his lack of visibility. Objections to the Vietnam War were strong on college campuses, and Dwyer liberally permitted priests to aid conscientious objectors. He was also open to ecumenism, had the archdiocese join the Ecumenical Ministries of Oregon, and served on its board of directors.[40]

Dwyer's activity in the realm of politics was very minimal. After Dwyer's installation, Leo Smith had continued to be the attorney for the archdiocese and its unpaid lobbyist in Salem; but when he called the archbishop's office for input on pending legislation, he received no response to his telephone calls. After he wrote a letter stating how important it was that he be able to present the Church's position—and received no reply—Smith ended his role as a spokesman for the archdiocese. Some low-profile political activity continued, however. For example, Father Alcuin E. Heibel, O.S.B., remained politically active in Salem, and Dwyer supported his efforts. Also, Dwyer entertained Catholic legislators at his home for dinner at least once, and in 1968 he wrote letters to three state senators—Thomas R. Mahoney, Anthony Ituri, and E.D. Potts—thanking them for "the service you have rendered to the Church and Christian decency" during the past session of the legislature.

In Dwyer's last year of office a concerted effort was made to promote Church lobbying. An archdiocesan coordinating team was set up, composed of the heads of all "duly recognized" Catholic organizations in the archdiocese. This political action group, with an almost entirely lay membership, was most active during the spring and summer of 1973. The organization's goals consisted of "combating issues or situations detrimental to the faith or morals of the people"; gathering and disseminating material on pertinent issues; and urging people to elect "candidates of high moral character and judgment." It evidently did not last long into Archbishop Cornelius M. Power's administration, although many of its focal issues continued to be of concern to the archdiocese, such as abortion, pornography, senior citizen concerns, lotteries, and taxes.[41]

Burdened by deteriorating health since his heart attack at the beginning of 1972, and by the frustrations of his administration, Dwyer submitted his resignation to Rome, which was accepted effective January 22, 1974. This action rounded out seven years abundant in controversy and change. His personal administrative style, temperament, and interests had merged uneasily with the demands of the expanding Portland chancery office. However, to his credit, Dwyer had recognized and accepted many of the changes taking place, either supporting or initiating actions to accommodate them within the scope of his beliefs. In hindsight, it could be speculated that had Dwyer had an auxiliary bishop to handle day-to-day functions, such as running the chancery office, hearing complaints, and making assignments—thus freeing the archbishop to visit parishes, write articles, and preach sermons—both Dwyer and the Catholics within his charge might have been more satisfied.[42]

His request for permission to retire in 1973 may also have been precipitated by his clash with the Holy Names Sisters and the catechism controversy with Harrington, both of which emphasized his strained relations with some of his religious and his general perception of what was happening to the Catholic Church in America. Soon after his retirement he apparently wrote Pope Paul VI a long, detailed letter with occasional evidences of suppressed emotion, lacking his customary elegance of style, about what he perceived as a gradual takeover of the Catholic Church in the United States by modernists and secularists, and as growing disobedience to the Holy See. In it he cited well known names and examples as illustrating this trend, with the United States Catholic Conference–National Conference of Catholic Bishops (USCC–NCCB) as a major culprit; however, he mentioned no names or incidents traceable to the Portland archdiocese. The letter was made public a year after he died, but it is unclear whether or not the Pope ever read it.[43]

Dwyer died of cancer in 1976, in Piedmont, California, two years after his retirement; his little dog, Minnie, perhaps his closest companion and greatest comfort during those trying years in Portland, died a few weeks prior to him. Despite the trials he had encountered in the Portland archdiocese, Dwyer had established warm ties with many of his priests; at his request his Requiem Mass took place in Portland at the Cathedral of the Immaculate Conception (St. Mary Cathedral) and internment was in Mount Calvary Cemetery so that he could be among his priests.[44]

Though Robert Joseph Dwyer was sensitive, liberal, and even innovative in regard to many social issues, it appears that he was not the right man to provide the kind of leadership the Church in Oregon needed in the turbulent '60s and '70s. Dwyer's public image—that of a rigidly orthodox, high-church prince—fitted poorly into the post-Vatican II Church in Oregon. Perhaps had Dwyer been younger and in better health, more active in making the rounds of parish functions, graduations, and banquets, and more at ease in conversing with ordinary people, he might have been perceived differently. After retirement, he seemed to relax in public somewhat, as if the constraints of the office he had held had been removed. Nevertheless, when he had been in charge, his formal and authoritarian leadership style alienated many Oregon Catholics, rather than bringing the archdiocese together to face its numerous challenges with solidarity.[45]

As the Oregon Catholic Church continued to march inexorably into the future, it would discover in its next archbishop a man with an understanding of the times, who would facilitate, rather than obstruct, the sometimes rough path to increased unity and maturity.

Cornelius Michael Power (1913–1997)
Archbishop of Portland in Oregon (1974–1986)
Oregon Catholic Press

Chapter Nine

Coming to Terms with Change

THE NEW ARCHBISHOP had a reputation as a soother of troubled waters. Archbishop Cornelius Michael Power, the first native Northwesterner to assume the position, was born in Seattle in December 1913 to devout parents who also contributed another son to the priesthood and two daughters to the Sisters of the Holy Names of Jesus and Mary. He attended St. Joseph Seminary in Mountain View, California, St. Patrick Seminary in Menlo Park, California, and St. Edward Seminary in Kenmore, Washington, before ordination, and afterwards obtained a doctorate in canon law from The Catholic University of America. Power had been a pastor of a large city parish, and then served as both vice-chancellor and chancellor in the Archdiocese of Seattle for over twenty-six years. After that, he was made bishop of the Yakima Diocese in Washington, where he mended the breach that had formed between the previous bishop and the flock there. Finding the diocese on the edge of bankruptcy, he restored it to financial health. Also while there, Power actively supported the efforts of Cesar Chavez to unionize migrant agricultural labor in the Yakima Valley. Coming to Oregon with this extensive background, he was installed as the seventh archbishop of Portland in Oregon on April 17, 1974.[1]

Power—sensitive, warm-hearted, approachable, and a man who refused to take himself too seriously—appeared as quite a contrast to his predecessor. He was a very pleasant person who made friends easily, perhaps even more easily than Howard had. He thoroughly enjoyed parish events and loved meeting and visiting with people. Many appreciated above all else that Power was always kind and readily expressed his appreciation for the efforts of others. The man possessed a gentle, quirky sense of humor that lightly flavored much of what he did and said. He was sometimes exasperatingly slow to make decisions, and quite diffident about expressing his views, very much in contrast with the assertive Dwyer. A reporter from the *Oregon Journal*, who interviewed Power in Yakima, described him as "relaxed and unpretentious…" and, while not evasive, "neither was he about to come out with ringing declarations of what he intended to do when he assumed his new office."

Power's appearance as well contrasted with that of his predecessor. A neat, almost dapper person, his bearing made him appear taller than Dwyer, and he had dark wavy hair atop a countenance that suggested that mirth was never very far below the surface. As if to try to counteract this, he wore dark-rimmed glasses, which gave him a faintly professorial demeanor.[2]

Power's style of living recalled the days of the former Oregon archbishops. He lived unpretentiously, frugally. After his installation, the archbishop lived in a guest apartment next to the convent of the Franciscan Sisters on Palatine Hill for four years. After that he took over an unfinished wing of the convent adjacent to La Salle High School in Milwaukie, a Portland suburb, and converted it into quarters for himself. It was a plain building, though large enough for guest accommodations and official functions. He even did most of his own cooking.

Breaking with long-standing practice, Power felt no pressing need to assert aggressively the primacy of the office of archbishop. He believed that the most important part of a bishop's administration was his relationship with his priests, because a bishop could not be very effective if his priests did not support him. When visited by priests, Power would greet them in the lobby and escort them cordially into his office, putting them at ease with casual conversation. During a priests' retreat at the University of Portland they would have a "morning with the archbishop," where, with many sitting on the floor around him, they just talked with him. When the superior of the Sisters of St. Mary of Oregon, Sister Fidelis Kreutzer, S.S.M.O., invited Power to conduct a canonical visit of their motherhouse, he declined, saying that Vatican II had rendered the procedure obsolete.

As Power admitted later, he never really liked "all the pomp and circumstance of being a bishop." He often concelebrated Mass as an equal among his fellow priests rather than as presiding archbishop, and on visits to parishes he refused to sit at the head of the table since that would displace the pastor. These actions prompted the criticism of some who felt that he was not insisting on proper deference to his position.[3]

✦

The church Dwyer had seen as being in deep trouble may not have been as weakened in reality as he had imagined, but some factors were disquieting.

During Dwyer's years, 1967–74, the number of active diocesan and religious priests had dropped from 475 to 444, and Catholic parochial and high school enrollment from 25,042 to 13,826, while the Catholic population had increased from 197,856 to 260,241. Just prior to Power's installation the Jesuits sold their novitiate in Sheridan because of a decline in novices, and later that same spring Marylhurst College announced that it was closing. In addition, the split between those eager to implement the decisions of Vatican II and those reluctant to change had widened from a hairline crack in Howard's time to an obvious breach during Dwyer's more exacting regime.[4]

The times seemed to indicate a need for building bridges, and Power was the man for it. With his past experience in church administration, he adapted easily to the role of archbishop, yet he felt comfortable with the greatly increased lay role in parish activities. He also smoothed out some ruffled feathers when, soon after he assumed office, he asked Father Emmet Harrington to return from Washington, D.C., to assume a parish in Eugene, which provided ample scope for his activities but kept him out of the Portland limelight for a time. Power's style of administration was along the lines of Archbishop Howard's: he tended to allow others to take initiative. Father Thomas J. Reese, S.J., in his study of modern bishops, places Power in a group he calls "laissez-faire" bishops, meaning those who believe that good initiatives will succeed while bad ones will fail without the leader's intervention.[5]

To an extent to which neither Howard nor Dwyer could have realized, Power settled into the role of a modern archbishop—one who is the chief executive of a complex organization, a sort of religious counterpart to a secular CEO. As such, he did not try to micromanage all the activities under his control, but rather set policy, made key decisions, and delegated authority. Power enjoyed being an administrator. A hard worker who took briefcase loads of paper home with him, he took pleasure in the details of administration, attended all the meetings he could—from the Priests' Senate to the Budget Committee—and conferred often with his subordinates. He brought with him to the office an even disposition, always friendly, smiling, and interested in the people around him. The contrast with his predecessor could hardly have been more pronounced.[6]

After assuming office, Power began a systematic realignment of lines of authority, delegating decision-making power to subordinates. Both the Personnel Board and the Priests' Senate operated freely, with his support and encouragement. The latter worked with him in restructuring the administration, but had some differences with him over the extent of its power. Without the fireworks that had marked disputes under Dwyer, Power was able to resolve conflicts, possessing an ability to be both gentle and firm.[7]

A year after taking office, in October 1975, Power concluded that the archdiocese needed an auxiliary bishop. Consequently, after consulting with priests, religious, lay organizations, and a committee he had appointed to look into the matter, he asked Rome to appoint one. He submitted, according to proper procedure, three names for consideration. In 1976, after consulting with other Northwest bishops and some of his priests, Power decided to ask for a second auxiliary bishop. Following a visit to the archdiocese by a representative of the apostolic delegate in Washington, D.C., he submitted another list of three names. Rome responded by approving two of the names on Power's combined lists: Father Paul E. Waldschmidt, C.S.C., president of the University of Portland, and Father Kenneth Steiner, pastor of St. Francis of Assisi parish in Roy. They were ordained bishops on March 2, 1979, in Portland's Civic Auditorium before an audience of almost 3,000. This ceremony was unusual in that it involved two candidates being consecrated as bishops at the same time.[8]

Auxiliary bishops Kenneth D. Steiner and Paul E. Waldschmidt, C.S.C., with Archbishop Power.
Oregon Catholic Press

In a further variation of the structure under his control, Power implemented additional vicariates. In 1971 Dwyer had organized the Hispanic Vicariate to minister more effectively to Hispanic ethnic groups, providing them with a resource outside the regular Euro-American-oriented parishes. In 1979 Power established vicariates to reorganize the bureaucratic functions of the chancery. This move delegated to the individuals named to head them authority over broad areas of Church activity, and reduced the number of persons who reported directly to the archbishop, although Powers continued to oversee all the activities of his archdiocese closely. The following year, 1980, he divided the archdiocese itself into area vicariates, giving the vicars in each geographic subdivision considerable discretion in how to draw together the parishes and missions in their jurisdictions.[9]

In the chancery office, the various agencies and bureaus that Power gathered under the episcopal vicars had been proliferating for a number of years at an increasing rate. During Howard's early administration the number and names of offices listed in the *Oregon Catholic Directory* had been fairly constant, and few in number. Reflecting the broadening scope of church activities, by 1955 the *Directory* listed diocesan agencies that ranged from study clubs to an office for radio and television. Under Dwyer the scope of interests reflected in the *Directory*'s listing of diocesan agencies continued to widen. During Power's administration, the *Directory* reflected what he considered important enough to be listed. A revised Senate of Priests made its appearance, along with a Personnel Board, Catholic Charities agencies in Marion, Polk, and Lane Counties, agencies for cemeteries, communications, refugee resettlement, an Office of Education that included all educational activities, a Marriage and Family Life Commission, and pro-life activities. Obviously, Power had a richly varied collection of agencies to consolidate under his episcopal vicars. Since then the *Directory* has listed more name changes than increases, although the issue for 1985 saw the addition of Special Services for the Handicapped (later changed to People with Disabilities). The first *Directory* issued in 1987 after the installation of Archbishop William J. Levada contained an organizational chart to help Catholics sort out the lines of authority among the many agencies of the chancery office, and in it the episcopal vicars became department directors. In 1990 those directors also appeared as members of the archbishop's cabinet, a way for him to keep in touch with the many activities of his administration. Over the years, particularly since the time of Howard, an increasing percentage of these agencies are being headed by members of the laity, who also make up increasing proportions of the various boards and commissions whose members' names are listed. Noting another of the continuing changes taking place for Oregon Catholics and their church, the 1991 issue listed as chancellor the name of Mary Jo Tully, the first woman and member of the laity to hold that office in the history of the archdiocese.[10]

History took another turn in 1981 when, after over a century of acquiring land—a practice at which archbishops Blanchet through Christie had been the most adept—Power undertook to sell several large parcels of it, mostly in the City of Beaverton and Washington County. Much of it had been acquired in the nineteenth century, including bequests from the estate of Levi Michael and Emma Anderson. Between 1981 and 1986, when Power retired, sales of the property netted the archdiocese about $24 million. This money became an endowment fund whose income was to be used to ease the archdiocesan assessments on parishes. With the annual fund drive and the endowment fund, the archdiocese freed itself from its sole dependence on parish assessments. Proliferating agencies and an increasingly complex and bureaucratic structure had made additional sources of income essential. During Power's administration Oregon Catholics began to be provided, through the *Sentinel,* with a yearly financial report. In line with practices beginning elsewhere, this further emphasized the business-like manner in which the archdiocese was now being managed.[11]

To further tighten business operations, the chancery office under Power required and audited parish budgets, maintained an in-house banking system for parishes, and tried to control insurance risks connected to parish activities. Thus, the business office became highly visible to parishes, which increasingly found themselves in the position of being branches on a corporate tree. Especially after its remodeling was completed in 1997, the chancery office—now renamed the Pastoral Center, with its wall-to-wall carpeting and many busy offices—radiates some of the atmosphere of a well-run corporate headquarters. Christie, who had stuffed chancery office business in a suitcase, would be thoroughly nonplussed.[12]

+≈+

By the 1970s Oregonians, including the Catholic population, had moved more into the American mainstream than ever before, issued there largely by the impact of post-World War II changes and the growth of communication technology.

Societal changes were clearly visible in Oregon parishes. By the early 1980s, many parish women were returning to college or taking jobs when their children left grade school; enrollment at the parish school was declining while religious education classes were growing. Parish activities now often included support groups for separated and divorced Catholics, and groups dealing with peace activities, scripture study, and prayer. St. Clare's Parish also set a precedent of sorts in 1975 when its pastor, Father Peter Krieg, O.F.M., allowed a girl to serve on the altar after she wrote the Pope asking permission and received no answer.[13]

Social awareness was extending well beyond parish boundaries. When St. Mary Star of the Sea parish in Astoria found itself with a convent too large for the seven sisters still teaching there, they leased it to the state and county to be used as a home for displaced girls. St. Charles parish in Portland, where the closing of its parish school left two surplus buildings, sold its convent to a group which used it to rehabilitate youths with alcohol problems, and rented its school to Portland Community College for its "Steps to Success" program to help the unemployed find jobs. St. Patrick's parish of Canby started a Loaves and Fishes Program in 1979, and donated food to the Mollala Area Food Bank in 1980. While the Catholic Daughters of America's Eugene Court continued many of its traditional activities, it also contributed funds to aid an abused child, to Birthright, and such ecumenical groups as Church Women United and the Interfaith Fellowship, as well as to most community fund drives. Entering the 1990s, St. Philip Neri parishioners in Portland worked with their neighborhood association and with Reach, a group that rehabilitates low-income housing. The parish also converted its former convent into a home for unwed mothers, provided offices for a Christian counseling center, and sponsored Alcoholics Anonymous and Narcotics Anonymous groups.[14]

Shifts also were occurring in the pietistic practices of Oregon Catholics. In step with a national trend, use of novenas and rosaries declined, while the number of Bible study groups increased. The Rite of Christian Initiation for Adults, started in the late 1970s, had as one of its goals to involve the entire parish community in the preparation and acceptance of converts. In a pastoral letter published on August 5, 1977, Power decided to permit the reception of Holy Communion in the hand; and two years later parish priests were informed they could also offer Communion from the cup to their parishioners. Increasingly, Catholics were (and are) trying to see through rituals, lovely as they may be, to the foundations behind them.[15]

Marriage Encounter was another means of making faith meaningful in the lives of many Catholics. More dramatic in its impact on the Church, the Charismatic Movement continued to grow throughout the 1970s and 1980s, providing a forum for the expression of a spirituality radically different from that with which most Catholics were accustomed. Unlike his predecessor, Power voiced no criticism of charismatics. In 1975 he wrote a letter welcoming the delegates attending a Northwest Charismatic Renewal Service

Conference at the University of Portland, and telling them he saw the Charismatic Movement as "a genuine blessing for many Catholics…providing them with a spirituality for which they have been longing." His successor, Archbishop William J. Levada, continued this policy of acceptance by establishing personal contact with the group through Father Thomas Bill, C.S.C., who had brought the movement to Oregon.[16]

+⇒≡⇐+

What can be considered radical changes in parish governance continued to spread throughout the archdiocese, as pastors relinquished more of the activities they had previously dominated. The belief that "Father knows best" rapidly faded as a well-educated laity emerged, and as parish councils and lay ministers took on more and more responsibility for decisions. Some pastors resisted while others, faced with a scarcity of assistant priests, were happy to share responsibility for secular concerns. Regarding the incorporation of laity in ministry, Archbishop Power noted: "To a large extent we needed to do this long before we did," and added that it made sense to involve the laity in doing things they could do much better than the priest.[17]

Canon Law changes in 1983 directed parishes to establish two councils. The parish council was designated to advise on what a parish should and should not do, how to do it, and to set priorities and goals. The second was to be a financial or administrative council to assist in such concerns as fundraising, accounting procedures, building maintenance, and an annual budget in line with goals established by the parish council. When Power called for the establishment of these councils, some parishes—like St. Clare's in Portland and a year later, St. Philip Benizi in Redland—responded promptly. Others took longer, notably Cathedral Parish in Portland, which, after an unsuccessful attempt in the early 1970s (following a directive by Archbishop Dwyer), did not install the two councils until 1992.

The growing shortage of priests precipitated an unprecedented move in the Oregon archdiocese in 1984: Power appointed the first lay administrator of a parish, Sister Eunice Hittner, O.S.F., at St. Rose of Lima, Monroe. A year later Joan Dotter was appointed the lay administrator of St. Mary's Parish, Vernonia.

As the roles of bishop and laity changed, they in turn affected the role of the parish priest, the traditional backbone of church structure. All three roles became more institutionalized: the bishop operated as chief executive, laymen and women as participants in parish government, and the parish priest as the official in charge of a subdivision of the organization. Many parish priests became painfully aware of this change as they tried to cope with the weekly mail containing directives, programs, appeals, and instructions from a bureaucratized chancery office. Another major change for priests occurred in 1983, when, with Power's approval, a tenure policy for pastors was initiated. The policy allowed a term of five years (later changed to six years), renewable once, and promulgated requirements for retirement. This was a considerable departure from the earlier practice of the archbishop deciding, usually without consulting his priests, where, when, and how they should serve. Later, a Personnel Board was instituted to take on some of the responsibilities of appointing priests to their assignments, which some considered a mixed blessing because it weakened the bond between a priest and his bishop. On the other hand, the board gave a priest a chance to state his assignment preference, and would not appoint him to a parish if he adamantly opposed it. Still, adding an impersonal ruling on the duration of his stay in a parish to the already institutionalized assigning process made some priests feel they were being crushed between an emerging laity and a corporate bureaucracy. Ideas or suggestions they might have informally expressed to their archbishop, although that avenue was still open, were now usually expected to be passed on formally through their representatives on the Priests' Senate, which in accordance with the changes in Canon Law became the Presbyteral Council. The Presbyteral Council acquired clearly defined duties as an advisory group to the archbishop, who now is required to consult the council on certain topics. (Recent archbishops have regularly attended its meetings.)

Sensitive to the priests' needs for connection with him, Power, during whose administration much of this structure was implemented, inaugurated the annual Clergy Convention in 1982. In 1985 he endeavored to reach out to all Catholics—priests and laity—through an Archdiocesan Pastoral Convention.[18]

Transitions in Catholic educational leadership had been taking place over several years. When the Board of Education was first formed during Christie's administration, and throughout most of Howard's term, both superintendents of Catholic schools *and* board members were priests. Over time, nonpriests began to replace priests as board members. When Father Arthur Dernbach, the last priest to serve as superintendent, retired in 1979, Sister Janice Burke, S.N.J.M., assumed the position. She was followed by Xaverian Brother James Malone, and Sister Molly Giller, O.P. The first lay superintendent, Larry Thompson, followed Giller, and by the early 1990s the superintendent and almost all board members were lay. The same change occurred at the parochial school level where lay teachers replaced religious. In the fall of 1991, when eight new principals of Catholics schools were appointed, the four men and four women were all lay people.[19]

The first attempts to cope with declining enrollments by consolidating schools took place outside the Portland area. In 1971 in Eugene, Father Emil H. Kies, pastor of St. Mary's parish, converted his school to an area school, with a board of lay representatives from the surrounding parishes who had children in the school and who also subsidized the children they sent to it. It was renamed O'Hara Catholic School in honor of St. Mary's most famous pastor, and was the first area school in the archdiocese. Its example was soon followed in the Portland area where many parochial schools consolidated into area schools, such as Holy Cross and Holy Redeemer. Other schools closed. Even though east Multnomah County contained fast-growing Portland suburbs, during the 1970s most of its parish schools closed.[20]

Catholic high schools also began to feel the impact of declining enrollments. The first one to shut its doors, after Columbia Preparatory School, was Serra High School in Salem. It had opened in 1954 as attendance at Catholic schools was reaching its zenith, and it closed in 1969. Oregon's Department of Education leased the buildings until 1979 when the property was sold and the funds used to establish an endowment fund, the Salem Catholic Schools Foundation, which is helping to keep other Salem Catholic schools open.

Oregon's Catholic institutions of higher education had fewer problems than those at lower levels. When Marylhurst College closed in spring 1974 and reopened in the fall as a nontraditional institution appealing to adult men and women, it was quickly accredited, found ready acceptance, and prospered under Sister Veronica Ann Baxter, S.N.J.M.—proving that a small Catholic college could survive and serve the educational needs of the communities surrounding it.[21]

Catholic Charities also found the nature of its work changing. When the Vietnam War drew to a close, its agencies and experience with previous refugees helped Catholic Charities cope with the arrival of fleeing Catholic Vietnamese. According to its director, Father Morton E. Park, their experiences with Hispanics had taught them one thing: "Keep it simple, don't get complicated." Consequently, Catholic Charities set up a revolving fund through which it could funnel cash to arriving refugees for their immediate needs and later be reimbursed by the federal government. Housing was provided by an arrangement with the Halsey Square Apartments in Portland whereby Catholic Charities obtained some of its units with six-month rental agreements. Most Vietnamese were able to make their own living arrangements after six months. By 1981 enough Catholic Vietnamese and other Southeast Asians had settled in Oregon to warrant setting up a vicariate to serve their spiritual needs, similar to the situation with the Hispanics. Soon after the Southeast Asian Vicariate was formed, it moved into the building that had formerly housed the Holy Child Academy. When the Society of the Holy Child decided to sell the property, the entire Southeast Asian community joined to raise the money to buy it. Auxiliary Bishop Paul E. Waldschmidt, C.S.C., who was their mentor and advocate, worked with the archdiocese and the community to facilitate the purchase. Since its establishment, the vicariate has helped thousands of Laotians, Cambodians, Mien, Hmong, and Vietnamese adjust to a new culture and build a strong community of their own. Besides providing spiritual ministry and help through such services as English classes, emergency aid, counseling, and job training and placement, the vicariate has become a meeting place for youth and adult groups and has welcomed Southeast Asians of other religious affiliations. Bishop Waldschmidt also played a central role in the establishment of a church for Koreans, and after attending Korean Masses at St. Francis and St. Anthony's churches in Portland, they eventually acquired their own church on S.E. Powell Street in 1996.[22]

While many individual Catholics helped them get started, Southeast Asians moved quickly to supply their own needs and began to make their own contribution to the Catholic community. Since the early 1980s Vietnamese and other Southeastern Asian men and women have been entering seminaries and religious communities, and the Vietnamese Sister Adorers of the Holy Cross have established themselves in a convent rented from All Saints Parish to help other refugees. By 1984 enough Vietnamese had settled in St. Mary's Parish in Mt. Angel to celebrate their traditional Lunar New Year with a special Mass. Also, by the 1980s, sizeable numbers of Vietnamese had settled in St. Joseph's Parish in Salem, and around Immaculate Heart Church in Portland by the early 1990s. Catholic Charities' job of refugee resettlement began to taper off in the late 1980s and 1990s because of increased efforts to keep people in their own countries.[23]

While the Southeast Asian Vicariate has concentrated the majority of its activities in Portland, where most Asians had settled, the Hispanic Vicariate spread out through much of the archdiocese because the Catholics it serves work in agricultural jobs. In the late 1970s, Power divided it into five (later ten) *misiones*, quasi-parishes that covered a large area. By the early 1980s these *misiones* were served by priests, sisters, and lay workers who were permanently assigned to the vicariate.[24]

Another minority, with roots in the American Church and nation older than any of the refugees and most of the European and Hispanic immigrants, remained on the periphery of the Oregon Catholic community. African-Americans are only about 1.6% of the Catholic population of western Oregon. Only in Portland are there enough Catholics to engage in the kind of group activities that have helped make other minorities visible. In 1976 Portland saw the chartering of a Portland chapter of the National Black Catholic Lay Caucus, with Sam Jackson Jr. as convener and later president. Immaculate Heart Church in 1981 was the setting for the establishment of the St. Martin de Porres Council of the Knights of St. Peter Claver. Ironically, this was a church where blacks had not been encouraged to take part in parish life until the early 1970s. Gradually, African-American Catholics are becoming more visible participants in the Oregon Catholic family.[25]

Certain Catholic charitable services have ceased or shifted according to resources and needs in recent years. In Portland, St. Vincent de Paul Day Nursery, which had started as Blessed Martin DePorres Day Nursery fifty years before, closed its doors early in 1990. Although affordable care was still needed, insufficient funds were available to maintain the standard of care it had provided for the children of war workers during World War II, and later for those of single and poor parents, both black and white. The Downtown Chapel, officially St. Vincent de Paul parish, moved to N.W. 6th and Burnside Street in the 1970s, and its programs became more social-welfare oriented when it converted its basement to a cleanup area with showers and laundry facilities for skid row occupants. It opened a kitchen to provide hot meals for the increasing number of needy, and set up a Loaves and Fishes program for the elderly, along with a "Meals on Heels" program to take meals, usually by walking, to the homebound in the single-occupancy hotels in the area. When the cleanup area moved to nearby Burnside Projects (Transition Projects) in 1997, the basement of the Downtown Chapel temporarily was turned into an overnight facility for young transients; after that it became a senior center for elderly street people. It also provides a meeting place for Alcoholics Anonymous, a monthly Mass for disabled persons, and a base for other charitable services to the poor and homeless. Downtown Chapel is a prime example of how the Church has reached out in different ways to meet changing needs. Blanchet House, which was started in 1952 to serve meals to the homeless, has not changed its mission, but has expanded to meet increased need. In the early 1990s, Blanchet House was providing about 900 meals a day, the most ever. However, it was finding its mission threatened by the increasing gentrification of the neighborhood around it.[26]

In day-to-day operations, both the *Sentinel* and the Catholic Truth Society (CTS) came under lay control. As Dwyer's term approached its end, the Catholic Truth Society, which subsidizes the *Sentinel,* was losing money. By 1974 the banks refused to extend further credit. As of October 1, 1974, soon after Power became archbishop, its editor and executive director, Gorman Hogan, resigned. Power became president of the Catholic Truth Society, with Francis (Fritz) Meagher appointed as editor of the *Sentinel.* Fitting his administrative style, Power appointed people whom he trusted to carry out his policies and allowed them to operate the *Sentinel* without his close involvement. Owen Alstott became editor of *Today's Music* and composed music, including the Heritage Mass, infusing the whole operation with new life. Meagher moved up to become publisher of the CTS and the *Sentinel,* and Robert Pfohman, who had previous experience on Baker and Salem newspapers, became editor of the *Sentinel.* When Meagher retired, Alstott took his place. He was replaced by John Limb in 1992 after Alstott resigned his position as publisher. The operation of the Catholic publishing enterprise has changed greatly since the days when Father Charles M. Smith ran both the Catholic Truth Society and the *Sentinel* as a one-man (priest) operation. Though the archbishop is president of both operations, they are entirely lay staffed and administered, with the exception of some of the *Sentinel*'s columnists.[27]

Of the institutions established by Oregon Catholics to express their faith to the world around them, probably none has been transformed as radically as the Catholic Truth Society—renamed the Oregon Catholic Press in 1981. Almost sixty years earlier, at a time when anti-Catholicism was overt and strong in Oregon, the society had been organized to defend and explain the Catholic Church and its faith. However, its mission began to be transformed with the first printing of a pamphlet-style missal for the laity. Vatican II's emphasis on the laity as participants in the celebration of the Mass led to a need for more missals and new music. A small group of composers and musicians began to fill the need for new music, and the Catholic Truth Society became its publisher, along with enlarging its offerings in missals. Subsequently, the society began to publish pamphlets, sheet music, tapes, and recordings, as well as to commission new hymns. Now it is one of the major publishers of Catholic music in the world. Limited in its traditional market because of fewer Catholic parishes in the United States, the Oregon Catholic Press, as it is now called, has begun to interest Protestant churches in its music, to publish for the Hispanic market, and to establish foreign outlets. The board of directors of the Catholic Truth Society changed the name in

1981, recognizing that the publisher's original mission of defending the Church no longer defined its activities.[28]

✛══✠

Issues of human sexuality, sexual misconduct, and practicing their faith with purity in the midst of an increasing breakdown of accepted social mores has had its effect on the Oregon Church, just as elsewhere. In a Church whose members are as much afflicted with the taint of original sin as their secular contemporaries, adhering to a life-style in accord with their beliefs in a world where many do not share those beliefs is not easy for laity or clergy. Clerics, because of their particular commitment, vow of celibacy, and high visibility, have been especially challenged throughout history. It is a problem the Church has always encountered. Archbishops Christie and Howard employed a lay representative to discreetly contact clergymen who had quit the priesthood to try to bring them back into the fold. During Howard's later years the archdiocesan lawyer, Leo Smith, dealt with cases of priests involved with women, and others in trouble over gambling and drunk driving. In more recent years, at least two cases of priests embezzling have occurred. Dwyer started a counseling service for priests and religious, but even so, sexual misconduct continued to surface.

In one painful but instructive case, Power, who combined the efficiency of a CEO with an almost incompatible kindness, tried for too long to deal gently with a priest accused of child-molestation by moving him to different parishes. Finally, in August 1983, the parents of some of the children involved turned to the civil authorities. As a consequence, the archdiocese paid dearly in cost and publicity. Out of the experience came new methods for dealing with such problems. The *Sentinel* learned from the painful episode that at times it is wiser to print unpleasant news and present the whole story—so as to counteract the secular press's sensationalism—than to try to hide such an affair from the public. The parish that had suffered the highly publicized case of child abuse formed a committee of parishioners that issued a number of recommendations, including that the archdiocese take steps to ensure that all allegations of child abuse be reported immediately to civil authorities. The archdiocese followed up with a meeting of all priests within the archdiocese to inform them about pertinent laws and to issue guidelines for reporting suspected cases. The archdiocese also expanded counseling services to help priests deal with psychological, personality, and emotional problems, as well as ones caused by alcohol and drug dependency. Of course, the question of confidentiality, such a prominent part of priests' ministry, added complications, but the entire situation resulted in an increased awareness in the Catholic community that it was still very much part of the world around it.[29]

Archbishop Power's impact on that world was low-key, in keeping with his overall style; he did not write a regular column voicing his opinion on various topics as his predecessor had. However, when moved by current events, he spoke out. In 1984, he wrote pastoral letters deploring the United States government's friendly attitude toward the government of El Salvador and later that year urged a "no" vote on a ballot measure to reinstate the death penalty in Oregon. Realizing the need to restore a presence in Oregon's capital to voice the Church's position on pertinent legislation, Power formed an advisory board. Besides himself as president, the board included Leo Smith, former state legislator and the archdiocese's attorney and lobbyist; Diarmaid O'Scannlain, a prominent Republican attorney and later federal judge; and Bishop Thomas J. Connolly of Baker. The board met two or three times a year to discuss possible legislation touching on topics of concern, such as abortion and capital punishment, and it hired a lobbyist to represent the Church in Salem. In 1984 Power and Connolly of the Baker Diocese together created the Oregon Catholic Conference as a sort of state version of the United States Catholic Conference, consisting of the archbishop and bishops of Oregon. Robert Castagna, of the Portland archdiocese, was appointed its executive director and given the mandate to voice its concerns on pertinent issues of public policy to government officials, agencies, and legislatures at local and national levels. Issues included aid for two-parent poor families; clergy-penitent confidentiality; abortion; euthanasia; child education; and the issuance of information on birth-control devices at public high school health clinics in Portland.[30]

In addition to making its positions known in government circles, the archdiocese increasingly became involved in ecumenical activities, particularly as a member of the Ecumenical Ministries of Oregon. Within individual parishes, community concerns also led to a broadening of ecumenical activities. Holy Cross parish in North Portland shared responsibility with Pioneer United Methodist Church for staffing North Portland's only family shelter for the homeless, housed in the Methodist Church, and also began joining with St. Andrew Episcopal Church in prayers during the annual Week of Prayer for Christian Unity. In 1991 St. Clare's parish sold its convent to Ecumenical Ministries of Oregon. It became known as Clare House, a residential treatment center for pregnant women with drug addictions. Parishes in Northeast Portland, among them All Saints and St. Charles, joined the Portland Organizing Project (POP), an ecumenical group of churches dedicated to improving neighborhoods on Portland's east side. Beginning in 1986, POP worked to close down neighborhood crack houses, to pressure banks to extend loans to homeowners in poorer neighborhoods, and to persuade the city to reduce charges for sewer hookups to homes.[31]

A very interesting exercise in ecumenism began in late July 1986, just prior to Power's retirement. About twenty families from St. Anthony's parish in Tigard joined with families from Atonement Lutheran Church to form a community that would worship, study, and perform ministry work together in the Progress area of Beaverton and Tigard. Through their Mission of the Atonement, their meeting place, they provided a new dimension to ecumenism in Oregon—giving expression to their faith in worship and ministry together while remaining true to their separate beliefs and traditions.[32]

Satisfied that his archdiocese was coming to terms with the changes surrounding it and achieving higher visibility and positive community relations throughout Oregon, Archbishop Power decided in 1986 that the time had come for him to resign. He was just a little short of his 75th birthday, at which time retirement was mandatory. In a pre-retirement interview with *Sentinel* reporter Jim Magmer, Power listed among his accomplishments the tenure policy for priests, and the calling of the Archdiocesan Pastoral Convention in 1985. The Convention had involved priests and laity in a discussion of the Church's needs. Power spoke about the nature of the Church, and in delineating the pattern of changes that had taken place, he summarized the effects of his administration. Lay involvement, he noted, changed the way in which an archbishop uses his authority. Previously, bishops ruled like monarchs who, out of their own vision, background, and study built the Church as they believed it should be. Now pastoral and administrative planning come not from the bishop alone, but "from an almost endless variety" of priests and laity who are just as interested as the archbishop in making the Church "everything Christ wants it to be." This, he felt, had to produce better priorities and decisions "than any that came from the bishop alone." He did not find it hard to change the bishop's role from that of autocrat to one requiring greater patience, tolerance, and willingness to accept new ideas from others. Nor did he believe that the bishop's authority was diluted, but rather that now the whole family was invited to contribute to the Church's mission, encouraging people to feel that they were the Church, not the Church's "children who should be seen and not heard." What was happening had nothing to do with the priest shortage: "The positions into which they [laity] are moving are rightfully theirs—have been all along." He added that the Church was showing its maturity—a conclusion that reflects back upon its leader.

By the time of his retirement, Power had quieted troubled waters and brought the Church and the Catholics it served onto the threshold of the closing years the twentieth century. After retiring, Power continued to live in Portland another ten years. He received the opportunity to minister in a way he had always enjoyed, just being a priest again (as he expressed it). He filled in at parishes wherever there was a need, and discovered a new ministry to enjoy: hosting retreats. Power died on May 22, 1997.[33]

Chapter Ten

The Church in Oregon: A Perspective

N THE CLOSING DECADES of the 20th century, the Catholic community experienced a pace of change unimaginable by Power's predecessors. Still, those predecessors who had served the Catholic
Church in Oregon since 1846 had each influenced and helped
shape the Church's present course. As the pioneer missionary who almost
single-handedly created the second archdiocese in the United States, Francis
Norbert Blanchet laid the foundation for an archdiocese that only now is
bringing his dream to reality. His successor, the unrequited missionary Charles
John Seghers, led the Oregon church out of the pioneer era, consolidated its
boundaries within those of the state, and introduced administrative order.
Oregon's first American-born archbishop, William Hickley Gross, C.Ss.R.,
drew the Oregon church into the mainstream of the American Catholic
Church, welcomed many new religious communities, and saw the start of
many institutions and religious observances in Oregon. Alexander Christie
oversaw an explosive growth of parishes and institutions, while the long administration of Edward Daniel Howard brought new and expanded institutions, increased social awareness, greater lay activity, and culminated in the
changes of Vatican II. In an administration marked by transitional turmoil and
continued progress, Robert J. Dwyer struggled to try to maintain historical
Church structure and doctrine while facing school closures and a major decline
in numbers of priests and religious, and trying to be sensitive to the social pressures on the Church. Cornelius M. Power quieted the turmoil with his gentle
demeanor and openness to all Catholics, while restructuring the Church's ex-
ploding bureaucracy and delegating authority with the competency of a modern CEO. His leadership ushered Oregon Catholics into an era of even greater
changes than those recorded in the past century and a half.

The challenges of the coming years may not be as formidable as they seem
because Oregon's hierarchy has found a powerful ally in the laity. Indeed, it was

a layman, John McLoughlin, who was responsible for requesting the first missionaries to come to the Oregon Country. Blanchet, Demers, and other early missionaries might have expected to evangelize Native Americans, but they found that the already-baptized laity especially required their ministry. The creation of an improbable archdiocese in the wilderness did not include lay contribution, but its fragile nature was exposed when the California gold rush lured away much of its meager supply of parishioners, as well as many of the religious who served them. As European ethnic groups, a smattering of Catholics among them, settled on the lands vacated by dying and forceably removed Native Americans, archbishops and priests scrambled to create a spiritual shelter for them. Extant records tell the story of the construction of the institutional church. More difficult to quantify is the role of the laity, who were often the ones who chose where a church should be located, sometimes in the face of the reluctance and even opposition of the archbishop. A lay group, the Society of St. Vincent de Paul, was responsible for the establishment of Oregon's first hospital, and laymen established, owned or partly owned, and ran the archdiocese's newspaper for almost fifty years, and are managing it again. Lay women's groups were involved in social work before the start of the twentieth century. In an archdiocese always short of priests, lay organizations have been indispensable in the formation and running of parishes as communities of believers.

Archbishop Howard, the first to enjoy the luxury of a substantially completed church infrastructure in place when he arrived, encouraged lay organizations, from the revival of the Society of St. Vincent de Paul to the establishment of the Legion of Mary in the archdiocese. He also encouraged lay people to examine their faith and its expression through study clubs. Howard's administration saw the beginning of lay participation in the liturgy in the years leading up to Vatican II.

Friction among archbishops, priests, and laity has flared—at times hot enough to produce sparks—among human beings caught in the stressful conditions of a young, still-forming society. Yet, somehow their common faith has kept them on track, even as they have struggled with new challenges, such as the assimilation of new and non-European ethnic groups, continued financial burdens, and the pressures of an increasingly strident secular society.

As more individual Catholics have begun to view themselves as the Church, many have become involved in church administration, in councils, and ministry. Similarly, lay Catholics now feel free to fill important roles in political, civic, and social activities in the state, carrying their faith into the larger community. Oregon Catholics have come to realize that they themselves can add a religious dimension to the region as they continue adapting in Eden.

Chapter Notes

Abbreviations

Chapter 1

1. Zephyrin Englehardt, O.F.M., *The Missions and Missionaries of California* (San Francisco: James H. Barry, 1912), 2:154; Francis N. Blanchet, *Historical Sketches of the Catholic Church in Oregon,* ed. Edward J. Kowrach (Fairfield, Wash.: Ye Galleon Press, 1978), 14.
2. Richard G. Montgomery, *The White-Headed Eagle: John McLoughlin, Builder of an Empire* (New York: Macmillan, 1934), 2; Maude E. Abbott, *History of Medicine in the Province of Quebec* (Ottawa: Magill University Press, 1931), 256-257; Gyndwr Williams, "Highlights of the First 200 Years of the Hudson's Bay Company: Simpson and McLoughlin," *The Beaver* 301 (autumn 1970): 49-55; George Simpson, *Fur Trade and Empire: George Simpson's Journal, 1824-1825,* ed. Frederick Merk (Cambridge: Harvard University Press, 1931), 215-217.
3. Blanchet, *Historical Sketches,* 75.
4. Dorothy Johansen and Charles M. Gates, *Empire of the Columbia* (New York: Harper & Row, 1967), 159; Herbert Beaver, *Reports and Letters,* ed. Thomas E. Jessett (Portland: Champoeg Press, 1959), xiii.
5. Harvey McKay, *St. Paul Oregon, 1830-1890* (Portland: Binford & Mort, 1980), 3; John McLoughlin to Thomas Maguire, Fort Vancouver, 1833, *United States Documents in the Propaganda Fide Archives: A Calendar,* ed. Finbar Kenneally, O.F.M. (Washington, D.C.: Academy of American Franciscan History, 1966), 1:246, item 1555; Edwin V. O'Hara, *Pioneer Catholic History of Oregon,* centennial ed. (Paterson, N.J.: St. Anthony Guild Press, 1939), 23-24; Edwin V. O'Hara, "Catholic Pioneers of the Oregon Country," *Catholic Historical Review*

3 (1917): 189; Sister Letitia M. Lyons, S.N.J.M., *Francis Norbert Blanchet and the Founding of the Oregon Missions, 1838-1848* (Washington, D.C.: Catholic University of America Press, 1940), 25; Blanchet, *Historical Sketches,* 77. It appears that there were at least two other letters from French Prairie, one in 1836, cited in *CCRPN: St. Paul, Oregon, 1839-1898, Volumes I, II and III,* comp. Harriet D. Munnick, collab. Mikell D. Warner (Portland: Binford & Mort, 1979), xvii, and another mentioned in a letter of Blanchet to Simpson, 15 November 1841, cited in Lyons, *Blanchet,* 54.

6. Gilbert J. Garraghan, S.J., *The Jesuits of the Middle United States* (New York: America Press, 1938), 2:243-44; Robert J. Loewenberg, *Equality on the Oregon Frontier* (Seattle: University of Washington Press, 1976), 79.

7. Daniel Lee and Joseph Frost, *Ten Years in Oregon* (Fairfield, Wash.: Ye Galleon Press, 1968), 127; Burt B. Barker, *The McLoughlin Empire and Its Rulers* (Glendale, Cal.: Arthur H. Clarke Co., 1959), 328.

8. Johansen, *Empire of the Columbia,* 173; Blanchet, *Historical Sketches,* 45; O'Hara, *Pioneer Catholic History,* 25.

9. Blanchet, *Historical Sketches,* 46, 65; Lyons, *Blanchet,* 2-4.

10. Lyons, *Blanchet,* 5.

11. Lyons, *Blanchet,* 6-7, 10; Francis N. Blanchet, Journal of M. F. N. Blanchet, V. G., from Montreal to Oregon during 1838, trans. Baxter Murray, Francis N. Blanchet Papers, AAPO, 4-5; Émilien Lamirande, O.M.I., "L'implantation de l'Église catholique en Colombie-Britannique, 1838-1848," *Revue de l'Université d'Ottawa* 28 (1958): 332; Blanchet, *Historical Sketches,* 145.

12. Lyons, *Blanchet,* 10.

13. Blanchet, *Historical Sketches,* 47-48, 49-50.

14. Blanchet, *Historical Sketches,* 71, 51; Lyons, *Blanchet,* 19-20.

15. Blanchet, *Historical Sketches,* 77.

16. Blanchet, *Historical Sketches,* 78-80.

17. Blanchet, *Historical Sketches,* 80, 81.

18. Blanchet, *Historical Sketches,* 91, 92.

19. O'Hara, *Pioneer Catholic History,* 45; *CCRPN: Vancouver Volumes I and II and Stellamaris Mission,* trans. Mikell Warner, ann. Harriet Munnick (St. Paul, Ore.: French Prairie Press, 1972), 11:6; James W. Barnes, "The Conversion of Dr. John McLoughlin" (master's thesis, Mount Angel Seminary, 1979), 10.

20. Blanchet, *Historical Sketches,* 74; Lyons, *Blanchet,* 30-34.

21. Philip M. Hanley, *History of the Catholic Ladder,* ed. Edward J. Kowrach (Fairfield, Wash.: Ye Galleon Press, 1993), 17-18; Blanchet, *Historical Sketches,* 83-84.

22. Lyons, *Blanchet,* 42.

23. *Notices and Voyages of the Famed Quebec Mission to the Pacific Northwest,* ed. Carl Landerholm (Portland: Oregon Historical Society, 1956), 84.

24. Blanchet, *Historic Sketches,* 104, 113-114; Lyons, *Blanchet,* 42-43.

25. Lyons, *Blanchet,* 87, 93; Loewenberg, *Equality,* 144, 149; David C. Duniway and Neil R. Riggs, eds., "The Oregon Archives, 1841-1843," *OHQ* 60 (1959): 216; John A. Hussey, *Champoeg: Place of Transition* (Portland: Oregon Historical Society, 1956), 136; F. G. Young, "Ewing Young and His Estate," *Quarterly of the OHS* 21 (1920): 191-315; Ray Billington, *Westward Expansion: A History of the American Frontier,* 3rd ed. (New York: Macmillan, 1967), 529.

26. Blanchet, *Historical Sketches,* 123; Lyons, *Blanchet,* 95; Charles Wilkes, *Narrative of the United States Exploring Expedition during the Years 1838, 1839, 1840, 1841, 1842* (Philadelphia: Lea & Blanchard, 1849), 2:352-353; Hussey, *Champoeg,* 140-141; Cornelius Brosnan, *Jason Lee, Prophet of the New Oregon* (Rutland, Vt.: Academy Books, 1985), 218.

27. Hussey, *Champoeg,* 155-156; Loewenberg, *Equality,* 227; Robert C. Clark, "How British and American Subjects Unite in a Common Government for Oregon Territory in 1844," *Quarterly of the OHS* 13 (1912): 140-159; John McLoughlin, *McLoughlin's Fort Vancouver Letters,*

Second series, 1838-44, ed E. E. Rich (London: Hudson's Bay Record Society, 1943), 199; J. N. Barry, "The Champoeg Meeting of March 4, 1844," *OHQ* 38 (1937): 425.

28. *Notices and Voyages,* 235-36; Lyons, *Blanchet,* 178; Barker, *The McLoughlin Empire,* 330-333.
29. Hussey, *Champoeg,* 116, 168, 191.
30. *Notices and Voyages,* 76; Blanchet, *Historical Sketches,* 101-102; Garraghan, *Jesuits,* 2:274, 252.
31. Lawrence B. Palladino, S.J., *Indian and White in the Northwest* (Baltimore: J. Murphy, 1894), 39; Blanchet, *Historical Sketches,* 109; Garraghan, *Jesuits,* 2:278. Vicariate Apostolic is a term used to describe a mission territory. The vicar apostolic who administers it has the status and title of bishop.
32. Lyons, *Blanchet,* 46, 53.
33. Lyons, *Blanchet,* 60-61; Blanchet, *Historical Sketches,* 110; O'Hara, *Pioneer Catholic History,* 90; J. B. Z. Bolduc, *Mission of the Columbia,* ed. and trans. Edward J. Kowrach (Fairfield, Wash.: Ye Galleon Press, 1979), 90.
34. Bolduc, *Mission,* 129; *Notices and Voyages,* 147, 145, 235; Lyons, *Blanchet,* 176-177.
35. *Notices and Voyages,* 139-142; Lyons, *Blanchet,* 130-132, 142-145; Garraghan, *Jesuits,* 2: 281-282.
36. Blanchet, *Historical Sketches,* 115, 118; Lyons, *Blanchet,* 146-147.
37. Sr. M. Dominica McNamee, S.N.D., *Willamette Interlude* (Palo Alto: Pacific Books, 1959), 63-103; Patricia Brandt, "Nuns' Journey to Oregon in 1844 No Picnic," *CS,* 24 November 1995, 7.
38. Blanchet, *Historical Sketches,* 114; O'Hara, *Pioneer Catholic History,* 117-118; George T. Brown, "Illegitimate Child Prompts Funds for Education," *CS,* 15 March 1996, 6.
39. Blanchet, *Historical Sketches,* 117-118; Garraghan, *Jesuits,* 2:277, 297-298.
40. McNamee, *Willamette Interlude,* 149, 173-174, 200-201; Blanchet, *Historical Sketches,* 139; O'Hara, *Pioneer Catholic History,* 119; Garraghan, *Jesuits,* 2:371.
41. Blanchet, *Historical Sketches, 75,* 113, 112, 116; O'Hara, *Pioneer Catholic History,* 118, 124; Theodore Bernards, *St. John's Parish, Oregon City, 1844-1957* (n.p.: n.p., 1957), 23.
42. O'Hara, *Pioneer Catholic History,* 57; Lyons, *Blanchet,* 171-172; Blanchet, *Historical Sketches,* 123-124, 113.
43. Lyons, *Blanchet,* 174; *Notices and Voyages,* 236; Blanchet, *Historical Sketches,* 139.
44. *CCRPN: St. Louis Register, Volume I (1845-1868), St. Louis Register, Volume II (1869-1900), Gervais Register (1875-1893), Brooks Register (1893-1909),* comp. Harriet D. Munnick (Portland: Binford & Mort, 1982), xv; O'Hara, *Pioneer Catholic History,* 86-87, 129; Lyons, *Blanchet,* 172-173.
45. Blanchet, *Historical Sketches,* 118; McNamee, *Willamette Interlude,* 155-156; George T. Brown, *St. Paul on the Wallamette: A Man—His Church—Its Treasure* (St. Paul, Ore.: George T. Brown, 1992), 7; Lyons, *Blanchet,* 150-151, 172.
46. Blanchet, *Historical Sketches,* 125; O'Hara, *Pioneer Catholic History,* 96; Lyons, Blanchet, 159.
47. Lamirande, "L'implantation," 480; *Notices and Voyages,* 211-233; Lyons, *Blanchet,* 162-164; Patricia Brandt, "Archbishop Blanchet's Memoire," *OCHSN* 10 (summer 1998): 7-8.
48. Blanchet to Propaganda Fide, Rome, 21 January 1846, *U. S. Documents,* 7:105-6, item 670; Propaganda Fide to Cardinals, Rome, 19 March 1846, *U. S. Documents,* 4:134, item 896; G. Brunelli to J. Mezzofanti, Rome, 20 March 1846, *U. S. Documents,* 3:141, item 886; Jean Leflon, *Eugene de Mazenod,* trans. Francis D. Flanagan, O.M.I. (New York: Fordham University Press, 1968), 4: 103; Blanchet, *Historical Sketches,* 126; Lyons, *Blanchet,* 164-166, xx.
49. Lyons, *Blanchet,* 166; Blanchet to Samuel Eccleston, Paris, 16 September 1846, Blanchet Letter Book 1:50 a, Blanchet Papers.
50. Lamirande, "L'implantation," 483-484.
51. Blanchet to G. Fransoni, Paris, 6 October 1846, Blanchet Letter Book I:32 a, Blanchet Papers; Lyons, *Blanchet,* 161, 172-174, 183; Blanchet, *Historical Sketches,* 123; Brown, *St. Paul,* 10; Augustine M. A. Blanchet, *Journal of a Catholic Bishop on the Oregon Trail,* ed. Edward J. Kowrach (Fairfield, Wash.: Ye Galleon Press, 1978), 53.

52. Etienne Catta and Tony Catta, *Basil Anthony Mary Moreau*, trans. Edward L. Heston, C.S.C. (Milwaukee: Bruce, 1955), 1: 577-579; Joseph Kehoe, C.S.C., *Holy Cross in Oregon* (Notre Dame, Ind.: Province Archives Center, 1982), 3; Blanchet, *Historical Sketches,* 127-128. The remains of St. Victoria are still on display in a reliquary at St. Paul Church.

53. Blanchet, *Historical Sketches,* 128-129; Lyons, *Blanchet,* 178-179; O'Hara, *Pioneer Catholic History,* 130-131.

54. A. M. A. Blanchet, *Journal,* 67, 77-78, 83-84; J. B. A. Brouillet, *Authentic Account of the Murder of Dr. Whitman and Other Missionaries by the Cayuse Indians of Oregon in 1847* in *Early Oregon Missions,* ed. Clarence B. Bagley (Seattle: Lowman & Hanford, 1932), 1:195-196, 209-210; Blanchet, *Historical Sketches,* 130-135.

55. Garraghan, *Jesuits,* 2:341-342; Blanchet, *Historical Sketches,* 136, 139-141; O'Hara, *Pioneer Catholic History,* 139-140.

56. A. M. A. Blanchet, *Journal,* 90; Lyons, *Blanchet,* 186-187; Blanchet, *Historical Sketches,* 139; O'Hara, *Pioneer Catholic History,* 146-147; Bertram F. Griffin, *The Provincial Councils of Portland* (Rome: Pontificia Universitatis Lateranensis, 1964), 5-9, 15.

57. A. M. A. Blanchet, *Journal,* 96-97; Blanchet, *Historical Sketches,* 135.

58. Griffin, *Provincial Councils,* 15, 18; Propaganda Fide General Council, Rome, 22 April 1850, *U. S. Documents,* 6:99, item 579; Blanchet, *Historical Sketches,* 141.

59. G. Franzoni to Blanchet, Rome, 10 September 1851, Blanchet Letter Book 1:215-216, Blanchet Papers; F. P. Kenrick to Propaganda Fide, Baltimore, 4 March 1852, *U. S. Documents,* 2:89, item *557;* Peter Guilday, *A History of the Councils of Baltimore (1791-1884)* (New York: Macmillan, 1932), 175.

60. George M. Waggett, O.M.I., "The Oblates of Mary Immaculate in the Pacific Northwest, 1847-1878," *Records of the American Catholic Historical Society* 64 (1953): 79; Cyprian Bradley, O.S.B. and Edward Kelly, *History of the Diocese of Boise* (Boise: Caxton, 1953), 88-89.

61. Garraghan, *Jesuits,* 2:399; Blanchet, *Historical Sketches,* 140.

62. McNamee, *Willamette Interlude,* 202; Garraghan, *Jesuits,* 2: 293; O'Hara, *Pioneer Catholic History,* 123.

63. McNamee, *Willamette Interlude,* 253; O'Hara, *Pioneer Catholic History,* 123; *CS,* 16 April 1908; Wilfred P. Schoenberg, S.J., *A History of the Catholic Church in the Pacific Northwest, 1743-1983* (Washington, D.C.: Pastoral Press, 1987), 147-148; Waggett, "Oblates," 89.

64. O'Hara, *Pioneer Catholic History,* 109-110, 150; *In Harvest Fields by Sunset Shores: The Work of the Sisters of Notre Dame on the Pacific Coast* (San Francisco: n.p., 1926), 124-126.

65. Charles M. Smith, *Centenary of Cathedral Parish, 1851-1951* (Portland: n.p., 1951), 17, 19; O'Hara, Pioneer Catholic History, 155.

66. William McLeod, *Souvenir, 1858-1958* (Medford: n.p., 1958), 1; O'Hara, *Pioneer Catholic History,* 166-167.

67. O'Hara, *Pioneer Catholic History,* 150-152; Blanchet to A. Barnabo, Portland, 30 May 1858, Blanchet Letter Book 1:309-311, Blanchet Papers.

68. Smith, *Centenary of Cathedral Parish,* 27, 29.

69. O'Hara, *Pioneer Catholic History,* 167; *CCRPN: Roseburg Register and Missions (1853-1911), Portland Register (1852-1871),* comp. Harriet D. Munnick (Portland: Binford & Mort, 1986), Roseburg II: 2; *CCRPN: Oregon City Register (1842-1890), Salem Register (1864-1885), Jacksonville Register (1854-1885),* comp. Harriet D. Munnick (Portland: Binford & Mort, 1984), Jacksonville, Al.

Chapter 2

1. Edwin V. O'Hara, *Pioneer Catholic History of Oregon,* centennial ed. (Paterson, N.J.: St. Anthony Guild Press, 1939), 159; *Gleanings of Fifty Years: The Sisters of the Holy Names of Jesus and Mary in the Northwest, 1859-1909* (Portland: Glass & Prudhomme, 1909), 59-72.

2. *Gleanings,* 69, 81, 84.
3. Charles Smith, *Centenary of Cathedral Parish, Portland, Oregon, 1851-1951* (Portland: n.p., 1951), 35; *Gleanings,* 89.
4. *Gleanings,* 91-92.
5. Sara J. McLellan, ed., "Chronicles of Sacred Heart Academy, Salem, 1863-1873, Part 1," *OHQ* 80 (1979): 343, 345-346; *Gleanings,* 98-99, 103.
6. Gleanings, 105; McClellan, "Chronicles I," 353, 354; Sara J. McLellan, ed., "Chronicles of Sacred Heart Academy, Salem, 1863-1873, Part II," *OHQ* 81(1980): 93.
7. *Gleanings,* 106, 107; Dominic O'Connor, O.F.M., Cap., *Brief History of the Diocese of Baker City* (St. Benedict, Ore.: Benedictine Press, 1966), 147.
8. *Gleanings,* 123, 124, 127.
9. *Gleanings,* 110, 130-132; Blanchet to A. Barnabo, Portland, 2 August 1865, Blanchet Letter Book 1:478-81; Blanchet to A. Barnabo, Portland, 2 Sept 1869, Blanchet Letter Book 1:583-84, Francis N. Blanchet Papers, AAPO; McLellan, "Chronicles, II," 79-80; *Hope of the Harvest, by a Sister of the Holy Names* (Portland: Press of Kilham Stationary & Printing, 1944), 252.
10. *Gleanings,* 142-144.
11. Smith, *Centenary of Cathedral Parish,* 49; Willis Whalen, "The Pioneer Period of the Catholic Church in Portland, Oregon, 1851-1881" (master's thesis, University of Portland, 1950), 50; *CS,* 14 August 1874, 8 December 1898.
12. *CS,* 4 September 1874, 18 April 1878; O'Connor, Brief History, 50; Gerard G. Steckler, S.J., *Charles John Seghers, Priest and Bishop in the Pacific Northwest, 1839-1886: A Biography* (Fairfield, Wash.: Ye Galleon Press, 1986), 133; Peter De Roo to Sister Superior, Baker City, 5 March 1877, Peter De Roo Papers, AMAA.
13. *Gleanings,* 121, 116.
14. *CS,* 6 October 1960, Sec. 3, 24; Daniel T. McColgan, *A Century of Charity: The First One Hundred Years of the Society of St Vincent De Paul in the United States* (Milwaukee: Bruce, 1951), 1:288; Whalen, "Pioneer Period," 63; Sister Mary of the Blessed Sacrament McCrosson, F.C.S.P., *The Bell and the River* (Palo Alto: Pacific Books, 1957), 226.
15. Whalen, "Pioneer Period," 78; Ellis Lucia, *Cornerstone: The Story of St. Vincent—Oregon's First Permanent Hospital, Its Formative Years* (Portland: St. Vincent Medical Foundation, 1975), 47, 51.
16. *CS,* 21 October 1871, 25 April 1873; Whalen, "Pioneer Period," 63, 64, 61.
17. John B. McGloin, S.J., *The Eloquent Indian* (Stanford: Stanford University Press, 1949), 138, 221, 223, 220, 230.
18. Wilfred P. Schoenberg, S.J., *Defender of the Faith: The History of the Catholic Sentinel, 1870-1990* (Portland: Oregon Catholic Press, 1993), 12-13, 16-17.
19. Schoenberg, *Defender,* 64.
20. Blanchet to E. S. Parker, Portland, 27 January 1871, Blanchet Letter Book 3:6, Blanchet Papers; Blanchet to E.S. Parker, Portland, 12 February 1871, U. S. Dept. of the Interior, Appointment Papers, Roll 9, Box 3, RG 48, NA (microfilm); Peter J. Rahill, *The Catholic Indian Missions and Grant's Peace Policy* (Washington, D.C.: Catholic University of America Press, 1953), 42; Gilbert J. Garraghan, S. J., *The Jesuits of the Middle United States* (New York: America Press, 1938), 2:561.
21. Rahill, *Catholic* 52, 58, 69; Schoenberg, *Defender,* 37, 43-44.
22. Martinus Cawley, O.C.S.O., *Father Crockett of Grand Ronde* (Lafayette, Ore.: Guadalupe Translations, 1985), 12-16; Joseph Van der Heyden, "Monsignor Adrien J. Croquet, Indian Missionary, 1818-1902," *RACHS* 16 (1905): 138, 152; *CCRPN: Grand Ronde Register 1(1860-1885), Grand Ronde Register 11(1886-1898), St. Michael the Archangel Parish, Grand Ronde Reservation, Oregon, St. Patrick's Parish, Muddy Valley Oregon,* ed. and ann. Harriet D. Munnick and Stephen Dow Beckham (Portland: Binford & Mort, 1987), Grand Ronde Register 1, 4; Martinus Cawley, O.C.S.O., *Saint James Parish, McMinnville, Oregon* (Portland: Glass-Dahlstrom Printing, 1977), 4, 7, 11.

23. Amos Harvey to J. W. Huntington, Grand Ronde Agency, 1 October 1865, U. S. Bureau of Indian Affairs, Letters received, Oregon Superintendency, M2, Roll 22, RG *75,* NA (microfilm); *Gleanings,* 140.

24. Blanchet to Vermeersch, 17 October 1865, Blanchet Letter Book 1:485-486, Blanchet Papers; O'Connor, *Brief History,* 125, 50; Blanchet to Bertram Orth, Narcisse Cornoyer, 20 December 1874, Blanchet Letter Book 3:131-132, Blanchet Papers; J. B. A. Brouillet to Blanchet, Washington, D.C., 10 February 1876, Umatilla file, BCIM.

25. Francis X. Blanchet, *Ten Years on the Pacific Coast,* ed. Edward J. Kowrach (Fairfield, Wash.: Ye Galleon Press, 1982), 36; Sister Mary Evangela Henthorne, B.V.M., *The Irish Catholic Colonial Association of the United States* (Champaign, Ill.: Twin Cities Printing Co., 1932), 13.

26. Robert S. Neugebauer, *Diamond Jubilee, Visitation Church, Verboort, Oregon, 1875-1950* (Verboort, Ore.: n.p., 1950), 5-6; Blanchet to Edward Herman, 15 October 1876, Blanchet Letter Book 3:203, Blanchet Papers.

27. *CS,* 23 May 1878; James D. Shand, "Portland's German Parish," *Oregon Catholic Historical Society Newsletter* 4 (summer 1992): 8.

28. Francis Leipzig, "Early-Day Portlander Left Legacy of Civic, Religious Activities," *CS,* 2 September 1977, 15; Schoenberg, *Defender,* 56-60.

29. *CCRPN: Roseburg Register and Missions (1853-1911), Portland Register (1852-1871),* comp. Harriet D. Munnick (Portland: Binford & Mort, 1986), Roseburg, 5-6, 11-13, 7.

30. Cyprian Bradley, O.S.B., and Edward Kelly, *History of the Diocese of Boise* (Boise: Caxton, 1953), 111; Cyril Van der Donckt, "Founders of the Church in Idaho," *American Ecclesiastical Review* 32 (1905): 17.

31. Cawley, *Father Crockett,* 1, 7; Joseph Van der Heyden, *Louvain American College* (Louvain: C. & R. Ceuterick, 1909), 133; Blanchet to A. Barnabo, Portland, 21 September 1862, Blanchet Letter Book 1:397-398, Blanchet Papers; L. Dieleman to Blanchet, Baker City, 31 January 1871, Blanchet Papers.

32. John P. Marschall, "Diocesan and Religious Clergy," in *The Catholic Priest in the United States: Historical Interpretations,* ed. John Tracy Ellis (Collegeville, Minn.: St. John's University Press, 1971), 303, 393, 402; J. B. A. Brouillet to Propaganda Fide, Walla Walla, 20 September 1850, *U. S. Documents,* 2:64, item 420; Clergy of Oregon to Propaganda Fide, Oregon, 19 October 1850, *U. S. Documents,* 2:65, item 427.

33. Thomas O'Loughlin, "The Demand and Supply of Priests to the United States from All Hallows College, Ireland, between 1842 and 1860," *RACHS* 94 (1983): 39, 55, 59, 54; Richard J. Purcell, "Missionaries from All Hallows (Dublin) to the United States, 1842-1865," *RACHS* 53 (1942): 238.

34. Patricia Brandt, "The Belgian Bulge: The Oregon Priesthood from 1860-1900," *OCHSN* 4 (summer 1992): 4.

35. Sister M. Dominica McNamee, S.N.D., *Willamette Interlude* (Palo Alto: Pacific Books, 1959), 260; *Gleanings,* 88, 53.

36. Blanchet to A. Barnabo, Portland, 21 September 1862, Blanchet Letter Book 1:397-398; Blanchet to A. Barnabo, Portland, 14 January 1863, Blanchet Letter Book 1:399-400; A. Barnabo to Blanchet. Rome, 18 April 1863, Blanchet Letter Book 1:418-419; A. Barnabo to Blanchet, Rome, 29 November 1863, Blanchet Letter Book 1:441; A. Barnabo to Blanchet, Rome, 21 January 1864, Blanchet Letter Book 1:441-442, Blanchet Papers; Propaganda Fide Audience Schedule, Rome, 25 January 1863, *U. S. Documents,* 8:247, item 1714; Smith, *Centenary of Cathedral Parish,* 33.

37. McGloin, *Eloquent Indian,* 221; Blanchet to J. F. Fierens, Portland, 1 October 1863, Blanchet Letter Book 1:425-426; Blanchet to P. Mackin, 5 October 1865, 20 October 1865, Blanchet Letter Book 1:487, 488-489, Blanchet Papers.

38. Olga S. Freeman, *A Guide to Early Oregon Churches* (Eugene, n. p., 1976), 23; *CS,* 28 May 1878, 8 April 1879; Patricia Brandt "Bishop's House Proves Older Than Believed," *CS,* 13 September 1996, 6.

Chapter Notes 179

39. William McLeod, comp., *Souvenir, 1858-1958* (Medford, Ore.: n.p., 1958), 21; *CCRPN: Oregon City Register*, Jacksonville A 2; *CS*, 19 November 1878; Francie Lichtenwaler, "Church History Shows Courage, Dedication," *CS*, 22 March 1996, 7.
40. *CS*, 28 September 1876, 16 October 1874; *The Centenary: 100 Years of the Catholic Church in the Oregon Country* (Portland: Catholic Sentinel, 1939), 51; *CCRPN: Oregon City Register (1842-1890), Salem Register (1864-1885), Jacksonville Register*, Jacksonville, 1; L. Dieleman to Blanchet, Canyon City, 26 April 1872, Blanchet Papers; *CCRPN. St. Louis Register, Volume I (1845-1863), St. Louis Register, Volume II (1869-1900), Gervais Register (1875-1893), Brooks Register (1893-1909)*, comp. Harriet D. Munnick (Portland: Binford & Mort, 1982), Gervais, 1.
41. O'Connor, *Brief History*, 114, 50, 25-27.
42. Peter Guilday, *History of the Councils of Baltimore (1791-1884)* (New York: Macmillan, 1932), 201; Bertram F. Griffin, *The Provincial Councils of Portland in Oregon* (Rome: Pontificia Universitatis Lateranensis, 1964), 26-27.
43. O'Hara, *Pioneer Catholic History*, 188-190; James Hennesey, S.J., *The First Council of the Vatican: The American Experience* (New York: Herder and Herder, 1963), 296-299; Griffin, *Provincial Councils*, 27.
44. Bradley and Kelly, *History*, 88-92.
45. Blanchet to A. Barnabo, Montreal, 6 November 1866, Blanchet Letter Book 1:518, Blanchet Papers; L. Lootens to Propaganda Fide, Rome, 14 June 1870, *U. S. Documents*, 9:285-286, item 2259; Blanchet to Propaganda Fide, Rome, 27 September 1870, *U. S. Documents*, 9:286, item 2262; A. Franchi to Blanchet, Rome, 23 November 1875, Blanchet Letter Book 3:162-163; Blanchet to clergy of Idaho, Portland, 14 August 1876, Blanchet Letter Book 3:196, Blanchet Papers; Bradley and Kelly, *History*, 97, 137, 182.
46. *CS*, 12 August 1871, 2 July 1873, 19 September 1873; E. Laveille, S.J., *The Life of Father De Smet, S. J.*, trans. Marian Lindsay (New York: Kenedy, 1915), 385.
47. M. Leona Nichols, *The Mantle of Elias* (Portland: Binfords & Mort, 1941), 250; J. F. Fierens to P. De Roo, Portland, 19 February 1877, De Roo Papers; J. F. Fierens to P. De Roo, Portland, 17 October 1876, De Roo Papers; Francis X. Blanchet, *Ten Years*, 29.
48. Blanchet to A. Barnabo, Portland, 21 September 1862, Blanchet Letter Book 1:397-398; Blanchet to Archbishops of the U.S., Portland, 4 March 1877, Blanchet Letter Book 3:221; G. Simeoni to Blanchet, 13 January 1879, Blanchet Letter Book 3:270-271, Blanchet Papers; *CS*, 8 May 1879; Steckler, *Seghers*, 111.
49. Garraghan, *Jesuits*, 2:289.

Chapter 3

1. Maurice De Baets, *The Apostle of Alaska*, trans. Sister Mary Mildred, S.S.A. (Paterson, N.J.: St. Anthony Guild, 1943), 155; Gerard G. Steckler, S.J., "Charles John Seghers: Missionary Bishop in the American Northwest, 1839-1886" (Ph.D. diss., University of Washington, 1963), 186, 200.
2. De Baets, *Apostle*, 13-14; Steckler, "Seghers," 2-3.
3. De Baets, *Apostle*, 94-95; Steckler, "Seghers," 71-72.
4. Steckler, "Seghers," 94, 106-192, passim; De Baets, *Apostle*, 96, 101-109, 118-155.
5. *CS*, 24 July 1879.
6. De Baets, *Apostle*, 174; Steckler, "Seghers," 286.
7. Steckler, "Seghers," 314.
8. Steckler, "Seghers," 247-250; *CS*, 3 March 1881.
9. Steckler, "Seghers," 57, 243, 298-299; Seghers to John Heinrich, Portland, 13 July 1883, Seghers Letter Book 3:130, Charles Seghers Papers, AAPO.
10. Steckler, "Seghers," 229-231.
11. Steckler, "Seghers," 260, 267-268.

180   *Adapting in Eden*

12. Steckler, "Seghers," 253-257; Sister M. Grace McDonald, O.S.B., *With Lamps Burning* (St. Joseph, Minn.: St. Benedict's Priory Press, 1957), 124.
13. Colman J. Barry, O.S.B., *Worship and Work* (Collegeville, Minn.: St. John's Abbey, 1956), 408; Steckler "Seghers," 260-261.
14. Barry, *Worship and Work,* 151; Steckler, "Seghers," 272-275, 279.
15. Joel Rippinger, O.S.B., *The Benedictine Order in the United States, An Interpretive History* (Collegeville, Minn.: Liturgical Press, 1990), 56-58; Steckler, "Seghers," 262-263.
16. Adelhelm Odermatt, O.S.B., "The Founding of Mt. Angel Abbey: A Letter of 1883," ed. Ambrose Zenner, O.S.B., *Marion County History* 4 (1938): 13-14.
17. Sister M. Agnes Voth, O.S.B., *Green Olive Branch,* ed. M. Raymond (Chicago: Franciscan Herald Press, 1973), 41-42; Odermatt, "Founding," 14.
18. Sister M. Ildephonse Nuxoll, O.S.B., *Idaho Benedictine* (Cottonwood, Idaho: St. Gertrude's Convent, 1976), 6-7, 10, 27.
19. *St. Mary's Parish, Mt. Angel, Oregon, 1880-1980* (Salem, Ore.: Panther Printing Co., 1979), 17-18; Odermatt, "Founding," 14; Martin Pollard, O.S.B., and Hugh Feiss, O.S.B., *Mount of Communion: Mount Angel Abbey 1882-1982,* rev. ed. (St. Benedict, Ore.: Mount Angel Abbey, 1985), 34.
20. J. B. A. Brouillet to Sister Ignatius, Washington, D.C., 17 May 1882, Grand Ronde file, BCIM; Seghers to J. B. A. Brouillet, Portland, 11 January 1882, Umatilla file, BCIM; Steckler, "Seghers," 269-270, 337-339.
21. Seghers to J. B. A. Brouillet, Portland, 19 December 1882, Seghers Letter Book 1:414, Seghers Papers; J. B. A. Brouillet to Seghers, Washington, D.C., 13 January 1883, Umatilla file, BCIM.
22. Dominic O'Connor, O.F.M., Cap., *Brief History of the Diocese of Baker* (St. Benedict, Ore.: Benedictine Press, 1966), 125.
23. Bertram F. Griffin, *The Provincial Councils of Portland in Oregon* (Rome: Pontificia Universitatis Lateranensis, 1964), 23; Steckler, "Seghers," 298-299; De Baets, *Apostle,* 182.
24. Steckler, "Seghers," 327-328, 344-346, 409-412; Patricia Brandt, "The Viatorian Mission in Oregon," *OCHSN* 3 (summer 1991): 7.
25. De Baets, *Apostle,* 187-191; Steckler, "Seghers," 311-327, 330-333.
26. Steckler, "Seghers," 355-357; Lillian Pereyra, "The Shrinking Archdiocese," *OCHSN* 6 (summer 1994): 7-8.
27. Cyprian Bradley, O.S.B., and Edward Kelly, *History of the Diocese of Boise* (Boise: Caxton, 1953), 204; Steckler, "Seghers," 359-361.
28. Steckler, "Seghers," 287-288.
29. *Gleanings of Fifty Years: The Sisters of the Holy Names of Jesus and Mary in the Northwest, 1859-1909* (Portland, Ore.: Glass & Prudhomme Co., 1909), 175-176; De Baets, *Apostle,* 192; Steckler, "Seghers," 367-369; *CS,* 21 June 1883.
30. Steckler, "Seghers," 56; Patricia Brandt, "The Belgian Bulge: the Oregon Priesthood from 1860-1900," *OCHSN* 4 (summer 1992): 4.
31. Wilfred P. Schoenberg, S.J., *Defender of the Faith: The History of the* Catholic Sentinel, *1870-1990* (Portland: Oregon Catholic Press, 1993), 73-74, 83-84, 90, 92.
32. *Portland City Directory* (Portland: S. J. McCormick, 1874, 1875); Charles Ewing to Carl Schurz, Washington, D.C., 25 May 1880, Umatilla file, BCIM; Martinus Cawley, O.C.S.O., *Father Crockett of Grand Ronde* (Lafayette, Ore.: Guadalupe Translations, 1985), 47.
33. Mark Schmid, O.S.B., *Sublimity, The Story of an Oregon Countryside, 1850-1950* (St. Benedict, Ore.: Library Bookstore, 1951), 67; *CS,* 21 October 1880, 5; Blanchet memo, 24 February 1880, Blanchet Papers; *St. Mary's Parish, Mt. Angel,* 13; Steckler, "Seghers," 245, 264, 375, 351, 376-377, 330-332; Scott Vandehey and Steve Greif, *A History of Oregon's South Coast Vicariate Including Holy Redeemer's 75 Years* (North Bend, Ore.: Holy Redeemer Parish, 1981), 17, 27; Charles M. Smith, *Centenary of Cathedral Parish, 1851-1951* (Portland: n.p., 1951), 59.

34. Steckler, "Seghers," 234, 308, 374, 349; Cawley, *Father Crockett,* 31; Willis W. Whalen, "The Pioneer Period of the Catholic Church in Portland, Oregon, 1851-1881" (master's thesis, University of Portland, 1950), 89-90.
35. *The Centenary: 100 Years of the Catholic Church in the Oregon Country* (Portland: Catholic Sentinel, 1939), 63; *St. Mary's Parish, Mt. Angel,* 18; Steckler, "Seghers," 377.
36. Sister Mary of the Blessed Sacrament McCrosson, F.C.S.P., *The Bell and the River* (Palo Alto: Pacific Books, 1957), 236; Steckler, "Seghers," 248; *CS,* 8 June 1882.
37. *CS,* 11 August 1881, 18 August 1881; De Baets, *Apostle,* 179-181; Steckler, "Seghers," 302-306, 376, 372; Griffin, *Provincial Councils,* 28-46; John T. Ellis, *The Life of James Cardinal Gibbons, Archbishop of Baltimore, 1834-1921* (Milwaukee: Bruce, 1952), 2:215.
38. De Baets, *Apostle,* 197; Steckler, "Seghers," 388-391; S. L., "Romewards with Archbishop Seghers," *Messenger of the Sacred Heart* 1 (January 1897): 16; *CS,* 17 April 1884.
39. *The Memorial Volume: A History of the Third Plenary Council of Baltimore, November 9- December 7, 1884* (Baltimore: Baltimore Publishing Co., 1885), 114-119, 71-74; *CS,* 2 April 1885.

Chapter 4

1. Michael J. Brady, C.Ss.R., "Most Reverend William Hickley Gross, C.Ss.R., D.D., Third Archbishop of Oregon City, 1885-1898" (paper, Mt. St. Alphonsus Seminary, 1981), 5.
2. Andrew H. Skeabeck, C.Ss.R. "Most Rev. William Gross, Missionary Bishop of the South," *RACHS* 65 (1954): 108, 66 (1955): 44-45; *CS,* 22 September 1986.
3. Chloe M. Ryan, "William H. Gross, Missionary Archbishop, Archbishop of Oregon City, 1885-1898" (paper, Marylhurst College, 1952), 15; Andrew Skeabeck, "Most Rev.," *RACHS* 66 (1955): 49; Charles W. Currier, "History of the Church of Our Lady of Perpetual Succor in Boston," *RACHS* 2 (1887): 211; Brady, "Most Reverend," 21; Gross to Rev. Dear Confrere, on Steamer, 30 September 1886, William H. Gross Papers, AAPO; Gross to Joseph Wuest, Portland, 28 January 1888, Gross Papers. This is the picture, incorrectly reputed to be 300 years old, which was stolen from the Cathedral in 1992.
4. Ryan, "William H. Gross," 19; Wilfred P. Schoenberg, S.J., *These Valiant Women: History of the Sisters of St. Mary of Oregon, 1886-1986* (Portland: Sisters of St. Mary of Oregon, 1986), 344; *CS,* 28 May 1885.
5. Gross to James Gibbons, Portland, 27 August 1887, Gross Papers; John Tracy Ellis, *The Life of James Cardinal Gibbons, Archbishop of Baltimore, 1834-1921* (Milwaukee: Bruce, 1952), 1:325-326.
6. *CS,* 13 October 1887.
7. Gross to James Gibbons, St. Paul, Oregon, 28 July 1885, Gross Papers; *CS,* 13 October 1887.
8. Gross to P. De Roo, Portland, 5 May 1887, Peter De Roo Papers, AMAA.
9. Skeabeck, "Most Rev.," 66 (1955): 139.
10. Ryan, "William H. Gross," 4; Skeabeck, "Most Rev.," 65 (1954): 106.
11. Ryan, "William H. Gross," 26, 29, 44; *CS,* 9 July 1885; Gross to James Gibbons, Oregon City, 26 June 1890, Gross Papers.
12. *CS,* 8 October 1885; Wilfred P. Schoenberg, S.J., *Defender of the Faith: The History of the Catholic Sentinel, 1870-1990* (Portland: Oregon Catholic Press, 1992), 100, 113, 114, 123; Mark Gross to P. De Roo, Portland, 3 October 1893, De Roo Papers; Mark Gross to James Gibbons, Portland, 4 March 1893, Gross Papers.
13. Steven W. Harmon, *The St. Josephs Blatt, 1896-1919* (New York: Peter Lang, 1989), 3-5; P. De Roo to Gross, Verboort, 15 May 1894, De Roo Papers; William Lucey, S.J., "Catholic Magazines, 1890-1893," *RACHS* 63 (1952): 214; Eugene P. Willging and Herta Hatzfeld, "Catholic Serials of the Nineteenth Century in Oregon," *RACHS* 72 (1961): 50; Schoenberg, *Defender,* 125.

14. Bertram F. Griffin, *The Provincial Councils of Portland in Oregon* (Rome, Pontificia Universitatis Lateranensis, 1964), 52-53.
15. Griffin, *Provincial Councils,* 68-69, 82-83.
16. Martin Cawley, O.C.S.O. *Father Crockett of Grand Ronde* (Lafayette, Ore.: Guadalupe Translations, 1985), 61; For example, U.S. Commissioner of Indian Affairs *Annual Report, 1885,* in U.S. Secretary of the Interior *Annual Report, 1885* (Washington, D.C.: Government Printing Office, 1885) Serial 2379, 396 (hereafter cited as C.I.A.); *Pendleton Tribune, 3* July 1885, 31 July 1885, 28 August 1885.
17. For example, Gross to Cleveland, Portland, 11 August 1886, U. S. Dept. of the Interior, Appointment Papers, Roll 9, Box 3, RG 48, NA (microfilm); D. S. Otis, *The Dawes Act and the Allotment of Indian Land,* new ed. (Norman: University of Oklahoma Press, 1973), 45.
18. *Pendleton East Oregonian,* 7 July 1885; C.I.A., *Annual Report, 1886,* Serial 2467, 437-438; C.I.A. *Annual Report,* 1887, Serial 2542, 275; *CS,* 23 December 1886.
19. See issues of *CS* and *Oregonian* during December, 1886.
20. Joseph Stephan to Martin Marty, O.S.B., Washington, 31 January 1887, Umatilla file, BCIM; Henry Stanton to A.B. Upshaw, Pendleton, 1 April 1887, U. S. Bureau of Indian Affairs, Letters received, 1887-9084, RG 75, NA; *Oregonian,* 12 September 1911.
21. Dominic O'Connor, O.F.M., Cap., *Brief History of the Diocese of Baker* (St. Benedict, Ore.: Benedictine Press, 1966), 104, 126, 142; Wilfred P. Schoenberg, S.J., *Paths to the Northwest: A Jesuit History of the Oregon Province* (Chicago: Loyola University Press, 1982), 164; Francis P. Prucha, S.J., "Indian Policy Reform and American Protestantism, 1880-1900," in *People of the Plains and Mountains,* ed. Ray Billington (Westport, Conn.: Greenwood, 1973), 137-138.
22. "Sisters of the Third Order of St. Francis, 1855-1928, by a member of the Sisterhood," *RACHS* 40 (1929): 231,232-4; O'Connor, Brief History, 139-140, 144.
23. *The Centenary: 100 Years of the Catholic Church in the Oregon Country* (Portland: Catholic Sentinel, 1939), 61.
24. Brady, "Most Reverend," 29; Sister Pia Backus, O.P., *Her Days Unfolded: Mother Pia Backus, of the Dominican Sisters of Mission San Jose,* trans. and ed. Mother Bernardine Michael, O.P. (St. Benedict, Ore.: Benedictine Press, 1952), 65, 70, 91, 93; Schoenberg, *These Valiant Women,* 351, 179.
25. *St. Mary's Parish, 1880-1980, Mt. Angel, Oregon* (Salem: Panther Printing Co., 1979), 22, 125; Sister Ida M. Annen, O.S.B., "Mt. Angel College," *Marion County History* 4 (1958): 47; "Sisters' Ministries Form Lengthy List," *Oregon Catholic History Newsletter* 4 (winter 1981-1982): 8; *CS, 7* Feb. 1889.
26. Ryan, "William H. Gross," 45; *Gleanings of Fifty Years: The Sisters of the Holy Names of Jesus and Mary in the Northwest, 1859-1909* (Portland, Ore.: Glass & Prudhomme Co., 1909), 191-193, 168.
27. Schoenberg, *These Valiant Women,* 96-97; Reports of Parishes, 1895: Sublimity, AAPO.
28. Schoenberg, *These Valiant Women,* 108, 111.
29. Schoenberg, *These Valiant Women,* 116-117, 162; Mark Schmid, O.S.B., *Sublimity, The Story of an Oregon Countryside, 1850-1950* (St. Benedict, Ore.: Library Bookstore, 1951), 89; Skeabeck, "Most Rev.," 66 (1955): 88.
30. Schoenberg, *These Valiant Women,* 149, 151, 161, 185.
31. Gross to P. De Roo, Portland, 12 April 1887, 18 March 1886, 21 April 1886, De Roo Papers.
32. Ronald E. Isetti, F.S.C., *Called to the Pacific, A History of the Christian Brothers of the San Francisco District, 1868-1944* (Moraga, Calif.: St. Mary's College of California, 1979), 87-91, 149.
33. Patricia Brandt, "The Viatorian Mission in Oregon," *OCHSN* 3 (spring 1991): 7; Gerard G. Steckler, S.J., "Charles John Seghers: Missionary Bishop in the American Northwest, 1839-1886" (Ph.D. diss., University of Washington, 1963), 429-431.
34. Michael J. Curley, C.Ss.R., *The Provincial Story: A History of the Baltimore Province of the Congregation of the Most Holy Redeemer* (New York: Redemptorist Fathers, 1963), 219-220; "Manuscript History of St. Alphonsus Church and Convent, Portland, Oregon—The First Redemptorist Foundation on the Pacific Slope," undated, Gross Papers.

35. Gross to F. S. Vilanasa, O.P., Portland, 28 September 1885, Gross Papers; *Oregonian*, 31 July 1893; Francis P. Leipzig, "The Origin of Murphy's Hole," *CS*, 28 March 1975, 18.

36. Edward E. Malone, O.S.B., *Conception: A History of the First Century of the Conception Colony, 1858-1958* (Omaha: Interstate Printing Co., 1971), Appendix II; Brady, "Most Reverend," 11; *CS*, 31 October 1889; Martin J. Pollard, O.S.B., and Hugh Feiss, O.S.B., *Mount of Communion*, rev. ed. (St. Benedict, Ore.: Mount Angel Abbey, 1985), 4.

37. Gregory Robl, O.S.B., *Fiftieth Anniversary, Sacred Heart Parish, Portland, Oregon* (Portland: n.p., 1943), 12; Pollard and Feiss, *Mount*, 5, 14, 18; Ambrose Zenner, O.S.B., "Fire Twice Destroys Mt. Angel Abbey," *CS*, 6 Oct. 1960, sect. 3, p.18, 20; Brady, "Most Reverend," 11.

38. Pancratius Pfeiffer, S.D.S., *Father Francis Mary of the Cross Jordan*, trans. Winfrid Herbst (St. Nazianz, Wis.: Society of the Divine Savior, 1936), 336, 344; Jerome Schommer, S.D.S., *The Moment of Grace* (Milwaukee, Wis.: Society of the Divine Savior, 1994) 1:26.

39. *CS*, 28 April 1898; Gross to P. De Roo, McMinnville, 28 April 1890, De Roo Papers; Schoenberg, *These Valiant Women*, 150; Wilfred P. Schoenberg, S.J. *A Test of Time: History of St. Mary's Home, 1889-1989* (Beaverton: St. Mary's Home for Boys, 1989), 15-16; St. Mary's Home Association Letterbook, 1892-93, AAPO.

40. Sister Anne Berrigan, R.G.S., "The Work of the Sisters of the Good Shepherd in Oregon" (master's thesis, University of Portland, 1953), 13, 14, 16, 19; *CS*, 9 April 1891, 2 September 1897; *Oregonian*, 10 November 1896.

41. Kathleen O'Brien, R.S.M., *Journeys: A Pre-Amalgamation History of the Sisters of Mercy, Omaha Province* (Omaha: n.p., 1987), 545-546; *The Centenary*, 52, 18; *CS*, 11 February 1897, 11 Oct. 1897.

42. *Baker City Bedrock Democrat*, 19 April 1897; O'Connor, *Brief History*, 144; Ellis Lucia, *Cornerstone: The Story of St. Vincent—Oregon's First Permanent Hospital, Its Formative Years* (Portland: St. Vincent Medical Foundation, 1975), 85, 88, 91, 95.

43. *Report of Financial Standing of St. Joseph's Ecclesiastical Society of the Province of Oregon* (Portland: n.p., 1896), Gross to the Clergy, 23 April 1896, De Roo Papers.

44. Francis Leipzig, "Father Fierens Noted Early Portland Pastor, Builder," *CS*, 19 August 1977, 12; *CS*, 3 March 1887, 30 September 1885; Cawley, *Father Crockett*, 32; Steckler, "Seghers," 455, 499, 566.

45. *CS*, 8 August 1895; Francis Leipzig, "First Two Oregon-Born Priests Both Ordained in Same Year," *CS*, 11 May 1973, 22; *CS*, 10 September 1896; O'Connor, *Brief History*, 5; Cawley, *Father Crockett*, 31.

46. Gross to P. De Roo, 4 February 1892, De Roo Papers; S.G. McKenna, C.Ss.R., "Our Lady's Bishop," *Central Blatt and Social Justice* 24 (1931): 176; Allen S. Will, *Life of Cardinal Gibbons, Archbishop of Baltimore* (New York: E. P. Dutton, 1922)1:91; Skeabeck, "Most Rev.," 65 (1954): 151.

47. Schoenberg, *Defender*, 98-99, 109; Ellis Lucia, *The Saga of Ben Holladay* (New York: Hastings House, 1959), 348; *CS*, 14 July 1887; Patricia Brandt, "Benefactors Were Generous on the Sly," *CS*, 14 June 1996, 7.

48. Gross to P. De Roo, 17 September 1886, De Roo Papers; Gross to W. Comekamp, Salem, Oct. 3, 1885; Gross to Frederick Schauer, Baker City, 7 July 1886, Gross Papers.

49. Gross to Joseph Wuest, Portland, 9 June 1885, 13 December 1885, Gross Papers; *CS*, 16 December 1886, 6 January 1887, 20 January 1887; James D. Shand, "Portland's German Parish," *OCHSN* 4 (summer 1992): 8; Ryan, "William H. Gross," 40.

50. *CS*, 19 March 1893, 15 Sept. 1892, 14 March 1895; Fred A. Granata, *The Biography of a Parish: Saint Michael the Archangel Catholic Church, 1894-1994* (Portland: Dynagraphics, 1994), 10.

51. Olga Samuelson Freeman, *A Guide to Early Oregon Churches* (Eugene: Freeman, 1976), 27; *CS*, 12 March 1891.

52. Connie Lenzen, *St. Mary's Cemetery, Portland's Pioneer Catholic Cemetery* (Vancouver, Wash.: Clark Co. Genealogical Society, 1987), 6-7; *The Centenary*, 46.

53. *CS,* 21 January 1886, 25 August 1898, 9 June 1886, 2 June 1898; Charles M. Smith, *Centenary of Cathedral Parish, Portland, Oregon, 1851-1951* (Portland: n.p., 1952), 59.
54. O'Connor, *Brief History,* 103, 45, 116; *CS,* 24 March 1898.
55. *Centennial History, 1885-1985, Our Lady of Lourdes, Jordan, Oregon* (Jordan: North Santiam Newspapers, 1985), 13, 19; Report of parishes, 1895: Sublimity, AAPO; Patricia Brandt, "The Mystery of the Sisters of Mercy at Cedar Mill," *OCHSN* 11 (summer 1999): 8, 12.
56. *CS,* 20 August 1885; Francis Leipzig, "Financial Plight of Cathedral Faced Archbishop Gross in 1880s," *CS,* 8 December 1978, 14; Gross to James Gibbons, 23 June 1885, Gross Papers; Ryan, "William H. Gross," 52.
57. Gross to P. De Roo, Portland, 2 February 1893; Mark Gross to P. De Roo, Portland, 3 April 1893, De Roo Papers; *Oregonian,* 1 November 1891; *CS, 5* November 1891, 8 Nov. 1891; Gross to My Very Dear Confrere, Portland, 25 November 1891, Gross Papers; Gross to P. De Roo, Portland, 9 November 1891, De Roo Papers.
58. P. De Roo to Mark Gross, Pendleton, 2 October 1893; P. De Roo to Senior Bishop of Province, Centerville, 11 February 1896; J. Brondel to P. De Roo, Helena, 14 February 1896; P. De Roo to Gross, Centerville, 27 December 1897, De Roo Papers; Isetti, *Called,* 144.
59. Gross to P. De Roo, Portland, 5 February 1892, De Roo Papers; *Oregonian,* 1 October 1894, 23 April 1893, 25 February 1895; *CS,* 4 October 1894, 16 December 1894, 15 November 1894; Patricia Brandt, "Bishop's House Proves Older Than Believed," *CS,* 13 September 1996, 6.
60. *CS,* 23 September 1897, 28 April 1898, 2 June 1898; P. De Roo to Gross, Blanchet, Centerville P.O., 24 April 1898, De Roo Papers; Record Book of Society to Raise Funds to Build Residence, 1895, AAPO.
61. Skeabeck, "Most Rev.," 66 (1955): 82; Gross to George Dusold, C.Ss.R., Astoria, 11 April 1896, Gross Papers.
62. Gross to Frederick Schauer, C.Ss.R., Portland, 31 January 1888, Gross Papers; Gross to P. De Roo, Ilchester, Maryland, 4 November 1898, De Roo Papers; *CS,* 17 November 1898; Schoenberg, *These Valiant Women,* 167.
63. *CS,* 17 November 1898.

Chapter 5

1. Rev. John Larkin, interview by author, tape recording, OHS, 10 January 1989; Rev. Francis J. Schaefers, interview by author, tape recording, OHS, 30 January 1990; Rev. Martin Thielen, interview by author, tape recording, OHS, 13 January 1989; Wilfred P. Schoenberg, S.J., *A History of the Catholic Church in the Pacific Northwest, 1743-1993* (Washington, D.C.: Pastoral Press, 1987), 409; Wilfred P. Schoenberg, S.J., *A Test of Time: A History of St. Mary's Home, 1889-1989* (Beaverton, Ore.: St. Mary's Home for Boys, 1989), 47-48; Msgr. Edmund Van der Zanden, interview by author, tape recording, OHS, 4 May 1998; Rev. Alfred Williams, conversation with author, March 1988.
2. Rev. John R. Laidlaw, *The Catholic Church in Oregon and the Work of Its Archbishops* (Smithtown, N.Y.: Exposition Press, 1977), 22-24; Edwin V. O'Hara, *Pioneer Catholic History of Oregon,* centennial ed. (Paterson, N.J.: St. Anthony Guild Press, 1939), 205; Timothy Michael Dolan, *Some Seed Fell on Good Ground: The Life of Edwin V. O'Hara* (Washington, D.C.: Catholic University Press, 1992), 19; Schoenberg, *History,* 409-410.
3. Leo Smith, interview by author, tape recording, OHS, 17 October 1990; Sister Miriam Margaret O'Donnell, S.N.J.M., "In Faith and Kindness: The Life of Most Reverend Alexander Christie, D. D., Fourth Archbishop of Portland in Oregon," (master's thesis, University of Portland, 1945), 28, 102. Archbishop Robert Dwyer drew a delightful sketch of him: "Tall and rangy, impressive and oratund of address, with a pawky humor, he was never more at ease than with his priests, taking innocent (or perhaps not so innocent) delight in cheating a bit at poker and purloining any loose cigars that might be around," *CS,* 14 April 1974; Joseph

A. Schiwek Jr. recalls Father John R. Laidlaw telling him that Christie enjoyed getting boxes of cigars at Christmas from his priests, so much so that he would reduce the parish assessment upon receipt of them, and that he remembered seeing stacks of cigar boxes in Christie's room. Conversation with the author, September 1991; *CS,* 20 July 1916.

4. Schoenberg, *History,* 407-408; Laidlaw, *Catholic Church in Oregon,* 22; O'Hara, *Pioneer Catholic History,* 162; Gordon B. Dodds, *Oregon: A Bicentennial History* (New York: W.W. Norton, 1977), 116-117.

5. Jay P. Dolan, *The American Catholic Experience: A History from Colonial Times to the Present* (Garden City, N.Y.: Doubleday & Company, 1985), 43, 221-225; Dodds, *Oregon,* 149; an example of the nature of this authority might be indicated by the start of a Catholic Church in Stayton. In 1903 Catholics in the area acquired land but Christie refused to give permission to build a church. They built it anyway, and when presented with a completed church, Christie dedicated it. *Souvenir of Dedication* (Stayton, Ore.: Immaculate Conception Church, 1952), AAPO.

6. Peter De Roo to Archbishop Alexander Christie, 28 May 1899, 3 June 1899 and 18 June 1899, Christie to De Roo, 8 December 1899, De Roo to Christie, 9 December 1899, Peter De Roo Papers, AMAA; *CS,* 16 August 1991; *Centennial History, 1885-1985: Our Lady of Lourdes, Jordan, Oregon* (Jordan, Ore.: North Santiam Newspapers, 1985), 21-24, the monks were ultimately unsuccessful; form letter, 29 January 1902, Alexander Christie Papers, AAPO.

7. One possible reason for Christie's decision, which even the writer admits is a "rather frivolous interpretation," has it that once during a trip by stagecoach from Eastern Oregon, Christie suffered an attack of dysentery "whereupon he resolved to get rid of the vast arid and barren area ill favor of someone who was becoming too popular in Portland!" portion of a letter from Msgr. Hubert a Campo, Lincoln, Nebraska, no date, no signature, Christie Papers.

8. Schoenberg, *Test of Time,* 48; *CS,* 17 August 1991, *Tillamook (Oregon) Headlight-Herald,* 13 March 1991; Schell also became controversial in secular circles when he wrote a letter to the *Oregon Journal* in 1902 that "prominent men and politicians" were swindling the state out of timber lands. The letter led to an official investigation and involved a leading banker. Marshall N. Dana, *Newspaper Story, Fifty Years of the Oregon Journal, 1902-1952* (Portland: Binford & Mort, 1951), 79, 82.

9. Schoenberg, *History,* 432-433, 434-436; Laidlaw, *Catholic Church in Oregon,* 25, 26; O'Donnell, "In Faith and Kindness," 52-53; *CS,* 21, 28 July 1904; *Oregonian,* 27 June, 18 July 1904; portion of letter from Campo, Christie Papers; "Refutation of the Slanderous Attack Recently Made Upon Archbishop Christie, Bishop O'Reilly and Priests of Oregon," which includes a number of testimonials by priests and is signed by a long list of Catholic laymen, Christie Papers; *CS,* 21 July 1904; O'Donnell, "In Faith and Kindness," 54-58.

10. Jeffrey M. Burns, "Building the Best: A History of Catholic Parish Life in the Pacific States," in *The American Catholic Parish: A History from 1850 to the Present,* ed. Jay P. Dolan (Mahwah, N.J.: Paulist Press, 1987), 2:51; O'Meara, interview by author, tape recording, OHS, 11 November 1991; *CS,* 22 January 1920, 22 September 1992.

11. O'Donnell, "In Faith and Kindness," 87-89; Laidlaw, *Catholic Church in Oregon,* 27-28; *CS,* 30 April 1925.

12. Schoenberg, *History,* 461-463, 535; Wilfred P. Schoenberg, S.J., *Paths to the Northwest: A Jesuit History of the Oregon Province* (Chicago: Ill.: Loyola University Press, 1982), 241, 250, 265, 328; Laidlaw, *Catholic Church in Oregon,* 27; O'Donnell, "In Faith and Kindness," 93; O'Hara, *Pioneer Catholic History,* 208; *CS,* 16 April 1925; *The Centenary: 100 Years of the Catholic Church in the Oregon Country* (Portland: Catholic Sentinel, 1939), 79.

13. Schoenberg, *History,* 494-495; Rev. Edmond Bliven, interview by author, tape recording, OHS, 25 April 1996; *CS,* 9 April 1925; *The Centenary,* 79; Ronald Eugene Isetti, F.S.C., *Called to the Pacific: A History of the Christian Brothers of the San Francisco District, 1868-1977* (Moraga, Cal.: St. Mary's College, 1979), 202-206, 209.

14. Francis I. McKenna, University Land Company, to Rev. A. Christie, 3 October 1899, Christie Papers; Laidlaw, *Catholic Church in Oregon*, 25; Schoenberg, *History*, 415-418, 513-514.

15. "Marylhurst 1929…History and Jubilee," SHNPA, Marylhurst; "Annals of Sisters of the Holy Names, 1929-1930: The Foundation of Marylhurst College," transcribed Denise Meyer and Barbara Whittlesey-Hayes, 1979, SHNPA; O'Hara, *Pioneer Catholic History*, 207-208; Schoenberg, *History*, 464; *ACWR News* (Archivists for Congregations of Women Religious) 2 (August 1992): 2.

16. O'Donnell, "In Faith and Kindness," 94; Rev. Lucien Lauerman, Report, 1933, in Catholic Charities History folder, CCAPO; *CS*, 4 June 1900, 28 January 1909, 4 October 1917, 22 November 1917, 13 December 1917 and 22 January 1920; T. Dolan, *Some Seed Fell*, 21-22.

17. *CS*, 20 July 1899; Wilfred P. Schoenberg, S.J., *Defender of the Faith: The History of the* Catholic Sentinel, *1870-1990* (Portland: Oregon Catholic Press, 1993), 131-132, 135, 141-142, 147.

18. J. Dolan, *The American Catholic Experience*, 344; James Hennesey, S.J., *American Catholics: A History of the Roman Catholic Community in the United States* (New York: Oxford University Press, 1981), 225.

19. Arthur Wheeler, C.S.C., "Columbia University, 1914-1922," (paper presented at the Holy Cross History Conference, Portland, Oregon, June 6, 1992); James T. Covert, *A Point of Pride: The University of Portland Story* (Portland: University of Portland Press, 1976), 54.

20. Laidlaw, *Catholic Church in Oregon*, 28; Schoenberg, *History*, 503; Joseph A. Schiwek Jr., *Called to be Church: A Brief History of St. Charles Borromeo Parish* (Portland: n. p., 1989), 14; O'Donnell, "In Faith and Kindness," 108-109; Christopher J. Kauffman, *Faith and Fraternalism: The History of the Knights of Columbus, 1882-1982* (New York: Harper & Row, 1982), 200-202; Maurice F. Egan and John B. Kennedy, *The Knights of Columbus in Peace and War* (New Haven: Knights of Columbus, 1920), 2:33-34, 369, 379; "Catholic Daughters of America," in Catholic Daughters of America, Court 118 file, AAPO; *Oregonian*, 20 January 1918, 15 September 1918, 21 January 1919.

21. Arthur Wheeler, C.S.C., "Federal Investigation of Archbishop Christie," *OCHSN* 4 (Summer 1992): 7 and "Portland Irish in World War I," (paper presented at the 5th Annual Meeting of the Oregon Catholic Historical Society, Portland, Oregon, 25 September 1992). Christie, who apparently was aware of the investigation, was quickly and quietly exonerated, as were Father William A. Daly, pastor of Immaculate Heart Church, and Father George Thompson, pastor of The Madeleine Church. The Irish "troubles" were brought to the attention of Portland Catholics when Father James P. O'Flynn, while visiting relatives in Ireland, had his passport taken from him for a time by the British police, Schiwek, *Called to Be Church*, 14. In 1919 Eamon De Valera, a leader in the Irish independence movement, was a guest at the Cathedral rectory and "caused consternation by having something good to say about the Russian revolution," J. G. Shaw, *Edwin Vincent O'Hara, American Prelate* (New York: Farrar, Straus and Cudahy, 1957), 32. However, De Valera spoke at the University of Portland and other Catholic schools, several priests and prominent Catholic laymen were involved in his reception, the *Catholic Sentinel* gave his visit extensive coverage, and he met with Christie at least twice, Wheeler, "Columbia University, 1914-1922"; *CS*, 6 November 1919, 13 November 1919, 20 November 1919, 27 November 1919. Section Two devoted entirely to De Valera's speech in the Municipal Auditorium in Portland, and the Declaration of Irish Independence. A split in 1920 between supporters and opponents of De Valera's solution to Ireland's problems divided the Ancient Order of Hibernians in Portland and led to its decline, O'Meara, interview by author, tape recording, OHS, 1 November 1991.

22. Martin Pollard, O.S.B., and Hugh Feiss, O.S.B., *Mount of Communion: Mount Angel Abbey, 1882-1982*, rev. ed. (St. Benedict, Ore.: Mount Angel Abbey, 1985), 19; *Oregonian*, 14 May 1918, 15 May 1918, 17 May 1918.

23. *CS*, 27 July 1944, 23 September 1966.

24. Bertram F. Griffin, *The Provincial Councils of Portland in Oregon* (Rome: Pontificia Universitatis Lateranensis, 1964), 114; Schoenberg, *History*, 515-516; E. Kimbark MacColl, *Merchants, Money and Power: The Portland Establishment, 1843-1913* (Portland: Georgian Press, 1980), 443-444; Dodds, *Oregon*, 150; Shaw, *O'Hara*, 41-42, 45; A Statement by Reverend Jerome M. Schmitz to a New Board of Catholic Charities, at the Benson Hotel, June 20, 1966, in Catholic Services for Children History folder, CCAPO; Gloria M. Hauer, "A Woman of Vision: Caroline Gleason, 1886-1962" (term paper, University of Portland, 1992); Arthur S. Link and William B. Catton, *American Epoch* (New York: Alfred A. Knopf, 1973), 1:59.

25. Statement by Jerome M. Schmitz, 20 June 1966, Catholic Services for Children History folder, CCAPO (he describes the work as being started by Father O'Hara); T. Dolan, *Some Seed Fell*, 55; Shaw, *O'Hara*, 73, 90, 113, 138-144; Schoenberg, *History*, 517-518: Schoenberg, *Defender*, 171; John F. Piper Jr., *The American Churches in World War I* (Athens: Ohio University Press, 1985), 187.

26. *CS*, 25 March 1983; Hauer, "A Woman of Vision."

27. Thielen, interview; Patricia Brandt, "Oregon's Maria Monk: The Escaped Nun from Mt. Angel Convent," (paper presented for the celebration of 25 years of the Aalto Library, St. Benedict, Oregon, July 1995), 8-10 (paper in possession of author); Schoenberg, *History*, 468, 522; Pollard and Feiss, *Mount of Communion*, 19; *CS*, 8 June 1916, and 15 February 1917.

28. M. Paul Holsinger, "The Oregon School Bill Controversy," 37 *Pacific Historical Review* (August 1968): 328; Immaculate Heart parish experienced quite an influx of northern European immigrants during and right after World War I, and its young people's group, St. Mary's Club, had members from Russian, German, Irish, and Polish families, O'Meara, interview, 1 November 1991.

29. Smith, interview by author, tape recording, OHS, 17 October 1990; O'Meara, interview, 1 November 1991; Rev. Morton F. Park, interview by author, tape recording, OHS, 25 February 1993.

30. Frank Freidel, *America in the Twentieth Century*, 4th ed. (New York: Alfred A. Knopf, 1976), 133.

31. Smith, interview, 17 October 1990; Larkin, interview, 10 January 1989. According to Larkin, Columbia Prep won the football championship and the following day all the public high schools withdrew from the league, leaving Hill Military Academy and Columbia Prep as the only two schools in it; Smith, interview by author, tape recording, OHS, 17 October 1990 and 16 November 1990; Kenneth T. Jackson, *The Ku Klux Klan in the City, 1915-1930* (New York: Oxford University Press, 1967), 207, 213. In 1924 Gaten ran for mayor and came in a distant second behind George Baker, the incumbent and winner, but far ahead of the Klan candidate, John H. Rankin.

32. Schoenberg, *History*, 523-527, 531; Lawrence J. Saalfeld, *Forces of Prejudice in Oregon, 1920-1925* (Portland: Archdiocesan Historical Commission, 1984), 3, 19, 62, 66-71, 79-87; Sister Marian Dolores Robinson, S.N.J.M, interview by author, tape recording, OHS, 22 October 1992; Kauffman, *Faith and Fraternalism*, 281; Dudley G. Wooten, *Remember Oregon*, (Denver: American Publishing Society, n. d.), 1, 10.

33. Kauffman, *Faith and Fraternalism*, 282-283; David M. Chalmers, *Hooded Americans: The First Century of the Ku Klux Klan, 1865-1965* (Garden City, N.Y.: Doubleday, 1965), 85-86; Saalfeld, *Forces of Prejudice*, 89-92; Schoenberg, *History*, 527, 529 ; *CS*, 18 January 1923.

34. *CS*, 16 November 1922, 23 November 1922, 29 January 1925; O'Donnell, "In Faith and Kindness," 117. It apparently had a predecessor in the Catholic Defense Guild, started by Father John Bernards, also with the purpose of fighting the Compulsory School Bill, which ran a series of advertisements in the daily press on Catholic teachings. It was discontinued when the Catholic Truth Society came into existence, *CS*, 30 September 1937 and 10 November 1972, guest editorial by Francis P. Leipzig.

35. Schoenberg, *History*, 402, 514-515, 535-536; Romeo Lemire, interview by author, tape recording, OHS, 25 August 1987; Williams, interview by author, tape recording, OHS, 8

November 1988; *CS*, 14 May 1914; Larkin, interview, 10 January 1989; Wilfred P. Schoenberg, S.J., *These Valiant Women: History of the Sisters of St. Mary of Oregon, 1886-1986* (Portland: Sisters of St. Mary of Oregon, 1986), 217; according to one account, Christie insisted that the Cathedral's facade, with its columns, resemble that of a 1920s-era bank, hoping that would encourage reluctant banks to lend money to the archdiocese. Rev. Edmond Bliven, interview.

36. Larkin, interview by author, tape recording, OHS, 14 February 1989; Thielen, interview; Laidlaw, *Catholic Church in Oregon*, 24; O'Hara, *Pioneer Catholic History*, 207, 210; O'Donnell, "In Faith and Kindness," 71-72, 87, 104.

37. Francis P. Leipzig, *Extension in Oregon* (St. Benedict, Ore.: Benedictine Press, 1956), 41-59, 62, 69; Sister Caroline Gimpl, S.N.J.M., et al., *St. Mary's Parish Centennial* (Eugene, Ore.: n. p., 1987), 7-9; Larkin, interview, 14 February 1989; Schoenberg, *History*, 445, 478; O'Donnell, "In Faith and Kindness," 106, 108; *CS*, 21 January 1943.

38. Copy of letter "to all parishes," n.d., Christie Papers; one reason Christie may have had trouble raising money from the parishes was his willingness to accept whiskey and/or cigars in lieu of assessments, Rev. Edmond Bliven, interview by the author, tape recording, OHS, 4 June 1996.

39. O'Hara, *Pioneer Catholic History*, 207, 209; Christie to Peter De Roo, 8 December 1899 and 18 February 1900—someone has translated the words under each line of the first letter, and the second one contains a note from De Roo complaining that he cannot read the archbishop's handwriting, De Roo Papers; Schoenberg, *History*, 209, 413; O'Donnell, "In Faith and Kindness," 101-102.

40. *Oregonian*, 7 April 1925; Thielen, interview; *CS*, 2 February 1922 and 22 January 1920; Schoenberg, *A Test of Time*, 53.

41. Thomas J. Reese, S.J., *Archbishop, Inside the Power Structure of the American Catholic Church* (San Francisco: Harper & Row, 1989), 94-9.

42. Circular letter "Rev. and Dear Father," 21 December 1899, Christie Papers.

Chapter 6

1. Rev. John Larkin, interview by author, tape recording, OHS, 10 January 1989; Romeo Lemire, interview by author, tape recording, OHS, 25 August 1987: Rev. Msgr. Martin H. Thielen, interview by author, tape recording, OHS, 26 May 1989; *CS*, Special Edition, 5 November 1977, 7 January 1983; John R. Laidlaw, *The Catholic Church in Oregon and the Work of its Archbishops* (Smithtown, N.Y.: Exposition Press, 1980), 32-33; Wilfred P. Schoenberg, S.J., *A History of the Catholic Church in the Pacific Northwest, 1743-1983* (Washington, D.C.: Pastoral Press, 1987), 540-541.

2. Laidlaw, *Catholic Church in Oregon*, 31; Rev. Francis J. Schaefers, interview by author, tape recording, OHS, 30 January 1990; Schoenberg, *History*, 541; *CS*, 7 January 1983; Thielen, interviews by author, tape recording, OHS, 19 and 26 May 1989; Wilfred P. Schoenberg, S.J., *A Test of Time: A History of St. Mary's Home, 1889-1989* (Beaverton, Ore.: St. Mary's Home for Boys, 1989), 64-65; Edward F. O'Meara, interview by author, tape recording, OHS, 18 May 1992.

3. *CS*, 7 January 1983; Larkin, interview by author, tape recording, OHS, 14 February 1989.

4. Schaefers, interview, 30 January 1990; Rev. Morton B. Park, interview by author, tape recording, OHS, 25 February 1993; Sister Marian Dolores Robinson, S.N.J.M., interview by author, tape recording, OHS, 2 October 1992; Schoenberg, *Test of Time*, 64; Larkin, interview by author, tape recording, OHS, 14 February 1989; Rev. Emmet Harrington, interviews by author, tape recording, OHS, 26 and 28 July 1988; F. Leo Smith, interview by author, tape recording, OHS, 22 November 1990.

5. Park, interview; Thielen, interview, 19 May 1989; *CS*, 19 April 1974, 7 January 1983; Msgr. Edmund Van der Zanden, interview by author, tape recording, OHS, 3 March 1998.

6. *CS,* 7 January 1983; Rev. Alfred A. Williams, interview by author, tape recording, OHS, 8 November 1988; Thielen, interview by author, tape recording, OHS, 13 January 1989; *CS,* 13 August 1931, 7 January 1983; Park, interview; Rev. Edmund Bliven, interview by author, tape recording, OHS, 15 April 1997.

7. Larkin, interview, 14 February 1989; Thielen, interview, 26 May 1989; *The Centenary, 100 Years of the Catholic Church in the Oregon Country* (Portland: Catholic Sentinel, 1939), 60; Christie had had the archdiocese incorporated in 1909, letter from F. W. Benson, Secretary of State, State of Oregon, Salem, 6 April 1909, Alexander Christie Papers, AAPO.

8. Larkin, interview by author, tape recording, OHS, 7 March 1989; Laidlaw, *Catholic Church in Oregon,* 32; Schaefers, interview, 30 January 1990. In spite of Howard's directive on pew rents, St. Clare's parish in Portland continued to collect them from a few parish families as late as 1940. Jim Magmer, ed., *Celebration: St. Clare's Achievement from Mission to Post Vatican II Community, 1913-1988* (Wilsonville, Ore.: C&M Communications, 1988), 13; *Official Catholic Directory* (New York: J. P. Kenedy & Sons, 1905, 1911, 1912, 1913, 1916, 1922, 1923, 1924, 1925, 1926, 1927, 1928, 1929). In 1905 the Catholic population of Oregon was given as "about" 40,000, in 1916 it was 60,000 and remained at exactly that figure until 1927, during Howard's administration, when it was cited as 61,026; in 1928 a more realistic figure of 42,000 was settled upon. The statistics for births, marriages, and deaths were not supplied until 1928; Larkin, interview, 14 February 1989. Howard's version was a little different. He claimed that many of them had come out to Oregon because of their health, were working here temporarily, and eleven of them left during the first two years of his administration. Howard, interview by Brother David Martin, C.S.C., April 1970, Archives, University of Portland.

9. Wilfred P. Schoenberg, S.J., *Defender of the Faith: The History of the* Catholic Sentinel *1870-1990* (Portland: Oregon Catholic Press, 1993), 197, 202; Thielen, interview, 13 January 1989; *CS,* 30 September 1937, *The Centenary,* 38; Magmer, *Celebration, 30; Oregonian,* 18 September 1938; Schoenberg, *History,* 550-551; Bliven (who was on the editoral staff), interview by author, tape recording, OHS, 31 May 1996.

10. T. Timothy M. Dolan, *Some Seed Fell on Good Ground: The Life of Edwin V. O'Hara* (Washington, D. C.: Catholic University of America Press, 1992), 119; Thielen, interview, 19 May 1989.

11. Williams, interview by author, tape recording, OHS, 8 March 1988; Larkin, interview, 14 February 1989. Larkin accompanied Howard on many of his trips.

12. Arthur S. Link and William B. Catton, *American Epoch: A History of the United States Since 1900,* 4th ed. (New York: Alfred A. Knopf, 1973), 2:36; Sydney B. Ahlstrom, *A Religious History of the American People* (New Haven: Yale University Press, 1973), 639-640, 1004-1007; John F. Piper Jr., *The American Churches in World War I* (Athens: Ohio University Press, 1985), 187.

13. *New Catholic Encyclopedia,* s.v. "Catholic Action"; Jay P. Dolan, *The American Catholic Experience: A History from Colonial Times to the Present* (Garden City, N.Y., Doubleday, 1985), 408, 409, 415.

14. *CS,* 6 December 1928, 7 September 1939; *The Centenary,* 20; Father Lucian Lauerman, Report, 1933, in Catholic Charities History folder, CCAPO; Daniel T. McColgan, *A Century of Charity: The First One Hundred Years of the Society of St. Vincent De Paul in the United States* (Milwaukee: Bruce, 1951), 2:34-35, 36.

15. Father Valentine L. Moffenbeier, Report, 1950, in Catholic Charities History folder, CCAPO; Father Lucien Lauerman, Report, 1933, *CS,* 16 October 1930, 16 May 1935, and 22 January l965; Rev. Lucien Lauerman file in Diocesan Priests Files, AAPO; Articles of Incorporation of Catholic Charities, Inc., CCAPO; A Statement of Reverend Jerome M. Schmitz to a New Board of Catholic Charities at the Benson Hotel, 20 June 1966, in Catholic Services for Children folder, CCAPO; Park, interview by author, tape recording, OHS, 25 February 1993.

16. Father Jerome M. Schmitz, Outline of Reorganization Plan for Catholic Agencies and Institutions, 4 March 1952, in Policy folder, CCAPO; Statement of Jerome M. Schmitz, 20 June 1966; Father Valentine L. Moffenbeier, Report, 1950.
17. Brother Donald J. Stabrowki, C.S.C., "St Vincent de Paul Parish: A Half Century of Urban Ministry," *OCHSN* 3 (summer 1991): 9-10.
18. Lillian A. Pereyra, "The Catholic Church and Portland's Japanese: The Untimely St. Paul Miki School Project," *OHQ* 94 (winter 1993-1994): 399-434.
19. *CS,* 27 January 1929; Thielen, interview by author, tape recording, OHS, 3 March 1989; Schaefers, interview by author, tape recording, OHS, 25 January 1990.
20. Elizabeth McLagan, *A Peculiar Paradise: A History of Blacks in Oregon, 1788-1940* (Portland: Georgian Press, 1980), 140-142; *CS,* 28 September 1939, 15 February 1940, 23 May 1940, 14 May 1965, 30 March 1973, 3 March 1989, 21 April 1989, 9 February 1990. Thielen, telephone conversation with author, 31 August 1989.
21. Thielen, interview, 3 March 1989; Schaefers, interview, 25 January 1990; *CS,* 11 August 1938, 24 August 1939; Lillian A. Pereyra, "The Gospel on a Soapbox," *OCHSN* 2 (summer 1990): 1, 4.
22. Williams, interview, 8 March 1988; Sister Gertrude Schaefers, S.N.J.M., interview by author, tape recording, OHS, 1 August 1989; Rev. Alan Kennedy, interview by author, tape recording, OHS, 17 July 1997; Schoenberg, *Defender,* 244.
23. J. Dolan, *The American Catholic Experience,* 408; *CS,* 22 January 1931; McColgan, *A Century of Charity,* 2:35; Stabrowski, "St Vincent de Paul Parish," 10.
24. Williams, interview by author, tape recording, OHS, 8 October 1988; *Oregonian,* 25 January 1932; O'Meara, interview by author, tape recording, OHS, 26 October 1990; Schoenberg, *History,* 562-563.
25. Schoenberg, *History,* 551; Schaefers, interview, 25 January 1990; Thielen, interview by author, tape recording, OHS, 10 March 1989; *Oregonian,* 2 May 1938; O'Meara, interview by author, tape recording, OHS, 7 November 1991; Schoenberg, *Defender,* 233-234, 243, 257; *CS,* 11 August, 18 August, 15 September 1938; J. David Valaik, "American Catholic Dissenters and the Spanish Civil War," *Catholic Historical Review* 53 (January 1968): 540, 542; J. David Valaik, "Catholic Neutrality and the Spanish Embargo, 1933-1939," *Journal of American History* 54 (June 1967): 74-75, 84-85.
26. Schoenberg, *Defender,* 230; O'Meara, interview, 7 November 1991; Robinson, interview by author, tape recording, OHS, 22 October 1992; Dennis Joseph Black, *Star of the Sea Church, Brookings, Oregon, 1923-50-1973* (Brookings, Ore.: n.p., 1973), n.p.; Charles J. Tull, *Father Coughlin and the New Deal* (Syracuse, N.Y.: Syracuse University Press, 1965), 169, 247.
27. Thielen, interview, 10 March 1989.
28. Smith, interview by author, tape recording, OHS, 23 January 1991; CS, 1 August 1975, Special Edition, 5 November 1977; O'Meara, interview, 7 November 1991. According to O'Meara his rectory at All Saints smelled like a garlic and olive oil processing factory. In an interview with Gorman Hogan of the *Catholic Sentinel* upon his retirement, Tobin predicted that women would be ordained to the diaconate, would be similar to the deaconesses of the early church, and that married men would be ordained to the priesthood, *CS,* 26 June 1970; Park, interview, 25 February 1993; Rev. Bertram Griffin, interview by Sister Pauline Rose Waibel, S.S.M.O., tape recording, OHS, 20 November 1992.
29. Lauerman, Report, 1933, 51, 53; Knights of Columbus, Minute Books of Meetings, 1-1-36 to 5-17-37, 6-1-37 to 6-19-39, 8-4-41 to 10-5-42, Box 18, AAPO; Smith, interview by author, OHS, 26 October 1990; *CS,* 7 January 1983.
30. Edwin V. O'Hara, "Religious Study Clubs" report, Edward Howard Papers, Box 5, AAPO; T. Dolan, *Some Seed Fell,* 115; Bertram F. Griffin, *The Provincial Councils of Portland in Oregon* (Rome: Pontificia Universitatis Lateranensis, 1964), 112; Schoenberg, *Defender,* 226-227; Magmer, *Celebration,* 30; *The Centenary,* 46.
31. O'Meara, interview by author, tape recording, OHS, 1 November 1991; Lauerman, report, 1933.

32. Smith, interview by author, OHS, 17 October 1990; Larkin, interview, 7 March 1989; Thielen, interviews, 13 January, 10 March 1989; O'Meara, interview, 7 November 1989; *CS*, 24 September 1936.

33. Schoenberg, *History*, 562; Laidlaw, *Catholic Church in Oregon*, 32; *CS*, 12 May 1989; O'Meara, interview, 7 November 1991; Schaefers, interview, 25 January 1990; Thielen, interview by author, tape recording, OHS, 7 April 1989. The opening of Central Catholic High School had an immediate and continuing negative effect on enrollment at Columbia Preparatory School, Joseph Kehoe, C.S.C., "Columbia Preparatory School, 1934- 1955," (paper presented at the Holy Cross History Association Conference, Portland, Oregon, June, 1992), 4.

34. Schaefers, interviews, 25, 30 January 1990; Harrington, interview by author, tape recording, OHS, 28 July 1988; Thielen, interviews, 7 April, 19, 26 May 1989.

35. Schoenberg, *History*, 558-559; Larkin, interview, 10 January 1989; Thielen, interviews, 27 January, 7 April, 19 May 1989; Park, interview, 25 February 1993; Marion Burtchaell and Douris Connelly, "The Archbishop and the Ladies," paper described as a "brief and casual history of the Seminary Tea... prepared... for the 100th Birthday of Archbishop Howard," copy in possession of Arthur Schoenfeldt, C.S.C., University of Portland.

36. "Annals of Sisters of the Holy Names, 1929-1930: The Foundation of Marylhurst College," transcribed by Denise Meyer and Barbara Whittlesey-Hayes, 1979, 45-46, SHNPA; typed chronology, SHNPA; Robinson, interview by author, tape recording, OHS, 22 October 1992.

37. Thielen, interview, 10 March 1989; James T. Covert, *A Point of Pride: The University of Portland Story* (Portland: University of Portland Press, 1976), 73-74, 116-117; Winifred Dalgity and Philippa Mardesich, *St. Mary Star of the Sea Parish, Astoria, Oregon, 1874-1974* (Astoria, Ore.: Astoria Printing, 1974) n.p.; Schoenberg, *History*, 596-597; Schaefers, interview, 25 January 1990.

38. *CS*, 4 September, 11 December 1941, 17 September, 1 October, 18 December 1941, 4 March, 22 October, 24 December 1942, 18 February, 18 March, 18 September 1943, 1 February, 18 October, 1945, 26 June 1970, 13 December 1991, 11 August 1995; Bliven, interview by author, tape recording, OHS, 7 May 1996; List of Priests Who Served in Armed Forces in World War II file, AAPO; Edward F. O'Meara, *Continue to Prosper: The History of the First Half Century of All Saints Parish, Portland, Oregon* (Portland: n.p., n.d.), 57.

39. Larkin, interview by author, tape recording, OHS, 17 January 1989; Covert, *A Point of Pride*, 117; *Our Lady of Perpetual Help Parish (St Mary's)* (Albany, Ore.: n.p., 1972); Magmer, *Celebration*, 12; Sister Caroline Gimpl, S.N.J.M., et al., *St. Mary's Parish Centennial* (Eugene, Ore.: Express Press Printing and Graphics, 1987), 22; Dalgity and Mardesich, *St. Mary Star of the Sea Parish*, n.p.; Norma Haggerty, *Yesterday—125 Years at St Joseph's: A Historical Perspective, 1864 to 1989* (Salem: n.p., n.d), 17; *CS*, 29 January 1993; "Catholic Daughters of America, 3 October 1909" in Catholic Daughters of America Court Oregon 118 file, AAPO.

40. Thielen, interview, 10 March 1989; Schoenberg, *History*, 601; *CS*, 14 January, 25 February, 30 September 1943, 3 June 1948, 5 June 1992; Father Michael J. Raleigh, "Oregon Trail of '43," article, July, 1943, in Parishes: St. Catherine, AAPO.

Chapter 7

1. Sidney F. Ahlstrom, *A Religious History of the American People* (New Haven: Yale University Press, 1973), 952.

2. *Oregon Catholic Directory* (Portland: Oregon Catholic Press, 1945, 1950, 1955, 1960, 1992); on the other hand, in a 1977 interview, Archbishop Edward D. Howard said that much of the archdiocese's growth had come during the Depression and World War II when people left their homes in the East to seek jobs in the West, *CS*, 7 January 1983.

3. Rev. John B. Larkin, interview by author, tape recording, OHS, 14 February 1989; John R. Laidlaw, *The Catholic Church in Oregon and the Work of Its Archbishops* (Smithtown, N.Y.:

Exposition Press, 1980), 32; Rev. Francis J. Schaefers, interview by author, tape recording, OHS, 25 January 1990; Wilfred P. Schoenberg, S.J., *A History of the Catholic Church in the Pacific Northwest, 1743-1983* (Washington, D.C.: Pastoral Press, 1987), 624, 641; Wilfred P. Schoenberg, S.J., *A Test of Time: A History of St. Mary's Home, 1889-1989* (Beaverton, Ore.: St. Mary's Home for Boys, 1989), 106-114; *CS*, 13 December 1991; Sister Caroline Gimpl, S.N.J.M., et al., *St. Mary's Parish Centennial* (Eugene, Ore.: Express Press Printing & Graphics, 1987), 28.

4. *CS*, 9 April 1925, 16 September 1994; Timothy M. Dolan, *Some Seed Fell on Good Ground: The Life of Edwin V. O'Hara* (Washington, D.C.: Catholic University Press, 1992), 27-28; Edwin V. O'Hara, *Pioneer Catholic History of Oregon*, centennial ed. (Paterson, N.J.: St. Anthony Guild Press, 1939) 164-165; Rev. Martin H. Thielen, interview by author, tape recording, OHS, 21 April 1989. Thielen was superintendent of education from 1951 to 1968.

5. Jeffrey M. Burns, "Building the Best: A History of Catholic Parish Life in the Pacific States," in *The American Catholic Parish: A History from 1850 to the Present*, ed. Jay P. Dolan (Mahwah, N.J.: Paulist Press, 1987), 2:44; Thielen, interview, 21 April 1989; Jean O'Connell, et al., *The Spirit Within The Word—The Truth: St. Clare Newsletter in Celebration of 70 Years of Franciscan Heritage at St. Clare Parish, 1913-1992* (Portland: St. Clare Catholic Church, 1992), 7; Gimpl, et al., *St. Mary's Parish*, 23; Martin Cawley, O.C.S.O., *Saint James Parish, McMinnville, Oregon* (McMinnville, Ore.: Corel, Glass, Dahlstrom, 1977), 27-35.

6. F. Leo Smith, interview by author, tape recording, OHS, 22 November 1990: Rev. Morton E. Park, interview by author, tape recording, OHS, 25 February 1993; Thielen, interview by author, tape recording, OHS, 13 January 1989, tape #1; Tom Bannon, Kathryn Cowan and Kathleen Phillips, *One Hundred Years as a Parish: Holy Trinity Catholic Church, Bandon, Oregon, including St. John's Mission, Port Orford, Oregon* (Port Orford, Ore.: Holy Trinity Catholic Church, 1983), 23-24.

7. Smith, interviews by author, tape recording, OHS, 26 October 1990, 9 November 1990; Thielen, interview by author, tape recording, OHS, 27 January 1989, 21 April 1989; in Woodburn public school, buses came to the parochial school to pick the children up, although Woodburn was not "notoriously Catholic," Larkin, interview by author, tape recording, OHS, 17 January 1989.

8. Mother Mary Eucharista McNichols, S.H.C.J., "The History of Catholic Education in Oregon," 13, in Theses and Papers file, AAPO; Thielen, interview, 21 April 1989; Smith, interview by author, tape recording, OHS, 9 November 1990; Schoenberg, *History*, 591, 647-648; *Oregonian*, 6 April 1962; the Supreme Council of the Knights of Columbus financed the case for the archdiocese, in Church: Groups, Knights of Columbus Textbook Case file, AAPO.

9. Joseph Kehoe, C.S.C., "Columbia Preparatory School, 1934-1955" (paper presented at the Holy Cross History Association Conference, Portland, Oregon, June, 1991), 5, 7-8. Schoenberg, *History*, 634-635, 645; Wilfred P. Schoenberg, *Paths to the Northwest: A Jesuit History of the Oregon Province* (Chicago: Loyola University Press, 1982), 481; Thielen, interview, 21 April 1989; Schaefers, interview, 25 January 1990; Martin Pollard, O.S.B. and Hugh Feiss, O.S.B., *Mount of Communion, Mount Angel Abbey, 1882-1982*, rev. ed. (St. Benedict, Ore.: Mount Angel Abbey, 1985), 57; in 1968 the John F. Kennedy High School band played for Robert Kennedy at the Salem railroad station when his presidential campaign train passed through on the way down the coast to his fatal encounter in Los Angeles. Rev. Emmet Harrington, interview by author, tape recording, OHS, 28 July 1988; *CS*, 25 October 1991, 27 March 1992; Schoenberg, *History*, 674-675.

10. "Annals of the Sisters of the Holy Names, 1929-1930: The Foundation of Marylhurst College," transcribed by Denise Meyer and Barbara Whittlesey-Hayes, 1979, 51, SHNPA; James T. Covert, *A Point of Pride: The University of Portland Story* (Portland: University of Portland Press, 1976), 144-145, 214-215; Robinson, interview by author, tape recording, OHS, 29 October 1992.

11. Schoenberg, *History*, 641; Harrington, interview by author, tape recording, OHS, 26 July 1988; Griffin, interview by Sister Pauline Rose Waibel, S.S.M.O., tape recording, OHS, 18 July 1993; Park, interview, 25 February 1993.
12. A Statement of Reverend Jerome M. Schmitz to A New Board of Catholic Charities, at the Benson Hotel, June 20, 1966, 9-10 in Catholic Services for Children History file, CCAPO; Jerome M. Schmitz, Outline of Reorganization Plan for Catholic Agencies and Institutions, in Policy folder, CCAPO; Charter, signed by Archbishop Edward D. Howard on January 1, 1953, granted to Catholic Services for Children, and Articles of Incorporation for Catholic Services for Children, dated March 6, 1953, in Catholic Services for Children History file, CCAPO; Park, interview by author, tape recording. OHS, 4 March 1993; Gimpl, et al., *St. Mary's Parish*, 27, 37; Church: Groups, Catholic Charities Camp Howard file, AAPO.
13. *CS*, 22 February 1958, 5 March 1959, 14 May 1965, 27 January, 15 September 1972, 5 November 1977, 27 March 1992; Bertram F. Griffin, *The Provincial Councils of Portland in Oregon* (Rome: Pontificia Universitatis Lateranensis, 1964), 170-171; Brother Donald Stabrowski, C.S.C., "St. Vincent de Paul Parish: a Half Century of Urban Ministry, part II," *OCHSN* 4 (summer 1992):10; Keith D.Barger, "Hearing the Cry of the Poor: The Catholic Worker Communities in Oregon and Washington, 1940 to the Present" (senior thesis, University of Portland, 1992), 14-16; Ed Langlois, "'Everyone is Another Christ,'" *Portland* 12 (spring 1993): 38.
14. Harrington, interview, 28 July 1988; *CS,* 27 July 1950; Father James Edward Mosley, in Diocesan Priests file, AAPO.
15. Jay P. Dolan, *The American Catholic Experience: A History from Colonial Times to the Present* (Garden City, N.Y.: Doubleday, 1985), 157; Thielen, interview by author, tape recording, OHS, 19 November 1989; Jeffry M. Burns, "Building the Best," 2:37-38; *CS*, 24 November 1960.
16. *Oregonian*, 28 October 1945, 22 October 1946, 23 October 1946, 8 October 1957; *Oregon Journal*, 8 October 1957; Harrington, interview by author, tape recording, OHS, 3 August 1988; Edward F. O'Meara, interview by author, tape recording, OHS, 7 November 1991; the spirit of Tobin's conferences was continued in the Annual Tobin Lecture Series at All Saints parish which began in 1985, *CS*, 12 February 1993.
17. Burns, "Building the Best," 2:33-36; O'Meara, interview by author, tape recording, OHS, 1 November 1991; J. Dolan, *American Catholic Experience*, 384-355; Gimpl, et al., *St. Mary's Parish*, 35; Park, interview, 25 February 1993; *St. Mary's Parish, Mount Angel, Oregon, 1880-1980* (Salem: Panther Printing Co., 1979), 70.
18. Harrington, interview by author, tape recording, OHS, 13 September 1988; Larkin, interview by author, 14 January 1989; Church: Groups, Nocturnal Adoration Society file, AAPO; Burns, "Building the Best," 2:38: Schoenberg, *History*, 505, 605; Cawley, *Saint James Parish*, 49; Pollard and Feiss, *Mount of Communion*, 56-57.
19. Ahlstrom, *Religious History*, 960; John Tracy Ellis, *American Catholicism*, 2nd ed. (Chicago: University of Chicago Press, 1969), 137-138.
20. Smith, interview, 9 November 1990; *CS*, 7 January 1983; Edward F. O'Meara, *Continue to Prosper: The History of the First Half Century of All Saints Parish* (Portland: n.p., n.d.), 31, 54-56, 31; Wilfred P. Schoenberg, S.J., *Defender of the Faith: the History of the* Catholic Sentinel (Portland: Oregon Catholic Press, 1993), 265-266; O'Meara, *Continue to Prosper*, 31, 54-6; T. Dolan, *Some Seed Fell*, 181; Thielen, interview by author, tape recording, OHS, 19 May 1989.
21. Laidlaw, *The Catholic Church*, 34; Schoenberg, *History*, 166, 703; Griffin, interview by Sister Pauline Rose Waibel, tape recording, OHS, 20 November 1992; James Hennesey, S.J., *American Catholics: A History of the Roman Catholic Community in the United States* (New York: Oxford University Press, 1981), 314-315.
22. Griffin, interview by Sister Pauline Rose Waibel, tape recording, OHS, June 18, 1993; Jim Magmer, ed. *Celebration: St. Clare's Achievement from Mission to Post Vatican II Community, 1913-1988* (Wilsonville, Ore.: C & M Communications, 1988), 7, 34; *CS*, 23 April 1993.

23. Sister Pauline Rose Waibel, S.S.M.O., "A History of the Sisters of St. Mary of Oregon's Mission in Tamshiyacu, Peru, 1966-1973" (master's thesis, Portland State University, 1990), 5-8, 20; Gerald M. Costello, *Mission to Latin America: The Successes and Failures of a Twentieth Century Crusade* (Maryknoll, N.Y.: Obis Books, 1979), 35-38; William T. Pearsall, Boston, 6 January 1994, to William J. Levada, Levada Papers, AAPO.

24. Waibel, "Sisters of St. Mary of Oregon in Peru," 4, 26-27; *CS*, 17 October 1980; List in Missions of the Archdiocese, Peru file, AAPO; Father Brad Killingsworth went to Peru early in 1978, after joining the St. James Society, and was still serving there into the 1990s; Sister Yvette Chartrand, S.N.J.M., "Pages of History: Congregation of the Sisters of the Holy Names of Jesus and Mary, 1867-1967," trans. Sister J. Y. Peugnet, S.N.J.M., 1984, 84, 85, SHNPA.

25. Edward D. Howard, *The Ecumenical Movement* [Lenten Pastoral Letter] (Portland: Archdiocese of Portland in Oregon, 1965), Edward Howard Papers, AAPO; Griffin, interview, 18 July 1993; *CS*, 7 January 1993; Schoenberg, *Defender*, 287.

26. Smith, interview, 9 November 1990; Park, interview by author, tape recording, OHS, 4 November 1993; Thielen, interview by author, tape recording, OHS, 26 May 1989.

27. Smith, interview, 22 November 1990.

28. Smith, interview, 26 October 1990; Thielen, interview, 26 May 1989; Harrington, interview, 28 July 1988; O'Meara, interview by author, tape recording, 18 May 1992; Schaefers, interview by author, tape recording, OHS, 30 January 1990; Schoenberg, *History*, 634.

29. Smith, interview by author, tape recording, OHS, 16 November 1990; *Oregonian*, 6 April 1962; Schoenberg, *Defender*, 303; O'Meara, interview, 18 May 1992; Larkin, interview, 17 January 1989; *CS*, 14 June 1965.

30. Griffin, *Provincial Councils*, 175; Harrington, interview, 28 July 1988; O'Meara, interview, 18 May 1992.

31. *CS*, 7 January 1983; O'Meara, interview by author, tape recording, OHS, 2 July 1992; Schoenberg, *Defender*, 284-285, 313.

32. Rev. Alfred Williams, interview by author, tape recording, OHS, 8 November 1988; *Oregonian*, Letters to the Editor, letter from Thielen, 31 January 1974; Schoenberg, *History*, 661-662.

33. Larkin, interview, 14 February 1989; *CS*, 8 July 1966; Schaefers, interview, 30 January 1990, Schaefers was chairman of the Administrative Council on Finances and later Coordinator of Archbishop Dwyer's fund drive; Robert McQuarry, interview by author, tape recording, OHS, 29 June 1994, McQuarry served as archdiocesan business manager and then vicar for finances from 1968 to 1984. As far as the records show, Howard had never before asked Catholics to contribute directly to the archdiocese, apparently preferring to rely on their support through their parishes.

34. Schoenberg, *History*, 676; *CS*, 7 January 1983; J. Dolan, *American Catholic Experience*, 354-355; Thielen, interview, 26 May, 1989; Harrington, interview, 28 July 1988.

35. Wilfred P. Schoenberg, S.J., *These Valiant Women: History of the Sisters of St. Mary of Oregon, 1886-1986* (Portland: Sisters of St. Mary of Oregon, 1986), 290; *CS*, 7 January 1983; Howard Papers, Box #1, AAPO; Francis P. Leipzig. *Longevity and Historical Sketches of the American Hierarchy*, rev. ed. (Portland: *Catholic Sentinel*, 1978), 63. Two anecdotes, related by Griffin, interview by Sister Pauline Rose Waibel, tape recording, OHS, 29 November 1992, convey an idea of Howard's durability. While Pope John Paul II was in the United States in 1979, Howard was celebrating one of his birthdays, so the Pope called him on the phone to congratulate him, but was unable to get a word in edgewise. Another time Howard was invited to give the sermon at a Mass at St. Francis Church, and was so feeble he had to be helped down the aisle in the procession, and up into the pulpit. Once there, he suddenly straightened up, pushed the microphone away, and delivered a sermon from memory, quoting from McGuffey's Reader and Robert Frost's poetry. When it was over, two people had to assist him back to his chair.

Chapter 8

1. Father John P. Laidlaw, *The Catholic Church in Oregon and the Work of Its Archbishops* (Smithtown. N.Y.: Exposition Press, 1980), 36-37; Wilfred P. Schoenberg, S.J., *A History of the Catholic Church in the Pacific Northwest, 1743-1983* (Washington, D.C.: Pastoral Press, 1987), 678; *Oregonian,* 24 December 1966; Baxter Murray, interview by author, tape recording, OHS, 22 September 1992.
2. *Oregonian,* 1 January 1967, Northwest section; Rev. Emmet Harrington, interview by author, tape recording, OHS, 3 August 1988; Schoenberg, *History,* 679; Sister Marian Dolores Robinson. S.N.J.M., interview by author, tape recording, OHS, 5 November 1992; Robert McQuarry, interview by author, tape recording, OHS, 29 June 1994; Albert J. Steiss, *Ecclesiastes: The Book of Archbishop Robert Dwyer: A Selection of His Writings Edited by Albert J. Steiss and a Brief Life by the Editor and a Sketch from Memory by Isabel Piczek* (Los Angeles: National Catholic Register, 1982), 19, 21; one anecdote, probably apocryphal, tells about a priest who decided to increase his vocabulary, so every week he wrote down a word from Dwyer's column, looked it up and kept a list. After a few months he noticed that the list was alphabetical, Rev. Bertram Griffin, interview by Sister Pauline Rose Waibel, S.S.M.O., tape recording, OHS, 30 November 1992; Rev. Morton H. Park, interview by author, tape recording, OHS, 4 November 1993; Murray, interview, 22 September 1992; Wilfred P. Schoenberg, S.J., *Defender of the Faith: The History of the* Catholic Sentinel, *1870-1990* (Portland: Oregon Catholic Press, 1993), 338.
3. Edward R. Kantowicz, *Corporation Sole: Cardinal Mundelein and Chicago Catholicism* (Notre Dame: University of Notre Dame, 1983), 2-3.
4. *Oregon Journal,* 6 February 1967; *Oregonian,* 7 February 1967.
5. McQuarry, interview by author, tape recording, OHS, 13 July 1994; Murray, interview by author, tape recording, OHS, 29 September 1992; Dwyer was the first archbishop in the archdiocese to decline a salary. "He takes no remuneration from the Chancery Office," *Oregonian,* 28 July 1973; after Dwyer retired the archdiocese sold the house for $199,270, *CS,* 11 June 1976; Edward F. O'Meara, interview by author, tape recording, OHS, 18 May 1992.
6. Schoenberg, *Defender,* 319; *Oregonian,* 20 April 1969. The article describes some of Dwyer's art objects.
7. Steiss, *Ecclesiastes,* 21, 37, 166-174, 264-265; *Oregonian,* 1 January 1967, NW Section, 28 July 1973.
8. Murray, interview, 29 September 1992; Romeo Lemire, interview by author, tape recording, OHS, 1 September 1987.
9. Thielen, interview by author, tape recording, OHS, 26 May 1989: Harrington, interview by author, 23 August 1988; Larkin, interview by author, tape recording, 17 January 1989; *CS,* 29 March 1974; Organizations: Oregon Historical Society file, AAPO.
10. Thomas J. Reese, S.J., *Archbishop: Inside the Power Structure of the American Catholic Church* (San Francisco: Harper & Row, 1989), 99; Harrington, interview, 3 August 1988; Park, interview by author, tape recording, OHS, 4 March 1993; Schoenberg, *History,* 679; Steiss, *Ecclesiastes,* 19.
11. *Oregon Journal,* 24 March 1976; *Oregonian,* 23 January 1974; McQuarry, interviews by author, tape recordings, OHS, 29 June 1994, 6 July 1994, 13 July 1994; Rev. Edmund F. Bliven, interview by author, tape recording, OHS, 14 May 1996, 15 April 1997; *CS,* 26 April 1968.
12. O'Meara, interview by author, tape recording, OHS, 2 July 1992; Schoenberg, *Defender,* 286-287, 322.
13. Schaefers, interview by author, tape recording, OHS, 30 January 1990; Thielen, interview, 26 May 1989.
14. Murray, interview, 22 September 1992; Robinson, interview, 5 November 1992; *Oregonian,* 3 January 1972, 28 July 1973.

15. Larkin, interview by author, tape recording, 14 February 1989; E. Leo Smith, interview by author, tape recording, OHS, 22 November 1990; Schoenberg, *History*, 679; Murray, interview, 29 September 1992; *CS* 28, June 1968.

16. Harrington, interview, 3 August 1988; Park, interview, 4 March 1993; Rev. John Larkin, interview, 14 February 1989; Harrington, interview, 3 August 1988; *Oregonian*, 28 June 1967, 28 July 1973; Murray, interview, 22 September 1992; O'Meara, interview, 2 July 1992; Robinson, interview, 5 November 1992; In 1972 Dwyer applied for, and received, a grant from the Raskob Foundation for Catholic Activities, Inc. for a Consulting Service for Clergy and Religious, in Organizations: Raskob Foundation for Catholic Activities file, AAPO. Dwyer's interest in mental health went beyond his priests to St. Mary's Home for Boys, which he agreed to change to a treatment center for troubled boys with professional staff, Wilfred P. Schoenberg, S.J., *A Test of Time: A History of St. Mary's Home, 1889-1989* (Beaverton, Ore.: St. Mary's Home for Boys, 1989), 136, 140.

17. Jay P. Dolan, *The American Catholic Experience: A History from Colonial Times to the Present* (Garden City, N.Y.: Doubleday, 1985) 437; *Oregonian*, 28 July 1973; Park, interview by author, tape recording, OHS, 11 March 1993; Dwyer in an interview conceded he had had losses due to resignations and deaths "often untimely" of 23 priests, and pointed out, correctly, that the drop was more marked among religious clergy partly because of the closing of some of their institutions, *CS*, 5 April 1974; Griffin, interview by Sister Pauline Rose Waibel, S.S.M.O., tape recording, OHS, 18 January 1993.

18. *Oregonian*, 28 July 1973.

19. *CS*, 3 May 1962; A Statement of Reverend Jerome M. Schmitz Report to a New Board Catholic Charities at the Benson Hotel, June 20,1966, CCAPO; Margaret Godfrey, Report to the Board of Directors of Catholic Charities, ca. 1969, CCAPO.

20. Godfrey, Report to Catholic Charities, CCAPO; Park, interview, 4 November 1993.

21. Godfrey, Report to Catholic Charities, CCAPO; Erasmo Gamboa, *Mexican Labor and World War II: Braceros in the Pacific Northwest, 1942-1947* (Austin: University of Texas Press, 1990), 5-6; J. Dolan, *American Catholic Experience*, 371-372.

22. Erasmo Gamboa, "Oregon's Hispanic Heritage," *Oregon Humanities* (summer 1992): 6-7.

23. Jeffrey M. Burns, "Building the Best: A History of Catholic Parish Life in the Pacific States," in *The American Catholic Parish: A History from 1850 to the Present*, ed. Jay P. Dolan (Mahwah, N.J.: Paulist Press, 1987), 2:90-91; Larkin, interview by author, tape recording, OHS, 17 January 1989; Edward D. Howard, 12 January 1967 to Jose Gabriel Anaya y Diez de Bontilla, in Church: Groups, Confraternity of Christian Doctrine file, AAPO; Harrington, interview by author, tape recording, OHS, 28 July 1988; *St. Mary's Parish, Mount Angel, Oregon, 1880-1980* (Salem: Panther Printing Co., 1979), 114-115; Schoenberg, *History*, 695-696: Wilfred P. Schoenberg, S.J., *Paths to the Northwest: A Jesuit History of the Oregon Province* (Chicago: Loyola University Press, 1982), 527; *CS, 15* August 1957 and 7 November 1980. The latter article describes them as a people who have always considered themselves Catholic, but "are fragile in their faith," because they do not feel the need to go to Mass, partly because of the suppression of the Church in Mexico and partly because of the shabby treatment they often received from Catholics here. In Portland, ministry to the few Mexican families who had settled there began around 1962 when the Servite Sisters from Juarez, Mexico, came to serve at the Sanctuary of Our Sorrowful Mother (the Grotto).

24. Park, interview, 4 March 1993.

25. J. Dolan, *American Catholic Experience*, 371; Murray, interview by author, tape recording. OHS, 6 October 1992; Griffin, interview, 18 January 1993; Harrington, interview, 3 August 1988.

26. *CS*, 25 September 1972, letter to the editor; Keith D. Barger, "Hearing the Cry of the Poor: The Catholic Worker Communities in Oregon and Washington" (senior thesis, University of Portland, 1992), 19-33.

27. *CS*, 18 October 1917, notes that Rev. Edwin V. O'Hara, pastor of the Cathedral parish had consulted with the Parish Advisory Committee on the question of investing in Liberty Bonds,

suggesting that the idea of lay participation, at least in Oregon, was not that novel; *CS,* 22 April 1983; Lenore Warner and Mary Payne, *Saint Anthony's Parish, 1910-1985, Tigard* (Lake Oswego, Ore.: Lake Oswego Printing Co., 1985), n.p.; Thielen, interview by author, 19 May 1989, Tape #8, Side #1; McQuarry, interview, 29 June 1994; Joseph A. Schiwek Jr., *Called to be Church: A Brief History of St. Charles Borromeo Parish* (Portland: n.p., 1989), 35.

28. J. Dolan, *American Catholic Experience,* 431-432; Steiss, *Ecclesiastes,* 273-275; *CS,* 11 June 1976, 10 September 1992.

29. Paul Mouawad, *My Being Proclaims the Greatness of the Lord* (Portland: St. Sharbel Church, 1977), n.p.; *CS,* 12 November 1993.

30. *Oregonian,* 1 January 1967, Northwest Section, 7 February 1967; Murray, interview, 22 September 1992.

31. Griffin, interview by Sister Pauline Rose Waibel, S.S.M.O., tape recording, OHS, 18 June 1993; *Oregonian,* 23 January 1974; Robinson, interview, 5 November 1992; Wilfred P. Schoenberg, S.J., *These Valiant Women: History of the Sisters of St. Mary of Oregon, 1886-1986* (Beaverton, Ore.:, Sisters of St. Mary of Oregon, 1986), 270-272, 291; *CS,* 2 March 1973; "Annals of Sisters of the Holy Names, 1929-1930: The Foundation of Marylhurst College," transcribed by Denise Meyer and Barbara Whittlesey-Hayes, 1979, SHNPA.

32. *The Beacon* [University of Portland student newspaper], 12 May 1967; James T. Covert, *A Point of Pride: The University of Portland Story* (Portland: University of Portland Press, 1976), 226-229.

33. *Oregonian,* 7 March 1969, 24 April 1969, 9 October 1969, 13 August 1970, 11 February 1973, 11 April 1973, 16 November 1973, Northwest Report, 12 October 1981, 21 April 1983; *Oregon Journal,* 21 December 1972.

34. Griffin, interview, 18 June 1993.

35. Bliven, interview by author, tape recording, OHS, 4 June 1996.

36. Martin Pollard, O.S.B. and Hugh Feiss, O.S.B., *Mount of Communion: Mount Angel Abbey, 1882-1982,* rev. ed. (St. Benedict, Ore.: Mount Angel Abbey, 1985) 57, 74; *Oregonian,* 23 January 1974, 23:1-7; Schoenberg, *History,* 703.

37. Thielen, interview, 19 May 1989; Schoenberg, *These Valiant Women,* 284, 298-299, 315; *CS,* 24 May 1968, 25 July 1969, 15 December 1991; Burns, "Building the Best," 2: 107; Schoenberg, *History,* 702; *Our Lady of Perpetual Help Parish* (Albany, Ore.: n.p., 1972), n.p.

38. *Oregonian,* 28 June 1967; Murray, interview, 22 September 1992; O'Meara, interview, 18 May 1992; Robinson, interview, 5 November 1992; Harrington, interview, 3 August 1988; Park, interview by author, tape recording, OHS, 9 March 1993; *CS,* 14 November 1969; *Oregon Journal,* 31 July 1970. Dwyer also could inspire personal loyalty. A layman, Baxter Murray, and a priest, Rev. William Price, moved from Reno to Portland to be with him.

39. *Oregonian* and *Journal,* 22, 23, 25, 26, 27, 29 September 1972; Harrington, interview, 3 August 1988; Park, interview, 4 March 1993; Thielen, interview, 26 May 1989; Laidlaw, *Catholic Church in Oregon,* 40; Schoenberg, *History,* 710-711; Reese, *Archbishop,* 99.

40. Park, interview, 11 March 1993; Harrington, interview, 3 August 1988; Thielen, interview, 26 May 1989.

41. Smith, interview, 22 November 1990; McQuarry, interview, 13 July 1994; Robert J. Dwyer to Tom McCall, Portland, 20 June 1971, in "Church: Groups, Catholic Rural Life," AAPO; Robert J. Dwyer to Thomas R. Mahoney, Anthony Ituri, and E. D. Potts (identical letters), 3 January 1968, in Church: Groups, Legion of Decency file, AAPO; Minutes of the Archdiocesan Coordinating Team, 14 May 1993, 9 July 1973, 25 February 1974, and by-laws, final draft, 9 July 1973, in Church: Groups, Archdiocesan Coordinating Team file, AAPO.

42. Thielen, interview, 26 May 1989; Larkin, interview, 14 February 1989; Laidlaw, *Catholic Church in Oregon,* 39-40.

43. *Oregonian,* 26 March 1977, notes, with quotations from the letter, that Rev. Milan Mikulich, O.F.M., a priest of the Archdiocese of Portland in Oregon, claims that Dwyer made two unsuccessful attempts to deliver it personally to the Pope, that the archbishop then gave it to him

before his death, and that he had it published in *Orthodoxy of the Catholic Doctrine*, "a periodical review," hoping that the Pope would read it. It also was published in the *Wanderer*, 7 April 1977.

44. *Oregonian*, 2 April 1976; *CS*, 2 April 1976; Letter to William J. Levada from Tomi Tamagushi, Dwyer's adopted sister, 3 May 1988, Robert Dwyer Papers, AAPO.

45. O'Meara, interview, 18 May 1992, O'Meara also characterized Dwyer as "more of a Pius XII man than a John XXIII man"; Thielen, interview, 26 May 1989.

Chapter 9

1. Wilfred P. Schoenberg, S.J., *A History of the Catholic Church in the Pacific Northwest, 1743-1983* (Washington, D.C.: Pastoral Press, 1987), 691-692, 682-685; John R. Laidlaw, *The Catholic Church in Oregon and the Work of its Archbishops* (Smithtown, N.Y.: Exposition Press, 1980), 44; *Oregon Journal*, 22 January 1974; Archbishop Cornelius M. Power, interview by author, tape recording, OHS 12 October 1993.

2. Schoenberg, *History*, 692; Wilfred P. Schoenberg, S.J., *A Test of Time: A History of St. Mary's Home for Boys, 1889-1989* (Beaverton, Ore.: St. Mary's Home for Boys, 1989), 159; Sister Marian Dolores Robinson, S.N.J.M., interview by author, tape recording, OHS, 19 November 1992; Edward F. O'Meara, interview by author, tape recording, OHS, 18 May 1992; Rev. Francis Schaefers, interview by author, tape recording, OHS, 30 January 1990; Mrs. Julia Baker, interview by author, tape recording, OHS, 25 February 1998; *Oregonian*, 28 January 1974; *Oregon Journal*, 25 January 1974, Section 2; Archbishop Power's official motto, appropriately, was *Servite Domino in Laetitia* (Serve the Lord in Joy).

3. Laidlaw, *Catholic Church in Oregon*, 44; *Oregonian*, 9 December 1978; *CS* 1 December 1978 (includes picture of his residence), 26 May 1989; Power, interview by author, tape recording, OHS, 2 November 1993; Rev. Martin H. Thielen, interview by author, tape recording, OHS, 26 May 1989; Rev. Morton B. Park, interview by author, tape recording, OHS, 11 March 1993; Wilfred P. Schoenberg, S.J., *These Valiant Women: History of the Sisters of St. Mary of Oregon, 1886-1986* (Beaverton, Ore.: Sisters of St. Mary of Oregon, 1986), 314; Rev. Emmet Harrington, interview by author, tape recording, OHS, 23 August 1988.

4. *Official Catholic Directory* (New Providence, N.J.: P. J. Kenedy & Sons, 1967, 1975). The figures used are those submitted during Howard's last year in office and Power's first one because during Dwyer's term about 100 fewer active religious priests are listed, suggesting he may not have included some who were primarily teachers; Schoenberg, *History*, 692, 712-713; Wilfred P. Schoenberg, S.J., *Paths to the Northwest: A Jesuit History of the Oregon Province* (Chicago: Loyola University Press, 1982), 551; Harrington, interview, 23 August 1988; Power concluded that priests and sisters were more liberal than the laity, because they were more likely to be better educated in liturgical matters than the laity. Power, interview, 2 November 1993.

5. Thomas J. Reese, S.J., *Archbishop: Inside the Power Structure of the American Catholic Church* (San Franscisco: Harper & Row, 1989), 88, 96, 103; *Oregon Journal*, 25 January 1974, in an interview with a reporter just before his installation as archbishop, commenting on the turmoil in the Church and society, Power was reminded of a man he knew who worked in the freight yards and told him that the secret of staying on top of the freight cars as they rolled, stopped, and bumped, was to keep one's knees loose so that the jolting was absorbed in the legs, not conveyed to the rest of the body. "I think that's the way we have to walk these days," said Power.

6. Robert McQuarry, interview by author, tape recording, OHS, 13 July 1994.

7. Park, interview by author, tape recording, OHS, 11 November 1993; Power, interview by author, tape recording, OHS, 26 October 1993.

8. Harrington, interview, 23 August 1988; Cornelius Power "Memorandum to Priests, Religious and Heads of Lay Organizations. October 13, 1975," Cornelius Power Papers, AAPO;

Wilfred P. Schoenberg, S.J., *Defender of the Faith: The History of the* Catholic Sentinel, *1870-1990* (Portland: Oregon Catholic Press, 1993), 346; The extent to which Archbishop Power involved Oregon Catholics in the process appears, from available records and an oblique comment by Power in his "Memorandum," to have been unusual; *CS,* 2 March 1978, 10 March 1978: *Oregon Journal,* 3 March 1978; Power, interview, 26 October 1993; Thielen, interview, 26 May 1989.

9. *CS,* 2 March 1979; *Oregon Catholic Directory,* 1980 and 1981; McQuarry, interview, 13 July 1994, Tape #4, Side #1.

10. *Oregon Catholic Directory* (Portland: Oregon Catholic Press, 1955, 1974-1995), not all the agencies added or deleted were noted—just those that seem to indicate special interest or trends, and some of them had been in existence for various amounts of time before being listed.

11. Power, interviews, 26 October 1993, 2 November 1993; McQuarry, interview by author, tape recording, OHS, 6 July 1994; Rev. Wilfred P. Schoenberg, S.J., telephone conversation with author, 3 May 1993.

12. Thielen, interview, 26 May 1989; Power, interview, 2 November 1993; *CS,* 25 October 1991, 13 November 1987; Reese, *Archbishop,* 159, 165-6, 174, 170-171.

13. Jean O'Connell, et al., eds., *The Spirit Within: The Word—The Truth: St. Clare Newsletter in Celebration of 70 Years of Franciscan Heritage at St. Clare Parish, 1913-1992* (Portland: St. Clare Catholic Church, 1992), 8, 39.

14. Winifred Dalgity and Philippa Mardesich, *St. Mary Star of the Sea Parish, Astoria, Oregon, 1874-1974* (Astoria, Ore.: Astoria Publishing Co., 1974), n.p.; Joseph A. Schiwek Jr., conversation with author, 16 December 1993; *CS,* 1 July 1983, 4 June, 11 June, 27 August 1993; Jim Magmer, ed., *Celebration: St. Clare's Achievement from Mission to Post Vatican II Community, 1913-1988* (Wilsonville, Ore.: C & M Publications, 1988), 53; Martha Bradtl Elliott and Regina Etzel, *Saint Patrick's, 1884-1984: One Hundred Years of Progress* (Canby, Ore.: n.p., 1984), 18-20; Sister Caroline Gimpl, S.N.J.M., et al., *St. Mary's Parish Centennial* (Eugene, Ore.: Express Press Printing and Graphics, 1987), 36-37.

15. Jay P. Dolan, "The American Catholic Parish: A Historical Perspective, 1820-1980," in *The Parish in Transition: Proceedings of a Conference on the American Catholic Parish, May, 1985,* ed. David Byers (Washington, D.C.: United States Catholic Conference, 1986), 40; Harrington, interview by author, tape recording, OHS, 13 September 1988; *CS,* 5 August 1977, (pastoral letter), 5 June 1981; Park, interview, 11 March 1993.

16. J. Dolan, "The American Catholic Parish," 40; Harrington, interview, 13 September 1988; *CS,* 3 May 1985, 1 March 1991, 18 October 1991.

17. Magmer, *Celebration,* 8, 56; Harrington, interview, 13 September 1988; *CS,* 21 April 1983; Lawrence Saalfeld, et al., *History of St. Philip Benizi,* (Redlands, Ore.: n.p., 1991); Cathedral of the Immaculate Conception, Portland, Ore., *Sunday Bulletin,* 17 May 1992; St. Mary's parish in Eugene had had parish advisors since the arrival of Rev. Emil Kies as pastor in 1969, Gimpl, et al., *St. Mary's Parish,* 29; Power, interview, 2 November 1993.

18. Reese, *Archbishop,* 144; Dean Hoge, *Future of Catholic Leadership: Responses to the Priest Shortage* (New York: Sheed & Ward, 1987), 97-99; Burns, "Building the Best: A History of Catholic Parish Life in the Pacific States," in *The American Catholic Parish: A History from 1850 to the Present,* ed. Jay P. Dolan (Mahwah, N.Y.: Paulist Press, 1987), 118-119; *CS,* 26 November 1983, 30 May 1986, 2 July 1993; Saalfeld, et al., *History of St. Philip Benizi,* 27; Harrington, interview, 23 August 1988; Thielen, interview by author, tape recording, OHS, 19 May 1989; Park, interview, 11 March 1993; *Commemoration Booklet of the Installation of His Excellency Most Reverent William J. Levada, S.T.D, Eighth Archbishop of Portland in Oregon* (Portland: Archdiocese of Portland in Oregon, 1986), William Levada Papers, AAPO; Reese, *Archbishop,* 228, 236-239; Park, interview, OHS, 11 March 1993, some priests protested, at least once during Dwyer's administration, what they felt was treatment without due regard for their dignity when the Personnel Board sent out letters informing them of their new assignments but did not contact them personally; Rev. Bertram Griffin, interview by Sister Pauline Rose Waibel, S.S.M.O., tape recording, OHS, 20 November 1992, remembers not being

consulted about his first assignments after ordination in 1957, and being sent to Rome and told to study canon law; Robinson, interview by author, tape recording, OHS, 11 November 1992, sisters also felt a loss of dignity due to increased lay participation in education, a field in which they had predominated. They found themselves more equated with lay teachers, and as circumstances forced them to negotiate for salaries and such benefits as health care, they had a sense of decreased importance, which may have been a possible factor in some leaving religious communities.

19. Education, from 1980 on file, AAPO; *CS,* 30 August 1991.

20. Thielen, interview by author, tape recording, OHS, 14 May 1989; Joseph A. Schiwek Jr., *Called to be Church: A Brief History of St. Charles Borromeo Parish* (Portland: n.p., 1989), 30; *CS,* 22 March, 2 May, 1985, 29 August 1986, 13 March, 17 April, 29 May 1987; Gimpl, et al., *St. Mary's Parish,* 29.

21. *CS,* 5 October 1979, 15 December 1991; *The Mirror* [Marylhurst College] (fall 1984).

22. Park, interview by author, 4 March 1993; Julie Sly, "America's Vietnamese: Preserving their Heritage in a New Land," *St. Anthony's Messenger* 29 (February 1985): 36; *CS,* 12 July 1991, 9 October 1992, 12 July 1996.

23. Elliott and Etzel, *Saint Patrick's,* 16, 19; Warner and Payne, *Saint Anthony's Parish; St. Mary's Parish, Mount Angel, Oregon, 1880-1980* (Salem: Panther Printing Co., 1979), 112-113; Norma Haggerty, *Yesterday—125 Years at St. Joseph's, A Historical Perspective, 1864-1989* (Salem: n.p., n.d.); *CS,* 22 August 1992; Park, interview, 11 March 1993; *CS,* 12 July 1991; Julie Sly, "America's Vietnamese," 36.

24. J. Dolan, "The American Catholic Parish," 90-91.

25. *CS,* 9 July 1976, 20, 27 August, 14 September 1979.

26. *CS,* 4 August 1972, 3 December 1976, 11 July, 9 February 1990; Baker, interview by author, tape recording, OHS, 20 March 1998; Brother Donald Stabrowski, C.S.C., "St. Vincent de Paul Parish: A Half Century of Urban Ministry, Part II," *OCHSN* 4 (summer 1992): 10-11: Ed Langlois, "'Everyone is another Christ,'" *Portland* 12 (spring 1993): 43; At the end of 1994, Blanchet House—with the help of the Social Action Committee of St. James Parish, McMinnville—was in the process of reactivating its farm as a homeless shelter, *CS,* 23 December 1994.

27. Schoenberg, *Defender,* 339, 360-362, 364, 366, 369; Power, interview, 2 November 1993; O'Meara, interview, 2 July 1992.

28. O'Meara, interview, 2 July 1992; *Oregonian,* 24 December 1992; *CS,* 7 January 1983.

29. *Oregonian,* 30 August 1983, 31 August 1983; Smith, interview by author, tape recording, OHS, 22 November 1990; Robert McQuarry, interview, 13 July 1994; Thielen, interview, 26 May 1989; Bliven, interview by author, tape recording, OHS, 15 April 1997; Rev. Alan J. Kennedy, interview by author, tape recording, OHS, 17 July 1997; Baxter Murray, interview by author, tape recording, OHS, 6 October 1992; Park, interview, 11 March 1993; Schoenberg, *Defender,* 368; *CS,* 2 September, 19 August 1983.

30. F. Leo Smith, interview, 22 November 1990; *CS,* 16 March, 12 October 1984, 5 September 1986; Power, interview, 2 November 1993; William S. Stone, *The Cross in the Middle of Nowhere: A History of the Catholic Church in Eastern Oregon* (Bend, Ore.: W.S. Stone, 1993), 290-291.

31. Power, interview, 2 November 1993; *CS,* 6 March 1992; O'Connell, et al., *The Spirit Within the Word,* 8; Harrington, interview, 13 September 1988; Gimpl, et al., *St. Mary's Parish,* 36-37.

32. *CS,* 1 August 1986.

33. *CS,* 4 July, 22 August 1986, 26 May 1989; Power, interview by author, tape recording, OHS, 12 November 1993.

Bibliography

Abbreviations

CCRPN	*Catholic Church Records of the Pacific Northwest*
CS	*Catholic Sentinel*
OCHSN	*Oregon Catholic Historical Society Newsletter*
OHQ	*Oregon Historical Quarterly*
OHS	Oregon Historical Society
RACHS	*Records of the American Catholic Historical Society*

Manuscripts and Archival Material

ARCHIVES, ARCHDIOCESE OF PORTLAND IN OREGON, PORTLAND (AAPO)
   Archbishops' Papers: Francis N. Blanchet Papers; Charles Seghers Papers; William Gross Papers; Alexander Christie Papers; Edward Howard Papers; Robert Dwyer Papers; Cornelius Power Papers; William Levada Papers.
   Catholic Daughters of the Americas file.
   Church: Groups: Archdiocesan Coordinating Team; Catholic Charities Camp Howard; Catholic Rural Life; Confraternity of Christian Doctrine; Knights of Columbus; Legion of Decency; Nocturnal Adoration Society.
   Knights of Columbus, Portland, Oregon file.
   Miscellaneous Files: Education from 1980 on; Missions of the archdiocese: Peru; World War II: List of priests who served in armed forces.
   Organizations: Oregon Historical Society; Raskob Foundation for Catholic Activities.
   Parish Files: St. Catherine Parish.
   Priests' files: Lauerman, Lucian; Mosley, James Edward.
ARCHIVES, BUREAU OF CATHOLIC INDIAN MISSIONS, WASHINGTON, D.C. (BCIM)
   Correspondence, Grand Ronde File; Correspondence, Umatilla File.
ARCHIVES, MOUNT ANGEL ABBEY LIBRARY, ST. BENEDICT, OREGON (AMAA)
   Peter De Roo Papers.
NATIONAL ARCHIVES, WASHINGTON, D.C. (NA)
   RG48 Interior Dept. Appointment Papers. (Microfilm) Roll 9, Box 3; RG75 Bureau of Indian Affairs. Letters Received, Oregon Superintendency. (Microfilm) M2, Roll 22; RG75 Bureau of Indian Affairs. Letters Received.
SISTERS OF THE HOLY NAMES PROVINCIAL ARCHIVES, MARYLHURST, OREGON (SHNPA)
   Chartrand, Yvette, S.N.J.M., tr. J.Y. Peugnet, S.N.J.M. "Pages of History, Congregation of the Sisters of the Holy Names of Jesus and Mary, 1867-1967"; July, 1984; "Marylhurst 1929…History and Jubilee"; Meyer, Denise and Barbara Whittlesey-Hayes. "Annals of the Sisters of the Holy Names, 1929-1930: The Foundation of Marylhurst College," Unpublished paper, 1979.
THESES AND PAPERS
   Articles of Incorporation of Catholic Charities, Inc.; Catholic Charities History file; Lauerman, Lucien. Report, 1933; Moffenbeier, Valentine. Report, 1950; Catholic Services for Children History file; Schmitz, Jerome M. Statement to new Board of Catholic Charities, June 20, 1966; Godfrey, Margaret. Report to the Board of Directors of Catholic Charities, 1969;

Policy file: Schmitz, Jerome M. Outline of Reorganization Plan for Catholic Charities, March 4, 1952.
Catholic Charities, Inc. files (CCAPO)
McNichols, Mary Eucharista, S.H.C.J., "The History of Catholic Education in Oregon, 1843-1954." Paper.

Books and Pamphlets

Abbott, Maude E. *History of Medicine in the Province of Quebec.* Ottawa: Magill University Press, 1931.
ACWR News (Archivists for Congregations of Women Religious) 2 (August 1992): 2.
Ahlstrom, Sydney E. *A Religious History of the American People.* New Haven, Conn.: Yale University Press, 1973.
Annen, Sister M. Ida, O.S.B. "Mt. Angel College," *Marion County History* 4 (1958): 47-49.
Backus, Sister Pia, O.P. *Her Days Unfolded: Mother Pia Backus, of the Dominican Sisters of Mission San Jose.* Translated and edited by Mother Bernardine Michael, O.P. St. Benedict, Ore., Benedictine Press, 1952.
Bannon, Tom, Kathryn Cowan and Kathleen Phillips. *One Hundred Years as a Parish: Holy Trinity Catholic Church, Bandon, Oregon, including St. John's Mission, Port Orford, Oregon.* Bandon, Ore.: Holy Trinity Catholic Church, 1983.
Barger, Keith D. "Hearing the Cry of the Poor: The Catholic Worker Communities in Oregon and Washington, 1940 to the present." Senior thesis, University of Portland, 1992.
Barker, Burt B. *The McLoughlin Empire and Its Rulers.* Glendale, Cal.: Arthur H. Clarke, 1959.
Barnes, James W. "The Conversion of Dr. John McLoughlin." Master's thesis, Mount Angel Seminary, 1979.
Barry, Colman J., O.S.B. *Worship and Work: St. John's Abbey and University, 1856-1956.* Collegeville, Minn.: St. John's Abbey, 1956.
Barry, J. N. "The Champoeg Meeting of March 4, 1844." *OHQ* 38 (1937): 425-32.
Beaver, Herbert. *Reports and Letters.* Edited by Thomas E. Jessett. Portland: Champoeg Press, 1959.
Bernards, Theodore. *St. John's Parish, Oregon City, 1844-1957.* N.p.: n.p., 1957.
Berrigan, Sister Anne, R.G.S. "The Work of the Sisters of the Good Shepherd in Oregon." Master's thesis, University of Portland, 1953.
Billington, Ray. *Westward Expansion: A History of the American Frontier.* 3d ed. New York: Macmillan, 1967.
Black, Dennis Joseph. *Star of the Sea Church, Brookings Oregon, 1923-50-1973.* Brookings, Ore.: n.p., 1973.
Blanchet, Augustine M. A. *Journal of a Catholic Bishop on the Oregon Trail.* Edited by Edward J. Kowrach. Fairfield, Wash.: Ye Galleon Press, 1978.
Blanchet, Francis N. *Historical Sketches of the Catholic Church in Oregon.* Edited by Edward J. Kowrach. Fairfield, Wash.: Ye Galleon Press, 1983.
Blanchet, Francis Xavier. *Ten Years on the Pacific Coast.* Fairfield, Wash.: Ye Galleon Press, 1982.
Bolduc, J. B. Z. *Mission of the Columbia.* Edited and translated by Edward J. Kowrach. Fairfield, Wash.: Ye Galleon Press, 1979.
Bradley, Cyprian, O.S.B. and Edward Kelly. *History of the Diocese of Boise, 1863-1952.* Boise: Caxton, 1953.
Brady, Michael J. "Most Reverend William Hickley Gross, C.Ss.R., D.D., Third Archbishop of Oregon City, 1885-1898." Paper, Mt. St. Alphonsus Seminary, 1981.
Brandt, Patricia. "Archbishop Blanchet's Memoire." *OCHSN* 10 (summer 1998): 7-8.
_____. "The Belgian Bulge: The Oregon Priesthood from 1860-1900." *OCHSN* 4 (summer 1992): 4.
_____. "Benefactors Were Generous on the Sly." *CS,* 14 June 1996, 7.
_____. "Bishop's House Proves Older Than Believed." *CS,* 13 September 1996, 6.
_____. "The Mystery of the Sisters of Mercy at Cedar Mill." *OCHSN* 11 (summer 1999): 8, 12.
_____. "Nuns' Journey to Oregon in 1844 No Picnic. *CS* 24 November 1995, 7.
_____. "The Viatorian Mission in Oregon." *OCHSN* 3 (spring 1991): 7.
Brosnan, Cornelius. *Jason Lee, Prophet of the New Oregon.* New York: Macmillan, 1932.

Brouillet, John B. A. *Authentic Account of the Murder of Dr. Whitman by the Cayuse Indians in Oregon in 1847.* In *Early Catholic Missions in Old Oregon,* edited by C. R. Bagley. Vol. 1 Seattle: Lowman & Hanford, 1932.

Brown, George T. "Illegitimate Child Prompts Funds for Education." *CS,* 15 March 1996, 6.

____. *St. Paul on the Willamette: A Man—His Church—Its Treasure.* St. Paul, Ore.: George T. Brown, 1992.

Burns, Jeffrey M. "Building the Best: A History of Catholic Parish Life in the Pacific States." In *The American Catholic Parish: A History from 1850 to the Present,* edited by Jay P. Dolan. Vol. 2. Mahwah, N.Y.: Paulist Press, 1987.

Cathedral of the Immaculate Conception, Portland, Ore. *Sunday Bulletin,* 17 May 1992.

CCRPN: Grand Ronde Register I (1860-1885); Grand Ronde Register II (1886-1898); St. Michael the Archangel Parish, Grand Ronde Reservation, Oregon; St. Patrick's Parish, Muddy Valley, Oregon. Edited and annotated by Harriet D. Munnick and Stephen Dow Beckham. Portland: Binford & Mort, 1987.

CCPRN: Oregon City Register (1842-1890); Salem Register (1864-1885); Jacksonville Register (1854-1885). Compiled by Harriet D. Munnick. Portland: Binford & Mort, 1984.

CCPRN: Roseburg Register and Missions (1853-1911); Portland Register (1852-1871). Compiled by Harriet D. Munnick. Portland: Binford & Mort, 1986.

CCPRN: St. Louis Register, Volume I (1845-1868; St. Louis Register, Volume II (1869-1900); Gervais Register (1875-1893); Brooks Register (1893-1909). Compiled by Harriet D. Munnick. Portland: Binford & Mort, 1982.

CCRPN: St. Paul, Oregon, 1839-1898, Volumes I, II and III. Compiled by Harriet D. Munnick in collaboration with Mikell D. Warner. Portland: Binford & Mort, 1979.

CCRPN: Vancouver, Volumes I and II and Stellamaris Mission. Translated by Mikell D. Warner, annotated by Harriet D. Munnick. St. Paul, Oregon: French Prairie Press, 1972.

Catta, Etienne and Tony Catta. *Basil Anthony Mary Moreau.* Translated by Edward L. Heston, C.S.C. Vol. 1. Milwaukee: Bruce, 1955.

Cawley, Martin, O.C.S.O. *Father Crockett of Grand Ronde.* Lafayette, Ore.: Guadalupe Translations, 1985.

____. *Saint James Parish, McMinnville, Oregon.* Portland: Glass, Dahlstrom Printing, 1977.

The Centenary, 100 Years of the Catholic Church in the Oregon Country. Portland: CS, 1939.

Centennial History, 1885-1985; Our Lady of Lourdes, Jordan, Oregon. Jordan, Ore.: North Santiam Newspapers, 1985.

Chalmers, David M. *Hooded Americans: the First Century of the Ku Klux Klan, 1865-1965.* Garden City, N.Y.: Doubleday, 1965.

Clark, Robert C. "How British and American Subjects Unite in a Common Government for Oregon Territory in 1844." *Quarterly of the OHS* 13 (1912): 140-159.

Costello, Gerald M. *Mission to Latin America: The Successes and Failures of a Twentieth Century Crusade.* Maryknoll, N.Y.: Orbis Books, 1979.

Covert, James T. *A Point of Pride; The University of Portland Story.* Portland: University of Portland Press, 1976.

Curley, Michael J., C.Ss.R. *The Provincial Story: A History of the Baltimore Province of the Congregation of the Most Holy Redeemer.* New York: Redemptorist Fathers, 1963.

Currier, Charles W. "History of the Church of Our Lady of Perpetual Succor in Boston." *RACHS* 2 (1886-88): 206-224.

Dalgity, Winifred and Philippa Mardesich. *St. Mary Star of the Sea Parish, Astoria, Oregon, 1874-1974.* Astoria, Ore.: Astoria Printing Co., 1974.

Dana, Marshall N. *Newspaper Story: Fifty Years of the* Oregon Journal, *1902-1952.* Portland: Binford & Mort, 1951.

De Baets, Maurice. *The Apostle of Alaska.* Translated by Sister Mary Mildred, S.S.A. Paterson, N.J.: St. Anthony Guild Press, 1943.

Dodds, Gordon B. *Oregon: A Bicentennial History.* New York: W. W. Norton, 1977.

Dolan, Jay P. *The American Catholic Experience: A History from Colonial Times to the Present.* Garden City, N.Y.: Doubleday, 1985.

____. "The American Catholic Parish: A Historical Perspective, 1820-1980." In *The Parish in Transition: Proceedings of a Conference on the American Catholic Parish, May 1985,* edited by David Byers. Washington, D.C.: United States Catholic Conference, 1986.

Dolan, Timothy M. *Some Seed Fell on Good Ground; The Life of Edwin V. O'Hara.* Washington, D.C.: Catholic University Press, 1992.

Duniway, David C. and Neil R. Riggs, eds. "The Oregon Archives, 1841-1843." *OHQ* 60 (1959): 211-80.

Egan, Maurice Francis and John B. Kennedy. *The Knights of Columbus in Peace and War.* 2 vols. New Haven, Conn.: Knights of Columbus, 1920.

Elliott, Martha B. and Regina Etzel. *Saint Patrick's, 1884-1984: One Hundred Years of Progress.* Canby, Ore.: n.p., 1984.

Ellis, John Tracy. *American Catholicism.* 2nd Edition. Chicago: University of Chicago Press, 1969.

____. *The Life of James Cardinal Gibbons, Archbishop of Baltimore, 1834-1921.* 2 vols. Milwaukie: Bruce, 1952.

Engelhardt, Zephyrin. *The Missions and Missionaries of California.* Vol. 4. San Francisco: James H. Barry, 1912.

Freeman, Olga. S. *A Guide to Early Oregon Churches.* Eugene, Ore.: Freeman, 1976.

Freidel, Frank. *America in the Twentieth Century.* 4th Edition. New York: Alfred A. Knopf, 1976.

Gamboa, Erasmo. *Mexican Labor and World War II: Braceros in the Pacific Northwest, 1942-1947.* Austin: University of Texas Press, 1990.

____. "Oregon's Hispanic Heritage." *Oregon Humanities* (summer 1992): 6-7.

Garraghan, Gilbert J., S.J. *The Jesuits of the Middle United States.* Vol. 2. New York: America Press, 1938.

Gimpl, Sister Caroline, S.N.J.M., et al. *St. Mary's Parish Centennial.* Eugene, Ore.: Express Press Printing & Graphics, 1987.

Gleanings of Fifty Years: The Sisters of the Holy Names of Jesus and Mary in the Northwest, 1859-1907. Portland: Glass & Prudhomme, 1909.

Granata, Fred A. *The Biography of a Parish: Saint Michael the Archangel Catholic Church, 1894-1994.* Portland: Dynagraphics, 1991.

Griffin, Bertram F. *The Provincial Councils of Portland.* Rome: Pontificia Universitatis Lateranensis, 1964.

Guilday, Peter. *A History of the Councils of Baltimore (1791-1884).* New York: Macmillan, 1932.

Haggerty, Norma. *Yesterday—125 Years at St. Joseph's: A Historical Perspective, 1864 to 1989.* Salem: n.p., n.d.

Hanley, Philip. M. *History of the Catholic Ladder.* Edited by Edward J. Kowrach. Fairfield, Wash.: Ye Galleon Press, 1993.

Harmon, Steven W. *The St. Josephs Blatt, 1896-1919.* New York: Peter Lang, 1989.

Hauer, Gloria M. "A Woman of Vision: Caroline Gleason, 1886-1962." Term paper, University of Portland, 1992.

Hennesey, James, S.J. *American Catholics: A History of the Roman Catholic Community in the United States.* New York: Oxford University Press, 1981.

____. *The First Council of the Vatican: The American Experience.* New York: Herder and Herder, 1963.

Henthorne, Sister Mary Evangela, B.V.M. *The Irish Catholic Colonial Association of the United States.* Champaign, Ill.: Twin Cities Printing Co., 1932.

Hoge, Dean. *Future of Catholic Leadership: Responses to the Priest Shortage.* New York: Sheed & Ward, 1987.

Holsinger, M. Paul. "The Oregon School Bill Controversy." *Pacific Historical Review* 37 (1968): 327-341.

Hope of the Harvest, by a Sister of the Holy Names. Portland: Press of Kilham Stationery & Printing Co., 1944.

Hussey, John A. *Champoeg: Place of Transition.* Portland: Oregon Historical Society, 1967.

In Harvest Fields By Sunset Shores: The Work of the Sisters of Notre Dame on the Pacific Coast. San Francisco: Filmartin Co., 1926.

Isetti, Ronald E., F.S.C. *Called to the Pacific: A History of the Christian Brothers of the San Francisco District 1868-1977.* Moraga, Cal.: St. Mary's College of California, 1979.

Jackson, Kenneth T. *The Ku Klux Klan in the City, 1915-1930.* New York: Oxford University Press, 1967.

Johansen, Dorothy and Charles M. Gates. *Empire of the Columbia.* 2nd ed. New York: Harper & Row, 1967.

Kantowicz, Edward R. *Corporation Sole: Cardinal Mundelein and Chicago Catholicism.* Notre Dame: University of Notre Dame Press, 1983.

Kauffman, Christopher J. *Faith and Fraternalism: The History of the Knights of Columbus, 1882-1982.* New York: Harper & Row, 1982.

Kehoe, Joseph, C.S.C. "Columbia Preparatory School, 1934-1955." Paper presented at the Holy Cross History Association Conference, Portland, Oregon, June, 1992.

_____. *Holy Cross in Oregon, 1902-1980.* Notre Dame, Ind.: Province Archives Center, 1982.

Laidlaw, John R. *The Catholic Church in Oregon and the Work of its Archbishops.* Smithtown, N.Y.: Exposition Press, 1980.

Lamirande, Émilien, O.M.I. "L'implantation de l'Église catholique en Colombie-Britannique, 1838-1848." *Revue de l'Université d'Ottawa* 28 (1948): 213-25, 323-63, 453-489.

Langlois, Ed. "'Everyone is Another Christ.'" *Portland* 12 (spring 1993): 38.

Laveille, Eugene, S.J. *The Life of Father De Smet.* New York: P. J. Kenedy & Sons, 1915.

Lee, Daniel and Joseph Frost. *Ten Years in Oregon.* Fairfield, Wash.: Ye Galleon Press, 1968.

Leflon, Jean. *Eugene de Mazenod, Bishop of Marseilles, Founder of the Oblates of Mary Immaculate.* Translated by Francis D. Flanagan, O.M.I. Vol. 4. New York: Fordham University Press, 1968.

Leipzig, Francis P. "Early-Day Portlander Left Legacy of Civic, Religious Activities." *CS,* 2 September 1977, 15.

_____. *Extension in Oregon.* St. Benedict, Ore.: Benedictine Press, 1956.

_____. "Father Fierens Noted Early Portland Pastor, Builder." *CS,* 19 August 1977, 12.

_____. "Financial Plight of Cathedral Faced Archbishop Gross in 1880s." *CS,* 8 December 1978, 14.

_____. "First Two Oregon-Born Priests Both Ordained in Same Year." *CS,* 11 May 1973, 22.

_____. *Longevity and Historical Sketches of the American Hierarchy, August 15, 1790-December 31, 1978.* Revised Edition. Portland: Catholic Sentinel, 1978.

_____. "The Origin of Murphy's Hole." *CS,* 28 March 1975, 18.

Lenzen, Connie. *St. Mary's Cemetery, Portland's Pioneer Catholic Cemetery.* Vancouver, Wash.: Clark County Genealogical Society, 1987.

Lichtenwaler, Francie. "Church History Shows Courage, Dedication." *CS,* 22 March 1996, 7.

Link, Arthur S. and William B. Catton. *American Epoch.* 2 vols. New York: Alfred A. Knopf, 1973.

Loewenberg, Robert J. *Equality on the Oregon Frontier.* Seattle: University of Washington Press, 1976.

Lucey, William, S.J. "Catholic Magazines, 1890-1893." *RACHS* 63 (1952): 197-223.

Lucia, Ellis. *Cornerstone: The Story of St. Vincent—Oregon's First Permanent Hospital, Its Formative Years.* Portland: St. Vincent Medical Foundation, 1975.

_____. *The Saga of Ben Holladay.* New York: Hastings House, 1959.

Lyons, Sister Letitia M., S.N.J.M. *Francis Norbert Blanchet and the Founding of the Oregon Missions, 1838-1848.* Washington, D.C.: Catholic University of America Press, 1940.

McColgan, Daniel T. *A Century of Charity: The First One Hundred Years of the Society of St. Vincent de Paul in the United States.* 2 vols. Milwaukee, Wis.: Bruce, 1951.

MacColl, E. Kimbark, with Harry H. Stein. *Merchants, Money & Power; the Establishment, 1843-1913.* Portland: Georgian Press, 1988.

McCrosson, Sister Mary of the Blessed Sacrament, F.C.S.P. *The Bell and the River.* Palo Alto: Pacific Books, 1957.

McDonald, Sister M. Grace. *With Lamps Burning.* St. Joseph, Minn.: St. Benedict's Priory Press, 1957.

McGloin, John B., S.J. *The Eloquent Indian.* Stanford, Cal.: Stanford University Press, 1949.

McKay, Harvey. *St. Paul, Oregon, 1830-1890.* Portland: Binford & Mort, 1980.

McKenna, S. G., C.Ss.R. "Our Lady's Bishop." *Central Blatt and Social Justice* 24 (May 1931-January 1932) in 9 installments.

McLagan, Elizabeth. *A Peculiar Paradise: a History of Blacks in Oregon, 1788-1940.* Portland: Georgian Press, 1980.

McLellan, Sara J., ed. "Chronicles of Sacred Heart Academy, Salem, 1863-1873," part I-II. *OHQ* 80 (winter 1979): 341-64; 81 (spring 1980): 75-95.

McLeod, William. *Souvenir, 1858-1958.* Medford, Ore.: n.p., 1958.

McLoughlin, John. *Letters of John McLoughlin from Fort Vancouver to the Governor and Committee.* Second Series, 1838-44. Edited by E. E. Rich. London: Hudson's Bay Record Society, 1943.

McNamee, Sister M. Dominca, S.N.D. *Willamette Interlude.* Palo Alto: Pacific Books, 1959.

Magmer, Jim, ed. *Celebration: St. Clare's Achievement from Mission to Post Vatican II Community, 1913-1988.* Wilsonville, Ore.: C & M Communications, 1988.

Malone, Edward F. *Conception; A History of the First Century of the Conception Colony, 1858-1958.* Omaha, Neb.: Interstate Printing Co., 1971.

Marschall, John P. "Diocesan and Religious Clergy: The History of a Relationship." In *The Catholic Priest in the United States: Historical Interpretations,* edited by John Tracy Ellis. Collegeville, Minn.: St. John's University Press, 1971.

The Memorial Volume: A History of the Third Plenary Council of Baltimore, November 9-December 7, 1884. Baltimore: Baltimore Publishing Co., 1885.

The Mirror [(Marylhurst College] (fall 1984).

Montgomery, Richard G. *The White-Headed Eagle: John McLoughlin, Builder of an Empire.* New York: Macmillan, 1934.

Mouawad, Paul. *My Being Proclaims the Greatness of the Lord.* Portland: St. Sharbel Church, 1977.

Neugebauer, Robert S. *Diamond Jubilee Visitation Church, Verboort, Oregon, 1875 to 1950.* Verboort, Ore.: n.p., 1950.

Nichols, M. Leona. *The Mantle of Elias: The Story of Fathers Blanchet and Demers in Early Oregon.* Portland: Binfords & Mort, 1941.

Notices and Voyages of the Famed Quebec Mission to the Pacific Northwest. Edited by Carl Landerholm. Portland: Oregon Historical Society, 1956.

Nuxoll, Sister M. Ildephonse, O.S.B. *Idaho Benedictine.* Cottonwood, Idaho: St. Gertrude's Convent, 1976.

O'Brien, Sister Kathleen, R.S.M. *Journeys: A Pre-Amalgamation History of the Sisters of Mercy, Omaha Province.* Omaha: n.p., 1987.

O'Connell, Jean et al., eds. *The Spirit Within the Word—The Truth: St. Clare Newsletter in Celebration of 70 Years of Franciscan Heritage at St. Clare Parish, 1913-1992.* Portland: St. Clare Catholic Church, 1992.

O'Connor, Dominic. *Brief History of the Diocese of Baker City.* 2 vols. in 1. St. Benedict, Ore.: Benedictine Press, 1966.

Odermatt, Adelhelm, O.S.B. "The Founding of Mt. Angel Abbey: a letter of 1883." Edited by Ambrose Zenner, O.S.B. *Marion County History* 4 (1958): 11-17.

O'Donnell, Miriam Margaret, S.N.J.M. "In Faith and Kindness: The Life of Most Reverend Alexander Christie, D. D., Fourth Archbishop of Portland in Oregon." Master's thesis, University of Portland, 1945.

Official Catholic Directory. New York: P. J. Kenedy & Sons, 1905, 1911, 1912, 1913, 1916, 1922-1929, 1967, 1975.

O'Hara, Edwin V. "Catholic Pioneers of the Oregon Country." *Catholic Historical Review* 3 (July 1917): 187-201.

_____. *Pioneer Catholic History of Oregon.* Centennial ed. Paterson, N.J.: St. Anthony Guild Press, 1939.

O'Loughlin, Thomas. "The Demand and Supply of Priests to the United States from All Hallows College, Ireland, Between 1842 and 1860." *RACHS* 94 (1983): 39-60.

O'Meara, Edward F. *Continue to Prosper: The History of the First Half Century of All Saints Parish, Portland.* Portland: n.p., n.d.

Oregon Catholic Directory. Portland: Oregon Catholic Press, 1945, 1950, 1955, 1960, 1970-1995.

Otis, D.S. *The Dawes Act and the Allotment of Indian Lands.* New ed. Norman: University of Oklahoma Press, 1973.

Our Lady of Perpetual Help Parish (St. Mary's). Albany, Ore.: n.p., 1972.

Palladino, Lawrence B., S.J. *Indian and White in the Northwest.* Baltimore: J. Murphy, 1894.

Pereyra, Lillian A. "The Catholic Church and Portland's Japanese: The Untimely St. Paul Miki School Project." 94 *OHQ* (winter 1993-1994): 399-434.

_____. "The Gospel on a Soapbox." *OCHSN* 2 (summer 1990): 1, 4.

_____. "The Shrinking Archdiocese." *OCHSN* 6 (summer 1994): 7-8.

Pfeiffer, Pancratius. *Father Francis Mary of the Cross Jordan.* St. Nazianz, Wis.: Society of the Divine Savior, 1936.

Piper, John F. Jr. *The American Churches in World War I.* Athens: Ohio University Press, 1985.

Pollard, Martin and Hugh Feiss. *Mount of Communion: Mt. Angel Abbey 1882-1982.* Revised edition. St. Benedict, Ore.: Mt. Angel Abbey, 1985.

Portland (Oregon) City Directory. Portland: S. J. McCormick, 1874, 1875.

Prucha, Francis P. "Indian Policy Reform and American Protestantism, 1880-1900." In *People of the Plains and Mountains,* edited by Ray Billington. Westport, Conn.: Greenwood, 1973.

Purcell, Richard J. "Missionaries from All Hallows (Dublin) to the United States, 1842-1865." *RACHS* 53 (1942): 204-249.

Rahill, Peter J. *The Catholic Indian Missions and Grant's Peace Policy, 1870-1884.* Washington, D.C.: Catholic University of America Press, 1953.

Reese, Thomas J., S.J. *Archbishop: Inside the Power Structure of the American Catholic Church.* San Francisco: Harper & Row, 1989.

Rippinger, Joel. *The Benedictine Order in the United States, an Interpretive History.* Collegeville, Minn.: Liturgical Press, 1990.

Robl, Gregory, O.S.B. *Fiftieth Anniversary Sacred Heart Parish, Portland, Oregon.* Portland: n.p., 1943.

"Romewards with Archbishop Seghers: From the Diary of an American Student." *Messenger of the Sacred Heart* 1 (January 1897): 11-16.

Ryan, Chloe M. "William H. Gross, Missionary Archbishop, Archbishop of Oregon City, 1885-1898." Paper, Marylhurst College, 1952.

Saalfeld, Lawrence J. *Forces of Prejudice in Oregon, 1920-1925.* Portland: Archdiocesan Historical Commission, 1984.

_____ et al. *History of St. Phillip Benizi.* Redlands, Ore.: n.p., 1991.

St. Mary's Parish, 1880-1980, Mt. Angel, Oregon. Salem: Panther Printing Company, 1979.

Schiwek, Joseph A. Jr. *Called to be Church: A Brief History of St. Charles Borromeo Parish.* Portland: n.p., 1959.

Schmid, Mark, O.S.B. *Sublimity, The Story of an Oregon Countryside, 1850-1950.* St. Benedict, Ore.: Library Bookstore, 1951.

Schoenberg, Wilfred P., S.J. *Defender of the Faith: The History of the* Catholic Sentinel *1870-1990.* Portland: Oregon Catholic Press, 1993.

_____. *A History of the Catholic Church in the Pacific Northwest, 1743-1983.* Washington, D.C.: Pastoral Press, 1987.

_____. *Paths to the Northwest: A Jesuit History of the Oregon Province.* Chicago: Loyola University Press, 1982.

_____. *A Test of Time: History of St. Mary's Home, 1889-1989.* Beaverton: St. Mary's Home for Boys, 1989.

_____. *These Valiant Women: History of the Sisters of St. Mary of Oregon, 1886-1986.* Portland: Sisters of St. Mary of Oregon, 1986.

Schommer, Jerome, S.D.S. *The Moment of Grace.* Vol. 1. Milwaukee, Wis.: Society of the Divine Savior, 1994.

Shand, James. "Portland's German Parish." *OCHSN* 4 (summer 1992): 8-9.

Shaw, J.G. *Edwin Vincent O'Hara, American Prelate.* New York: Farrar, Straus and Cudahy, 1957.

Simpson, George. *Fur Trade and Empire: George Simpson's Journal, 1824-1825.* Edited by Frederick Merk. Cambridge: Harvard University Press, 1931.

"Sisters' Ministries Form Lengthy List." *OCHSN* 4 (Winter 1981-1982): 8.

"Sisters of the Third Order of St. Francis, 1855-1928 by a Member of the Sisterhood." *RACHS* 40 (1929): 226-248.

Skeabeck, Andrew, C.Ss.R. "Most Rev. William Gross, Missionary Bishop of the South." *RACHS* 65 (1954): 11-23, 102-115, 216-229; 66 (1955): 35-52, 78-94, 131-155.

Sly, Julie. "America's Vietnamese: Preserving Their Heritage in a New Land." *St. Anthony's Messenger* 29 (February 1985): 28-36.

Smith, Charles M. *Centenary of Cathedral Parish, Portland, Oregon, 1851 1951.* Portland: n.p., 1951.

Souvenir of Dedication. Stayton, Ore.: Immaculate Conception Church, 1952.

Stabrowski, Donald, C.S.C. "St. Vincent de Paul Parish: A Half Century of Urban Ministry, parts I and II." *OCHSN* 3 (summer 1991): 9-10; 4 (summer 1992): 1, 10-12.

Steckler, Gerard G., S.J. "Charles John Seghers: Missionary Bishop in the American Northwest, 1839-1886." Ph.D. diss., University of Washington, 1963.

____. *Charles John Seghers, Priest and Bishop in the Pacific Northwest, 1839-1886: A Biography.* Fairfield, Wash.: Ye Galleon Press, 1986.

Steiss, Albert J., ed. *Ecclesiastes: the Book of Archbishop Robert Dwyer; A Selection of His Writings edited by Albert J. Steiss and a Brief Life by the Editor, and a Sketch from Memory by Isabel Piczek.* Los Angeles: National Catholic Register, 1982.

Stone, William S. *The Cross in the Middle of Nowhere: A History of the Catholic Church in Eastern Oregon.* Bend, Ore.: Maverick Publications, 1993.

Tull, Charles J. *Father Coughlin and the New Deal.* Syracuse, N.Y.: Syracuse University Press, 1965.

U.S. Commissioner of Indian Affairs. *Annual Report.* In U.S. Dept. of the Interior *Annual Report.* Washington, D.C.: Government Printing Office, 1885, 1886, 1887. Serial 2379, 2467, 2542.

United States Documents in the Propaganda Fide Archives: A Calendar. 11 vols. Ed. by Finbar Kenneally. Washington, D.C.: Academy of American Franciscan History, 1966-1987.

Valaik, J. David. "American Catholic Dissenters and the Spanish Civil War." *Catholic Historical Review* 53 (1968): 537-555.

____. "Catholic, Neutrality, and the Spanish Embargo, 1937-1939." *Journal of American History* 54 (1967): 73-85.

Vandehey, Scott and Steve Greif. *A History of Oregon's South Coast Vicariate, Including Holy Redeemer's 75 years.* North Bend, Ore.: Holy Redeemer Parish, 1981.

Van der Donckt, Cyril. "Founders of the Church in Idaho." *American Ecclesiastical Review* 32 (1905): 1-19, 123-34, 280-91.

Van der Heyden, Joseph. *Louvain American College.* Louvain, Belgium: F. and R. Ceuterick, 1909.

____. "Monsignor Adrian J. Croquet, Indian Missionary, 1818-1902." *RACHS* 16 (1905): 121-61, 268-95, 456-462; 17 (1906): 86-96, 220-242, 267-288.

Voth, Sister M. Agnes, O.S.B. *Green Olive Branch.* Edited by M. Raymond. Chicago: Franciscan Herald Press, 1973.

Waggett, George M., O.M.I. "The Oblates of Mary Immaculate in the Pacific Northwest, 1847-1878." *RACHS* 64 (1953): 72-93.

Waibel, Pauline Rose, S.S.M.O. "A History of the Sisters of St. Mary of Oregon's Mission in Tamshiyacu, Peru, 1966-1973." Master's thesis, Portland State University, 1990.

Warner, Lenore and Mary Payne. *Saint Anthony's Parish, 1910-1985, Tigard.* Lake Oswego, Ore.: Lake Oswego Printing Co., 1985.

Whalen, Willis. "The Pioneer Period of the Catholic Church in Portland, Oregon, 1851-1881." Master's thesis, University of Portland, 1950.

Wheeler, Arthur, C.S.C. "Columbia University, 1914-1922." Paper presented at the Holy Cross History Conference, Portland, Oregon, June 6, 1992.

____. "Federal Investigation of Archbishop Christie." *OCHSN* 4 (summer 1992): 7.

____. "Portland Irish in World War I." Paper presented at the Fifth Annual Meeting of the Oregon Catholic Historical Society, Portland, Oregon 1992.

Wilkes, Charles. *Narrative of the United States Exploring Expedition During the Years 1838, 1839, 1849, 1841, 1842.* Vol. 2. Philadelphia: Lea & Blanchard, 1848.

Will, Allen S. *Life of Cardinal Gibbons, Archbishop of Baltimore.* Vol. 1. New York: E.P. Dutton, 1922.

Willging, Eugene P. and Herta Hatzfeld. "Catholic Serials of the Nineteenth Century in Oregon." *RACHS* 72 (1961): 46-61.

Williams, Gyndwr. "Highlights of the First 200 Years of the Hudson's Bay Company: Simpson and McLoughlin." *The Beaver* 301 (autumn 1970): 49-55.

Wooten, Dudley G. *Remember Portland.* Denver: American Publishing Society, n.d.

Young, F. G. "Ewing Young and His Estate." *Quarterly of the OHS* 21 (1920): 191-315.

Zenner, Ambrose, O.S.B. "Fire Twice Destroys Mt. Angel Abbey." *CS*, 6 October 1960, sect. 3, 18.

Interviews and Personal Communications

Baker, Mrs. Julia. Interviews by Lillian Pereyra. Tape recording, 25 February 1998, 20 March 1998. OHS.

Bliven, Rev. Edmond. Interviews by Lillian Pereyra. Tape recording, 25 April 1996, 7 May 1996, 14 May 1996, 31 May 1996, 4 June 1996, 15 April 1997. OHS.

Griffin, Rev. Bertram. Interviews by Sister Pauline Rose Waibel, S.S.M.O. Tape recording, 20 November 1992, 29 November 1992, 30 November 1992, 18 January 1993, 18 June 1993, 18 July 1993. OHS.

Harrington, Rev. Emmet. Interviews by Lillian Pereyra. Tape recording, 26 July 1988, 28 July 1988, 3 August 1988, 23 August 1993, 13 September 1988. OHS.

Howard, Edward D. Interview by Brother David Martin, C.S.C. Typed transcript, April 1970. University of Portland Archives.

Kennedy, Rev. Alan. Interview by Lillian Pereyra. Tape recording, 17 July 1997. OHS.

Larkin, John E. Interviews by Lillian Pereyra. Tape recording, 10 January 1989, 14 January 1989, 17 January 1989, 14 February 1989, 7 March 1989. OHS.

Lemire, Romeo. Interviews by Lillian Pereyra. Tape recording, 25 August 1987, 1 September 1987. OHS.

McQuarry, Robert. Interviews by Lillian Pereyra. Tape recording, 29 June 1994, 6 July 1994, 13 July 1994. OHS.

Murray, Baxter. Interviews by Lillian Pereyra. Tape recording, 22 September 1992, 29 September 1992, 6 October 1992. OHS.

O'Meara, Edward. Interviews by Lillian Pereyra. Tape recording, 26 October 1990, 1 November 1991, 7 November 1991, 18 May 1992, 2 July 1992. OHS.

Park, Rev. Morton E. Interviews by Lillian Pereyra. Tape recording, 25 February 1993, 4 March 1993, 9 March 1993, 11 March 1993, 4 November 1993. OHS.

Power, Archbishop Cornelius M. Interviews by Lillian Pereyra. Tape recording, 12 October 1993, 26 October 1993, 2 November 1993, 12 November 1993. OHS.

Robinson, Sr. Marian Dolores, S.N.J.M. Interviews by Lillian Pereyra. Tape recording, 2 October 1992, 22 October 1992, 19 October 1992, 5 November 1992, 11 November 1992, 19 November 1992. OHS.

Schaefers, Rev. Francis J. Interviews by Lillian Pereyra. Tape recording, 25 January 1990, 30 January 1990. OHS.

Schaefers, Sr. Gertrude, S.N.J.M. Interview by Lillian Pereyra. Tape recording, 1 August 1989. OHS.

Smith, Leo. Interviews by Lillian Pereyra. Tape recording, 17 October 1990, 26 October 1990, 9 November 1990, 16 November 1990, 22 November 1990, 23 January 1991. OHS.

Thielen, Rev. Martin. Interviews by Lillian Pereyra. Tape recording, 13 January 1989, 27 January 1989, 3 March 1989, 10 March 1989, 7 April 1989, 21 April 1989, 14 May 1989, 19 May 1989, 26 May 1989,19 November 1989. OHS.

Van der Zanden, Mrgr. Edmund. Interviews by Lillian Pereyra. Tape recording, 3 March 1998, 4 May 1998. OHS.

Williams, Rev. Alfred. Interviews by Lillian Pereyra. Tape recording, 8 March 1988, 8 October 1988, 8 November 1988. OHS.

Newspapers

The Beacon (University of Portland) 1967
Baker City Bedrock Democrat, 1874-1878.
Catholic Sentinel, 1870-1998
Pendleton East Oregonian, 1885-1893
Oregon Journal, 1902-1978
The Oregonian, 1860-1998
Pendleton Tribune, 1885
Tillamook Headlight-Herald, 1991
The Wanderer, 1977

DATE DUE